Successful Software Process Improvement

Hewlett-Packard Professional Books

Successful Software Process Improvement

Robert B. Grady

Hewlett-Packard Company

To join a Prentice Hall Internet mailing list,
point to http://www.prenhall.com/mail_lists.

Prentice Hall PTR, Upper Saddle River, New Jersey 07458
http://www.prenhall.com

Library of Congress Cataloging-in-Publication Data
Grady, Robert B., 1943-
    Successful software process improvement /Robert B. Grady
      p. cm.
    Includes bibliographical references and index.
    ISBN 0-13-626623-1 (hardcover)
    1. Computer software--Development
QA76.76.D47G75 1997
005--dc21   97-10734
                               CIP

Editorial/Production Supervision: *Joe Czerwinski*
Acquisitions Editor: *Greg Doench*
Editorial Assistant: *Mary Treacy*
Manufacturing Manager: *Alexis R. Heydt*
Cover Design Director: *Jerry Votta*
Cover Design: *Design Source*
Marketing Manager: *Miles Williams*
Manager, Hewlett-Packard Press: *Patricia Pekary*

© 1997 by Hewlett-Packard Company
Published by Prentice Hall PTR
Prentice-Hall, Inc.
A Division of Simon and Schuster
Upper Saddle River, NJ 07458

Prentice Hall books are widely used by corporations and government agencies for training, marketing, and resale. The publisher offers discounts on this book when ordered in bulk quantities. For more information, contact:

Corporate Sales Department
Phone: 800-382-3419
Fax: 201-236-7141
E-mail: corpsales@prenhall.com

Or write

Prentice Hall PTR
Corp. Sales Dept.
One Lake Street
Upper Saddle River, NJ 07458

Printed in the United States of America

10 9 8 7 6 5 4 3 2 1

ISBN: 0-13-626623-1

Prentice-Hall International (UK) Limited, *London*
Prentice-Hall of Australia Pty. Limited, *Sydney*
Prentice-Hall of Canada Inc., *Toronto*
Prentice-Hall Hispanoamericana, S.A., *Mexico*
Prentice-Hall of India Pte. Ltd., *New Delhi*
Prentice-Hall of Japan, Inc., *Tokyo*
Simon & Schuster Asia Pte. Ltd., *Singapore*
Editora Prentice-Hall do Brasil, Ltda., *Rio de Janeiro*

To three fantastic, loyal, ever-helpful, and enthusiastic friends who had the patience to read all the pieces of this book multiple times.

Jan Grady
Debbie Caswell
and
Cate Meyer

Thank you for your encouragement, support, and friendship.

Contents

Part One   PLAN: Identify and
                  Resolve Risks   **22**

     Putting a Stake in the Ground*   25

     A Range of Assessments, 26
     ISO 9001, ISO 9000-3, 26
     Capability Maturity Model (CMM), 27
     Software Quality and Productivity Assessment (SQPA), 29
     Quality Maturity System (QMS), 30
     Malcolm Baldrige National Quality Award, 31
     Choosing an Assessment, 33
     What Makes an Assessment Successful?, 36
     Conclusion, 37

3   *Planning for Software Core Competence*   39

     Creating a Software Core-Competence Plan, 41
     Management Leadership: Preplanning, 42
     The Nine Steps of a Core-Competence Plan, 43
     Implementing the Core-Competence Plan, 51
     Measuring Progress Toward Core Competence, 52
     Removing Barricades that Block the Road
        to Core Competence, 56
     Conclusion, 56

4   *An Investment Model for
     Software Process Improvement*   59

     Description of a Software Management Cost Model, 60
     New Development Components of the Model, 60
     Maintenance Components of the Model, 61
     Rework Components of the Model, 62
     The Complete Software Management Cost Model, 64
     Application of the Model, 65
     Setting Expectations for Improvements—The Case for Inspections, 66
     More Aggressive Expectations—The Case for Reuse, 67
     A Portfolio of Investment Choices, 68
     How Much Should You Invest?, 70
     Conclusion, 71

5   *Gaining Management Commitment*
    for Software Process Improvements   73

Part Two   DO: Train, Adapt,
                   Consult, Remove Barriers   **92**

6   *Moving Past Reasons Not to Succeed*   95

10 *Tracking and Reporting Process-Improvement Results—Mission Possible!* 169

Part Four ACT: Revise, Develop Next-Level Process, Convince Others 192

11 *Software Failure Analysis for High-Return Process-Improvement Decisions* 195

Appendices

ACKNOWLEDGMENTS

I'd like to thank the many Hewlett-Packard engineers and managers whom I've had the privilege to work with for many years now. Your curiosity and drive to do your jobs better, more easily, and to produce high-quality products has provided an exciting environment in which to work. Your challenges and openness to change have also encouraged me to continually evolve the ideas and models in this book to help us to improve some HP software processes. I particularly value the long-term support, encouragement, and sponsorship that Sheryl Root has given to me and her leadership in moving HP's software processes forward.

There are many people who have shared their excellent work and helped to shape the models and examples in this book. I want to thank these HP people for letting me share their examples: Paul Bartlett, David O. Blanchard, Dave Dickmann, Doug Doetz, Jan Grady, Jeannie Hollis, Wayne Lim, Jean MacLeod, Malcolm Rix, Paul Robinson, Glen Shirey, Sue Stetak, Marc Tischler, Lou Witkin, Brad Yackle, and Barbara Zimmer. A special thanks to Tom Van Slack who has led HP's inspections efforts for years now and who coauthored the original version of Chapter 13.

There are many groups outside HP who have encouraged improvements and published results. Without their work, we would not have been able to make the progress in HP that we have. Foremost among these are the Software Engineering Lab at NASA/Goddard and the Software Engineering Institute at Carnegie-Mellon University. Individuals whose software engineering results particularly influenced my process-improvement thinking over the years include Bill Agresti, Vic Basili, Barry Boehm, Dave Card, Bill Curtis, Tom DeMarco, Michael Fagan, Watts Humphrey, Frank McGarry, Mark Paulk, and Dieter Rombach.

The various chapters in the book went though a huge number of reviews. I would like to thank all these reviewers for their patience and their early comments and suggestions: John Alderete, Rand Barbano, Steven Bear, Debbie Caswell, Angela Chiasson, Dwight Cornwell, Patricia Cornwell, Guy Cox, Ron Crough, Nancy Federman, Ralph Goddi, Ron Grace, Jan Grady, Martin Griss, Joe Halpern, Bob Horenstein, Scott Ingraham, Emil Jandourek, Rod Juncker, Bert Laurence, Chuck Leath, Jean MacLeod, Rose Marchetti, Cate Meyer, Dan Miller, Nancy Near, Alan Padula, Jerry Peltz, Steve Rodriguez, Sheryl Root, Brian Sakai, Kevin Schofield, Fred Schurkus, Sue Stetak, Tom Van Slack, Bob Walstra, and Barbara Zimmer.

Finally, I would like to especially thank Debbie Caswell, Bob Glass, Jan Grady, Bob Horenstein, Shari Lawrence Pfleeger, Debra Mallette, Frank McGarry, Cate Meyer, Mark Paulk, Stan Rifkin, Sheryl Root, Howard Rubin, Fred Schurkus, and Ed Weller, who all read various versions of the book manuscript and gave me encouragement and valuable suggestions.

There are countless others who have helped me bring this book to where it is today. For those who I should have specifically mentioned and inadvertently missed, I apologize.

1

The Software Process- Improvement ━━ Land Rush ━━

When I was growing up, western movies were very popular. The story of early land rushes in the western United States left a strong impression on me. One particular image that I still remember was crowds of settlers on horseback, in wagons, and on foot. They were all lined up, waiting for a starting signal that caused them all to race each other to claim plots of land that they hadn't even seen. Later scenes would show wagons turning over, horses stumbling, and what appeared to be sheer madness of thousands.*

Is software development in a similar rush today? Our field has certainly been changing rapidly ever since it began. If you search for recent articles referencing software process that also discuss "improvements," their numbers have been constantly increasing (Figure 1-1; derived from an Inspec™ database search of abstracts). Yet these numbers miss a vital part of the story. A recent article by Tichy et al. compared computer science and software engineering research articles with ones from two other scientific fields. Of papers they felt should require some experimental validation, 40 percent of the computer

---

* Despite the cinematic popularity of the land-rush image, there were only a few such land rushes in the history of the U.S. settlement of the West. They all took place in Oklahoma between 1889 and 1893. The first one involved "thousands" of people and the largest was the one in 1893.

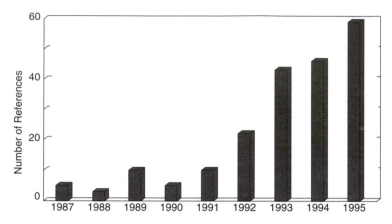

Figure 1-1 The increasing number of times that "Software Process (Improvement)" has been referenced in magazines/journals

science ones didn't. This compared to only 12 and 15 percent for the other two fields. They concluded: "On the whole, we consider this situation as unacceptable, even alarming. The results suggest that large parts of CS may not meet standards long established in the natural and engineering sciences." [1]

There is a great rush to encourage others to try new, unproven "improvements" (land they haven't seen yet) and benefits are proclaimed without any supporting evidence. Perhaps we are all involved in a "software process-improvement land rush," and this probably leads to some stumbling. Early stages of progress in most fields are fast-paced, so businesses involving software are caught up in a crowd moving forward, whether we like it or not. If we don't move with it, we'll be pushed aside and left behind.

This book is full of successful methods and tools that you can use to keep from overturning and getting trampled. Some will match your challenges, culture, and needs better than others, and you can use these immediately. Others may not seem to fit now, and that's ok. I've put them all here, because I want this book to be your most valuable resource for process-improvement advice for a long time.

Chapter 1 gives a Reader's Digest™ version (an abridgement) of the successful methods described throughout the book. These methods include carefully defining what you want, the path that you choose to follow, and the controls and feedback that will tell you if you are on track. In other words, this book will help you to control your own destiny.

A Process-Improvement Image

Let's start by combining two useful models into an image that we will return to throughout the book. The first is a simple, yet practical, improvement model (the Shewhart cycle) popularized by W. Edwards Deming: plan/do/check/act. [2] The second is a spiral model specially adapted for process improvements (Barry Boehm originally proposed a software development spiral model for some kinds of product projects [3]). Figure 1-2 is a new process improvement spiral model that shows things you will usually see as a practice is adopted and evolves.

You need to start your thinking in the middle of the model. However, you don't have to start implementing there. You can use your organization's maturity, existing skills, and infrastructure to begin at the most appropriate place.

The figure shows a progression from first-time practice usage (in the center, "project plans new practice") to widespread organizational adoption. Normal *product (development) projects* aren't organized to go through this entire spiral. At best, there may be a product-line architecture that could ideally do so if all the planned products were done. The figure gives some useful insights

Figure 1-2 Spiral model for process-improvement adoption

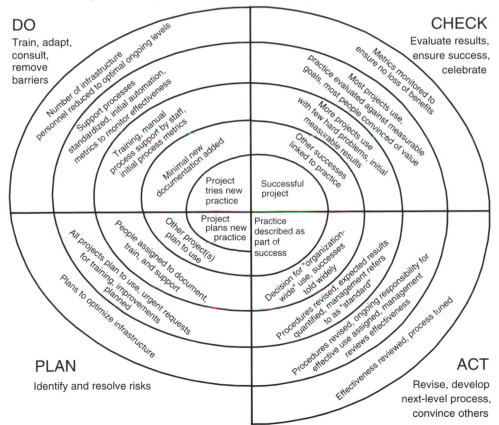

for *process improvement projects* that can help us assess to what extent an improvement has been adopted.

The model includes several patterns across the plan/do/check/act quadrants. These reflect

- increasing people and resource investments,
- greater management understanding, attention, and commitment, and
- better control with process metrics.

Let's briefly look at what outward movement within each separate quadrant suggests will happen as processes improve.

Plan - Most new improvements are first tried by one project team. When this appears to work, other project teams are convinced to try to duplicate the first project's success. As usage spreads, planning aspects of new adoptions include ways to provide better documentation, training, and support. Eventually, demand outpaces the ability of the people helping the new adopters to keep pace, and plans for an ongoing infrastructure are developed and tuned.

Do - Progress in this and the Check and Act quadrants parallels the stages described in Plan. Adoption by the second ring projects starts a trend to improve and adapt documentation and training. (I will use the term "spiral ring" for one helical progression around the spiral, with the "first" ring being the center one.) By the third ring, users have formed realistic expectations for the new process and use metrics to see how well those expectations are being met. They also continue to tune the process. In the outermost two rings, good support is common, automation (where feasible) improves process efficiency and quality, and the number of infrastructure personnel is finally reduced to optimal ongoing levels.

Check - After the first ring project team uses a new practice, they describe their "success" in terms that match whatever measurements they took. As a minimum, this probably means their project completed reasonably close to expected schedules, that initial customer reactions were good, and that the process improvement seemed to work. As other projects adopt the new process in later spiral rings, improvement metrics become more precise until process performance becomes well understood and is measured regularly to ensure optimum performance is maintained.

Act - The speed at which adoptions of a new practice occur will heavily depend on how credible early adopters are, how good a job they did of measuring their processes, how well they can communicate their success, and how well their improvement matches the readiness of the organization and its management team to make similar changes on other projects.

Gaining ever-increasing management commitment as you move outward on these segments suggests the critical elements of follow-through and "sales" that are necessary for process improvements. You can think of this sequence as pursuing "market share" for adopting a practice.

Before discussing useful techniques to use in each diagram quadrant in later sections, note how moving from the model's center to the outside suggests that process-improvement adoption is an evolutionary process. It is easier to imagine doing each ring sequentially than it is to imagine combining two or more rings into some kind of revolutionary jump. We are looking at a long journey, but software is a young, exciting field with many exciting successes along the trail. Some segments of the journey will be slow and others fast. However, the path cannot be random. Business survival depends on managing software development as a critical, long-term asset.

Organization of the Book

Whether you are a software developer, a project manager, a process-improvement manager, or a manager of an entire software business, you should be concerned about improving today's software practices. This book is designed to help you do just that. It is organized around the spiral model's plan/do/check/act quadrants. This organization isn't rigid. Discussions in some chapters go beyond their relevant quadrants. Also, the book isn't a cookbook that tells you what specific methods to apply at what specific spiral stages. You will have to adapt the methods to meet your organization's unique challenges.

The book's plan/do/check/act sections will help you focus on issues specific to identifiable stages of familiar projects. Also, the structure should make it easier to find help in the book when you need it. Most importantly, it reinforces both the spiral idea of evolving process improvements and the key role of plan/do/check/act.

The book includes a wide variety of models that capture significant successful practices. A broad range of success stories reinforces the use of these practices, and the rest of this chapter gives you a quick sampling. Each of its discussions is then expanded in later chapters that give practical examples and methods to organize for success and to recognize and overcome roadblocks you will encounter along the way. I hope you enjoy the ride!

PLAN: IDENTIFYING RISKS AND DECIDING WHAT TO DO

While plan/do/check/act always starts with some form of commitment, the nature and strength of that commitment is constantly challenged as plans solidify. Anticipating these challenges helps you to strengthen plans to help ensure success. Let's look at an example.

Imagine that you manage a business or an organization's software function. Outside consultants recently assessed your organization, and their recommendations are shown in Figure 1-3.

What should your action plan be? Your people have probably told you all this already. How has the assessment changed your views? Unlike practices you already fully understand and confidently use, you're not certain how much these suggestions will improve things. Can an outsider understand your business well enough to make high-return recommendations? And how will your people react to these suggestions? Don't they talk about how busy they are and how they can't handle more work?

Figure 1-3 Assessment recommendations for a software R&D organization

1. Maintain focused lab vision within the lab and sell it to division functional staff. Where possible, reduce number and length of lines of communication between groups.

2. Assign adequate resources to process improvement.

3. Build on current software engineering processes.
    Inspections and reviews - Train moderators. Expand use to include more formal design and requirements reviews. Log defects found during inspections and reviews.
    Quality planning - Continue use of quality plans and add measurable "FURPS+"* goals for all quality dimensions. Review quality plans. Measure quality early.
    Defect prevention/removal - Continue current test methods and measures. Consider use of earlier measures such as complexity and code stability. Capture defect data for root-cause analysis.
    Requirements analysis - Continue efforts to learn customer's needs, using QFD[†], customer visits, etc.

4. Add rigor to planning process.
    Estimation and scheduling - Develop realistic schedules based on detailed work breakdown input from engineers. Account for all engineering activities. Reestimate and reschedule at each phase and as changes occur. Consider using risk-based scheduling techniques.
    Life cycle and standards - Base project planning on a standard customizable life cycle with checklists and templates. Document current informal standards and procedures.
    Measures - Measure earlier in the life cycle, and use as a process-improvement basis. Track engineer time and effort by life cycle phase. Track and archive planned versus actual schedules.

5. Prepare for future needs.
    Actively manage third-party relationships. Build working relationships. Create checklists to manage. Plan to support increasingly complex configuration management and change control needs.

* FURPS+ functionality, usability, reliability, performance, supportability, and other business-specific attributes.
[†] QFD (quality function deployment) a way of rating the "voice of the customer" needs and comparing how well they are matched by planned product attributes. [4]

These assessment recommendations are typical of today's software management challenges. Imagining that you managed this business might have given you some ideas that a useful assessment must:

- Suggest some changes that make good business sense to you and link to your goals. The closer the tie they make between you and your competitive needs, the easier it will be for you to decide and act.
- Suggest the scope, timing, cost, and payback of each change. Without such scoping, you have no basis for comparing proposed process-improvement projects to any other urgent business proposals.
- Help you to understand your organization's readiness and enthusiasm for each proposed change. Your culture, your existing processes, and your people's underlying beliefs all affect changes. If you don't consider these aspects, even a simple process improvement can fail or not be cost effective.

Chapter 2 explores a variety of assessments, the role they play, and some of the advantages and disadvantages of specific types of assessments. Then, Chapters 3, 4, and 5 give you some useful ways to look at and plan around these key areas of business urgency, investment worth, and organizational readiness. Let's briefly discuss each key area.

The Business Urgency of Process Improvement

Many managers are used to viewing software development as a temporary crisis. Hewlett-Packard awareness of the business importance of this "temporary" crisis began over 15 years ago. As both the number of software developers and the clear product content significance of software increased, small first steps were finally taken to improve our software producing know-how. Today there is no denying software's strategic importance. A recent article has labelled such powerful know-how a "core competence." [5]

For several years, we have explicitly identified existing and desired core competencies with various HP divisions, and we have found that this new way of looking at business needs is very powerful. By thinking about those needs strategically, managers more easily tie improvement objectives to business needs. Such objectives are compelling and more likely to sustain management commitment than ones justified solely around some methodology or technology that is poorly understood by decision-making managers.

Chapter 3 shows you a model for a core-competence plan and how to develop and implement one, and it shows how *core-competence planning is just as important as business planning in setting an organization's long-term strategy*. The key results of the core-competence planning process are a set of clearly stated goals and action plans with clear links to business needs. With these plans and goals, you have a strategic framework that explains what software abilities your organization must develop to remain competitive, and you have a way to describe the business aspects of any process-improvement recommendations.

Whether you can get your organization to make a complete transition to preparing a core-competence plan initially or you just get them to better think in these terms, you will discover that your improvement goals will be clearer, more exciting, and more likely to be achieved.

The Investment Worth of Process Improvement

Knowing which competencies your organization needs provides a framework for strategic decisions. Just as you manage a personal "portfolio" of investments toward strategic investment goals, you also need to think of potential process-improvement projects as your organization's stocks and bonds of process improvement. Some projects are more costly, risky, timely, and so forth, than others. An investment model of your software processes will help you to evaluate trade-offs.

Software processes can be organized in many different ways. There are three major aspects that eventually affect all software development organizations. You can simplistically view each of these as roughly one-third of an average organization's costs.

- Development - This is usually further divided into requirements/specifications (18%), design (19%), implementation (34%), and test (29%). The parenthetical percentages are the averages for 132 HP software projects. [4]
- Maintenance - This is divided into enhancements (65%) and defect fixing (35%). Often, part of the enhancement work is included with development and uses much the same processes. There is a unique maintenance aspect called "knowledge recovery" or "program understanding." It becomes a major cost component as software ages (assume 50% of both enhancements and defect fixing).
- Rework - Roughly one-third of development and enhancement work is rework. All the nonknowledge recovery part of defect fixing is rework. Rework is also heavily affected by the type of defects, especially when they are found long after they were created. Late-found specifications defects cost more to fix than late-found design defects, which cost more than code defects.

A complete derivation of these cost components is given in Chapter 4. Table 1-1 summarizes them for an environment with 55 percent maintenance (and Appendix A shows how the model changes for high/low maintenance environments). Note that rework costs are associated with the development activity where defects were introduced, not where they are necessarily found.

Table 1-1 Estimated software development/maintenance cost percentages (55 percent maintenance environment)

	Development Work	Maintenance Work	Development Rework	Maintenance Rework
Requirements/ Specifications	5	2	8	9
Design	6	2	5	4
Coding	10	4	2	3
Test	9	3		
Knowledge Recovery		19		9
Total	30	30	15	25

Once you create a similar model of your costs, it is easier to match specific proposed improvements against modeled costs. Of course, challenges can be approached in either a tactical or strategic way. The short-term approach is to work overtime or to test longer. While this might relieve immediate problems, they will soon return, because you made no fundamental process change. Thinking in terms of an investment model focuses your actions on measurably reducing specific costs permanently.

Your Organization's Readiness for Process Improvement

No matter how well you analyze the business urgency of a particular process improvement and its investment value, your organization might just not be ready for it. If not, a decision to mandate people to make such changes could be very costly and ultimately unsuccessful. One approach here is to return to assessment results, if you did an assessment. A good subjective assessment should give you some sense of how widespread feelings are about key issue areas and how motivated people are to change.

Another approach is to directly evaluate the business and organizational forces that influence your organization's management commitment to potential improvements. Table 1-2 shows just one possible way to model many aspects that can be positive influences. Unfortunately, when they aren't positive, they can distract and undermine your manager's best intentions.

Table 1-2 Management commitment influencers

	Business	Organizational
Strategic	Vision Business Approach Core Competence	Organizational Maturity Process Improvement Infrastructure
Tactical	Customer Perceptions Market Share Product Cycle Time Profitability	Organizational Inertia Stability Cost/Time Alignment

You can probably remember situations when any one of these influencers has seemed to stop process-improvement progress in its tracks. Some more obvious examples include:

- Cost cutting due to declining profits *(profitability)*
- Reorganization that splits R&D into two different divisions or combines with another *(stability)*
- Improvement-project resources pulled to help shorten a development schedule due to a competitive product announcement *(product cycle time)*

Any one of the twelve aspects can temporarily slow or even stop process improvements. Thus, it is useful to consciously evaluate each one to understand potential risks in your organization. Chapter 5 discusses forces operating for and against each aspect, how to recognize negative symptoms, and steps to take to regain management commitment if it is threatened.

Our experience with looking at these influencers in many HP divisions suggests that none of the twelve are always weak or strong. Also, every organization seems to have pockets of strength, as well as weaknesses to work on. It is possible to suggest some generalities for the four parts of Table 1-2.

- *Strategic business aspects* most reflect leadership of your organization's management team.
- *Tactical business aspects* are a constant source of tension, since they are tied to commonly accepted evaluations of business health and are reviewed monthly.

- *Strategic organizational aspects* can be the strongest negative influencers. They are often victims of management responses to tactical business pressures. U.S. managers are especially vulnerable here, since U.S. businesses tend to focus more strongly on tactical results than on long-term ones.
- *Tactical organizational aspects* are the most controllable from lower in the organization. If any of these are negative influences, it is often possible to work around them.

There are many reasons to select various processes to improve. These include critical customer dissatisfiers, ease of solution, organizational readiness and enthusiasm, return on investment (ROI), and reinforcement of basic organizational values. A strong selection process with a well-thought-out balance of tactical and strategic projects with clearly defined goals shows people your rationale and helps to motivate them toward successful change.

DO: STRUCTURING FOR SUCCESS

After countless years of high pressure and late projects, software managers and engineers have a well-developed sense of urgency. They are also used to frequent and rapid changes. However, they seem to respond to many proposed process-improvement projects with skepticism. They've seen many improvements begun with perfectly good intentions that have died due to lack of management or organizational follow-through. What causes such breakdowns, and what can you do to help prevent them?

Skeptics will offer "reasons" why an improvement won't or can't succeed. When you hear this, you are hearing important information. The people who give these reasons are not necessarily *negative* people. Their experiences are real. Probing their reasons helps you and them to better understand what to do to move forward more quickly and successfully. Chapter 6 gives a variety of models and examples for working with people to move past reasons you hear when improvement programs slow down or get stuck. They hint at the experiences behind common hangups, and they are designed to expand your ability to try various approaches in similar situations.

One of the most powerful approaches is to work with people to mentally shift to a future desired state. When they make such a shift, they will use words like "can, might, should, or will." They will nod their head positively and might smile, and their gestures will be animated. The examples in Chapter 6 will help you in the same way. By seeing these techniques work in the examples, it will be easier for you to see yourself applying them equally effectively in your future.

Enlisting the Support of Key People

The spiral model shows that improvements progress by stages. The amount of management attention and influence also varies by stage. Chapter 7 discusses a variety of ways to structure successful projects. One aspect is the key people in an organization that require special attention.

Project Managers - They play a key role by ensuring that all the involved people work together productively. This takes positive feedback, open listening, a person the team can go to who will help to fairly resolve disagreements, and someone who can sense when people are stuck and get them unstuck.

Champion - A project manager is generally also the project's champion. The champion promotes a project, removes obstacles, enthusiastically supports implementers and users, and leads through active involvement.

Sponsor - A sponsor is a person in a higher organizational position who ensures funding and high-level public enthusiasm and encouragement. A sponsor also helps coach to keep things progressing smoothly.

Opinion Leader - Sometimes there are also less obvious technical leaders. Everett Rogers and others who have long researched technological adoption call these people "opinion leaders." [6] They may not be as vocal as many technical leaders, but before other people will even consider a change, they look to whether opinion leaders accept it.

Infrastructure Members - When people first work with a new process, ready access to someone to answer questions and remove roadblocks is invaluable. Later, these same key infrastructure members are continuing contact points to capture and exchange process adjustments and improvements.

Documenting Your Approach and Your Project Plan

Minimizing negative commitment influences and optimizing support from key people are already big challenges. What else will help you to implement changes? The single most important step you can take is to create and manage from a good process-improvement project plan. Chapter 7 also gives you an outline for one. This is even more necessary for a process-improvement project than it is for a regular development project.

Sometimes project plans aren't easy to do. A particularly successful format for presenting HP after-the-fact results has been the "TQC Storyboard" format. [7,8] A similar set of pictures and maps of where you plan to go is also a very useful way to start a project plan. Think in terms of a measurable framework and a clear picture of the intermediate steps that lead to widespread adoption. For example, a storyboard outline from Chapter 8 is shown in Figure 1-4. Chapter 8 continues by describing how to create a storyboard and by giving a complete example of one. Use the storyboard both to organize your plan/do/check/act thoughts and to create a slideset that you will evolve and present many times over the evolution and adoption of your process improvement.

Figure 1-4 Typical storyboard outline

The Rosetta Stone Knowledge Recovery Project	
■ DIV Situation, Challenges	*Plan*
■ Project Selection Criteria, Planned	
Changes, Objectives	
■ Cost/Benefit Analysis	
■ Project Milestones	*Do*
■ Methods for Measuring and Validating	*Check*
■ Approach for Standardizing Process	*Act*
Changes	

Structuring a process-improvement project for success is a big challenge. Fortunately, there are useful techniques that will help you to understand

- the forces in your organization and its business that influence improvement efforts,
- the people who are most likely to sponsor and lead the efforts and how to keep them motivated, and
- the best ways to plan and execute improvement projects to evolve specific processes and abilities into strategically important assets.

CHECK: MEASURING SUCCESS

Now imagine that your project is done and some managers from another company have asked you to discuss it. What will they want to know? What kinds of questions will they ask?

- "What kinds of savings did you get?"
- "What did it cost you?"
- "How does your project compare with others?"
- "What did you learn that should be passed on to other projects?"

If you started with a storyboard that included the "check" part, you are probably in good shape. If you didn't, then some of these questions might be tough to answer. Your answers will be no better than those from the "process-improvement" projects analyzed at the start (in the article by Tichy) who reported no experimental validation. Chapter 9 shows how to drive process improvements from key business goals and gives practical advice and a model for how to validate improvements.

Primitive Software Metrics

The amount of effort you might need to set up measures for your process-improvement project depends on what measures already exist in your organization. Four primitive software metrics form a basis for many specific results that you might want to understand. [4]

> *Non-Comment Source Statements (NCSS)* is a measure of the output of a software development process. There are certainly other measures that you could use, but it is important that you measure output so that you can normalize results in some believable way.
> *Engineering Months (EM)* is a key input measure. Your primary cost will be your people's efforts. While you won't need high accuracy for this measure, you will need enough information to tell you which tasks cost what.
> *Defects* are a necessary quality measure. Most improvement efforts will not succeed unless you have a clear definition of what defects are and how you expect to control and reduce them.
> *Calendar months* can be used as a process input measure similarly to EM. It can also be a significant output measure when time to market (TTM) is important.

If you don't measure these four primitive metrics, it will be difficult to frame expectations and even more difficult to describe success. If your organization doesn't already measure all four of these in some way, make sure that your process-improvement project does. If your organization already does, this part of your job is easier. Then make sure to complement existing measures with whatever more detail you need plus any project-specific metrics that might also be necessary.

Framing Expectations

You can't assume that currently collected organizational metrics will satisfy all your project needs. A useful technique is to assume your project is complete and that you have a set of metrics in front of you. Take these assumed values and summarize your improvement results.

For example, Figure 1-5 shows the defect source pattern for one HP division. The largest design defect category was user interface defects. One

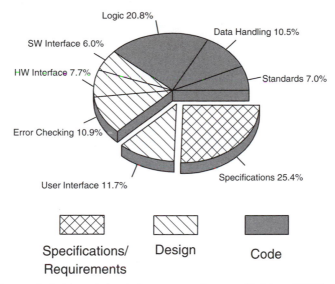

Figure 1-5 Top eight defect causes for one division (7/92)

project team at that division had experienced a disproportionately large number of these defects (over 20 percent for them compared with the division's 11.7 percent).

The team brainstormed ways to eliminate that defect type. They decided to create a user interface checklist that the team would use while they were doing designs, reviews, and tests. Let's imagine ourselves at that point. What do we think/hope will happen on the next project?

- We think the number of user interface defects will go down, say, from 20 percent to 5 percent.
- Assume the next project will produce about 25,000 NCSS and will require 6 people.
- Assume the project will take 1 year.
- Assume that rework takes about 33 percent of the total development time before the changes and that rework is where we will see a 15 percent reduction. -> 12 eng. mo./year × 6 eng. × .33 rework × .15 savings = 3.6 eng. mo. (× 160 eng. hrs/eng. mo. = 576 eng. hrs.)
- It will take some time to create the checklists, discuss them, and gain agreement, say, 3 people will take 8 hours each plus 1 hour for the project team of 6 people.
- The increased attention on interface designs will be accompanied by more desk checks and inspections, say, 10 hours more per person.

Table 1-3 summarizes the rough expectations from these assumptions. Notice what this exercise has told you about the measures you need to take. You need size data in order to compare your results against your previous project. You need effort and time data to see if you get your expected benefit. You need defect data to be sure that you really reduced the user interface defects.

Table 1-3 Cost/benefit analysis of user interface changes

ITEMS	COSTS	BENEFITS
Create UI checklists	24 Engineering hours	
Training	6 Engineering hours	
Increased deskchecks & inspections	60 Engineering hours	
Reduced defect find/fix time		576 Engineering hours
Reduced time to market		0.6 Months

ROI > 6:1 in first year and increases in subsequent years.

As you progress around the process-improvement spiral, this type of framing will help your team to better understand what the process-improvement goals are, and the measures will help you to track your progress toward those goals. The team will also be better able to spot related problem areas more quickly and help to provide course corrections.

Intermediate Results

Now let's return to what really happened on the project. The project team created its checklists and successfully completed their next project. The results of their changes were impressive. [9]

- They reduced the percentage of user-interface defects in test for their new, year-long project from their previous level of over 20 percent to roughly 5 percent of their total system test defects.
- Even though the project produced 34 percent *more* code, they spent 27 percent *less* time in test.

Of course, other improvement efforts also contributed to their success. But the clear user-interface defect reduction showed the team that their new guidelines and the attention they paid to their interfaces were major contributors. Finally, the best news is that the user interface pleased their customers, and product sales were very good.

This improvement seems like a wonderful success, but let's put it into the broader spiral context. It was a great success for one project team. However, the absence of a negative bar for user-interface defects when comparing the change in defects over a two-year period in Figure 1-6 suggests that the division still creates over 10 percent of those defects. It will take other actions listed in at least spirals 3, 4, and 5 (and probably 2, as well) to realize the total possible benefits. While there is little reason to believe that those efforts will be any less effective for the other project teams, such follow-on efforts are sometimes forgotten in the face of "other priorities." One reason for this is that people may not recognize or believe their own successes.

Figure 1-6 Results from focusing on the sources of defects (percentage defect type changes from 7/92 to 8/94)

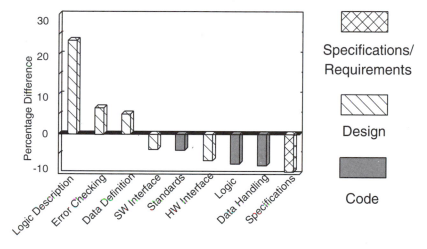

There are too few improvement projects that spend the minimal extra effort to evaluate their success measurably. This is largely because metrics aren't identified early enough in projects to track. Too often when this happens, efforts stop long before the improvement spiral is traversed enough times to fulfill an improvement's full strategic potential. Chapter 10 gives a brief snapshot of 11 other successful improvements that show the kinds of things you should measure and report for you to be successful.

ACT: LEVERAGING SUCCESS

In today's business environment of restructuring and downsizing, it seems especially hard to improve our software processes. Is there a formula for leveraging success? The essence of the "Act" step is to revise and spread improved processes.

A Powerful Way to Identify Improvement Areas

The user-interface defect improvement described in the previous section gave an excellent example of using defect data to do causal analysis to drive an improvement. Is this process generally applicable? Chapter 11 gives details for how this division used the process to not only attack their user-interface defects, but also to significantly cut their specifications defects.

Figure 1-5 showed that the sources of over 25 percent of this division's defects discovered in system test were attributed to specifications. It's not surprising that both the engineers and their managers were ready to try to eliminate some of these defects.

A cross-project team task force created two, 2-page specifications templates (one for user-interface oriented routines, one for software-interface oriented ones) that they felt would help them. Their initial efforts were modest, since changes affecting the specifications process can have widespread implications. Nevertheless, the data supporting the need for improvement and the process they used to gain organizational enthusiasm for the changes helped them to achieve impressive gains.

Figure 1-6 shows that after two years, they had significantly cut the number of specifications defects (from over 25 percent of their total to about 15 percent). This improvement is even more impressive when you consider that some of the data for that two-year period was from projects that had completed their specifications before the standard was created. These and other experiences suggest that such analyses can provide an accurate and powerful view of your processes. [4]

Spreading Successful Best Practices

Another key part of spreading successful practices is to describe them so that different audiences understand and get excited. Chapter 12 helps you to understand how people look at value, and how you can adjust your presentation of value to anticipate the needs of different audiences.

No process should ever be "final." This means we must

- model improvements on previous successes,
- create similar situations and environments, and
- reinforce behaviors that move people as quickly as possible to improved conditions.

The best example that we can look at and learn from in the software world is the adoption of software inspections. Their value has been documented many times, and yet their widespread effective usage is still limited. We specifically looked at HP's history of inspections adoption to learn from our experiences to try to create a model for increasing the rate of best-practice adoption. A summary of some of these learnings is shown in Table 1-4.

Table 1-4 Key contributors to successful HP divisional adoption of inspections and to making a transition to the next stage

	Experimental Stage	Initial Guidelines Stage	Widespread Belief and Adoption Stage
BUSINESS FACTORS		Compelling Vision (10X)	Recognition of need for core competence
ORGANIZATIONAL READINESS	Local improvement infrastructure	Company-wide infrastructure (productivity managers) Company-wide communications (SEPC)	Inspections infrastructure (company, group, divisional levels) and metrics Needs assessment - organizational plans, readiness, constraints Consulting to set stage for success
PEOPLE FACTORS	Visionary people (champions) No penalties for failures (sponsorship)	Management training (sponsors) Local adaptation	Proactive identification of champions and sponsors

The table has three stages that you can roughly think of as the first two rings, the third ring, and the fourth ring of the spiral model as you move outward. The business, organizational readiness, and people aspects are related to earlier discussions in the "Plan" and "Do" sections. A detailed discussion of each of the key learnings is in Chapter 13.

All the Table 1-4 entries came from specific examples in HP's inspections history. Many of them also have counter examples where we learned that their absence seemed just as tied to failure as their presence was tied to success. These are important messages in today's challenging business environment. We cannot forget to reward and reinforce process-improvement behaviors and infrastructures in our haste to downsize and cut costs. A process-improvement framework is one that values improving individuals' abilities and their pride in how they do their work. It encourages people not just to push to keep up, but also to figure out better ways to do things.

The best way to summarize what is needed to extend best-practice adoption and effective usage outward around the process-improvement spiral is

- proactively identify and seek support of process-improvement champions and sponsors,
- reinforce management awareness and commitment with a strong business case for each desired process improvement,
- build an infrastructure strong enough to achieve and hold software core competence, and
- measure the extent of adoption of each desired process improve-

ment until it is operating effectively, efficiently, and across all appropriate parts of the organization.

Your challenge is to change your management's thinking from solely tactically oriented process-improvement projects (or worse yet, sheer neglect) to include strategically oriented organizational capabilities. Such capabilities require business-decision makers to lead an evolution of key abilities from isolated individual knowledge to organizational processes and infrastructure that capture that knowledge.

CONCLUSION

To many in the Old West, the land rush seemed like the end point of their journey. In reality, it was just the beginning of another. The same is true of software process improvements. Each improvement is either another loop around the spiral of increasing understanding and perfection of critical abilities, or it is the foundation for the start of a new improvement spiral.

The challenges of software process improvements are complex and many-faceted. This chapter has given you a useful way of dividing your challenges into more manageable chunks. It has also briefly introduced you to many methods expanded on throughout the book that will help you to deal with your challenges. Finally, it has teased you with brief descriptions of some process-improvement successes. You will see more of these later.

Your job is to take some of the ideas that make the most sense to you and make them your own. Start using them in your own process-improvement spiral. Apply them to improve your own organization, and adjust them to improve your ability to help make constructive changes happen. Use the plan/do/check/act model to help you:

- Make sure you have clear goals and plans for what you want at the end of each of multiple spirals
- Understand how much you can expect to successfully do in stages
- Measure progress and results that emphasize your incremental successes
- Evaluate management and organizational commitment influencers and regularly reenlist and reinforce support on your continued exciting journey

Perhaps by applying these ideas you will be able to stay in front of the rush, not stumble, and successfully reach your destination.

BIBLIOGRAPHY

1. Quotation is reprinted by permission of the publisher from Tichy, W., P. Lukowicz, L. Prechelt, and E. Heinz, "Experimental Evaluation in Computer Science: A Quantitative Study," *J. Systems Software,* Vol. 28, (1995), pp. 9-18, Copyright 1995 by Elsevier Science, Inc.

2. Deming, W. E., *Out of the Crisis,* Cambridge, MA: MIT Center for Advanced Engineering Study, 1986, p. 88.

3. Boehm, B., "A Spiral Model of Software Development and Enhancement," Proc. IEEE 2nd Software Process Workshop, *ACM Software Engineering Notes,* Vol. 11, no. 4 (Aug. 1986), pp. 14-24.

4. Grady, R., *Practical Software Metrics for Project Management and Process Improvement,* Englewood Cliffs, NJ: Prentice-Hall, Inc., 1992, pp. 42, 122-157.

5. Prahalad, C., and G. Hamel, "The Core Competence of the Corporation," *Harvard Business Review,* (May-June 1990), pp. 79-91.

6. Rogers, E., *Diffusion of Innovations,* 3rd Edition, New York: Macmillan Publishing, 1983.

7. "TQC Storyboard Format," Corporate Quality Training and Development, (Oct. 1991). (Not available outside HP.)

8. Scholtes, P., *The Team Handbook,* Madison, WI.: Joiner Associates, Inc., 1988, Appendix 2.

9. Grady, R., "Successfully Applying Software Metrics," *IEEE Computer,* (Sept. 1994), pp. 18-25.

Part One

PLAN

Identify and Resolve Risks

Increasing Adoption

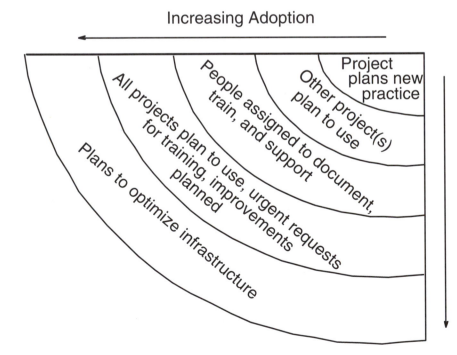

Project plans new practice

Other project(s) plan to use

People assigned to document, train, and support

All projects plan to use, urgent requests for training, improvements planned

Plans to optimize infrastructure

Chapter 1 loosely labeled planning as "identifying risks and deciding what to do." It then suggested that there are three critical planning areas to consider: *business urgency, investment worth,* and *organizational readiness.* The next four chapters expand on these aspects in ways that can be effectively used to varying degrees as you progress around the process-improvement spiral. The planning quadrant is repeated here to emphasize that you should adapt these methods to anticipate increasing scope and numbers of people to fully achieve adoption of any improvement.

Strictly speaking, assessments aren't part of planning, yet plans have to be based on something. Thus, I put "Software Process Assessments: Putting a Stake in the Ground" first. It looks at how various assessments can be used to model and motivate improvements. The motivational role of assessments can play a key part in understanding *organizational readiness.*

"Planning for Software Core Competence" then looks at the *business urgency* of process improvement and gives you a way to develop a strategic plan for necessary core competencies. This strategy addresses a weakness in many process-improvement efforts by providing a visible link to the management team's understanding of where the business is going. While all the chapters in the PLAN section are meant both to help you plan and to help you gain management commitment, this one is particularly targeted to help you work better with your management sponsors.

"An Investment Model for Software Process Improvement" builds on the core-competence discussion by deriving a practical process-improvement *investment model* that will help you to evaluate and present alternatives.

Finally, "Gaining Management Commitment for Software Process Improvements" introduces a force-field model to evaluate management and commitment influences—a key part of *organizational readiness.* It shows how to determine commitment level and summarizes steps you can take to strengthen commitment and continue to sustain it throughout your process-improvement project.

2

Software Process Assessments: Putting a Stake — in the Ground —

When you want to improve software processes, where do you start? One popular way is to do an assessment. What does the word "assessment" mean to you? For many of us, our first exposure to the word was in the game Monopoly®. One of the game's wild cards reads:

> "You are assessed for street repairs: $40 per house, $115 per hotel."

If you happened to have a lot of buildings on your properties and little cash on hand, then "assessed" left you with a very bad memory of quickly losing the game. If you were sitting on the other side of the table, you may have fond memories of the word.

An assessment is an evaluation of something. For Monopoly, it's the basis for a tax. A software-process assessment can be part of a much more positive experience. It can vary all the way from a brief postproject review to a lengthy, formal process based on something like the Software Engineering Institute's (SEI) Capability Maturity Model (CMM). It can even be a part of a broader business-process assessment. How do you decide which method to use? And what results will that method lead to in your organization?

Answers to these questions will be driven by your organization's business needs, investment willingness, and readiness for change.

It is crucial to create positive initial momentum with whatever assessment you choose. It's your chance to evaluate your current software processes as a starting point, a stake in the ground. It also is a way to model how desirable software processes might work for your organization and to motivate your people to make related changes. Let's look at some software and business assessments that companies have used.

A RANGE OF ASSESSMENTS

A postproject review is probably software's most familiar assessment. It is typically a single meeting with all of a project's key people. It can have several purposes: celebration, identification of items remaining, evaluation of changed processes, correction of problems, sharing of best practices, or simply an event that signals completion.

HP's postproject reviews tend to be informal, two-hour meetings that emphasize success and celebration. Several years ago, a significant HP variant was introduced that includes inexpensive capture of development-process information and a follow-up report. [1] Another useful HP variant is a postproject defect root-cause analysis (described in Chapter 11). Both of these variations on a postproject review change meetings from merely signalling closure into ones where attendees more proactively seek ways to do things better the next time. It is this philosophy that has driven the creation of a variety of general-purpose assessments, some of which are described below and then summarized in a table that compares them.

ISO 9001, ISO 9000-3

ISO 9001 is an international standard that "specifies quality system requirements for use where a contract between two parties requires the demonstration of a supplier's capability to design and supply product." [2] ISO 9000-3 guidelines clarify ISO 9001 use for software. [3] There currently is no single internationally accepted ISO 9001 software audit procedure or organization. Instead, some countries have formulated local requirements. For example, the U.K. accreditation body, NACCB, requires certification based on the TickIT scheme.

Preparing a company's quality system to be audited to ISO 9001 standards typically takes considerable effort and can cost several hundred thousand dollars. [4] Figure 2-1 shows the major software topics in ISO 9000-3. [3]

Quality System - Framework
Management responsibility
Quality system
Internal quality system audits

Quality System - Life Cycle Activities	Quality System - Supporting Activities
Contract review	Configuration management
Purchaser's requirements specification	Document control
Development planning	Quality records
Quality planning	Measurement
Design and implementation	Rules, practices, and conventions
Testing and validation	Tools and techniques
Acceptance	Purchasing
Replication, delivery, and installation	Included software product
Maintenance	Training

Figure 2-1 ISO 9000-3 guidelines for the application of ISO 9001 to the development, supply, and maintenance of software

The ISO 9000 certification process has been initially most popular in Europe. Initial ISO 9000 focus wasn't on software. Still, the guidelines were useful in getting better quality products from many countries, so it became a convenient basis for software quality discussions. In contrast, the CMM started in the U.S. several years before the software aspects of ISO 9001 were done. This made the CMM a more urgent business need for some U.S. companies, especially those working with U.S.military agencies.

It's possible that many U.S. companies were focused more on some U.S. domestic markets unlikely to require ISO certification. Since ISO certification doesn't necessarily ensure more competitive processes, many organizations prefer to invest in focused improvements. In fact, the need to solve pressing tactical problems is a major reason many organizations delay using either an ISO focus, a CMM assessment, or other possible strategic approaches.

Although over one hundred HP organizations are ISO 9000 (which includes ISO 9001, 9002, 9003) certified, few of them used such certification specifically to motivate software improvements. HP and other companies have also criticized moves by individual countries to require unique software accreditation. There are major concerns that the spread of similar country-specific accreditation adds unnecessary cost without adding more customer value.

Capability Maturity Model (CMM)

The SEI was created at Carnegie Mellon University in 1984 to advance the state of the practice of software engineering. A major SEI contribution is a five-level software development process model, the CMM. "Its purpose is to guide organizations in selecting process-improvement strategies by determining their current process maturity and identifying the few issues most critical to improving their software process and software quality." [5] [1] CMM experts do assessments, and they also train people in software supplier companies. These trainees then locally assess and guide improvements.

The CMM has evolved to include 18 Key Process Areas (KPAs). These are shown in the right-hand column of Figure 2-2. [5, 6] An assessment involves questionnaires, in-depth interviews of a moderate cross-section of an organization's management and engineers, and evaluation of project, process, and organizational documents. This typically takes a week. One of the reasons it involves so many people is to build support and consensus for final conclusions and recommendations.

The CMM has become a major influence on the thinking of U.S. software suppliers. One reason for this is pressure from buying organizations for evidence of certain levels of process maturity before contracting. [7] The CMM has clearly opened the door to healthy questions. Also, evidence has built that shows that increased maturity does create improved cost, quality, and schedule performance. [8-12]

Figure 2-2 Capability maturity model for software*

Level	Focus	Key Process Areas	
5 Optimizing	Continuous process improvement	Defect prevention Technology change management Process change management	
4 Managed	Product and process quality	Quantitative process management Software quality management	
3 Defined	Engineering process	Organization process focus Organization process defn. Peer reviews Training program	Intergroup coordination Software product engineering Integrated software mgmt.
2 Repeatable	Project management	Software project planning Software project tracking Software subcontract mgmt.	Software quality assurance Software configuration mgmt. Requirements mgmt.
1 Initial	Heroes		

*Reprinted from Information and Software Technology, vol. 35, no. 6–7. B. Curtis and M. Paulk, "Creating a Software Process Improvement Program," pp. 381–386, 1993 with kind permission of Elsevier Science - NL, Sara Burgerhartstraat 25, 1055 KV Amsterdam, The Netherlands

---

1. M. Paulk, C. Weber, B. Curtis, M. Chrissis, *The Capability Maturity Model*, (page 5), ©1994 Addison-Wesley Publishing Company Inc. Reprinted by permission of Addison-Wesley Longman Inc.

Software Quality and Productivity Assessment (SQPA)

HP used an assessment called SQPA from 1987 to 1991. It was based on a process created by Capers Jones of Software Productivity Research. Reviewers used a standard survey to ask managers and engineers about their software processes. They organized results around the eight major areas in Figure 2-3. Because each category was numerically rated, groups could easily compare their average ratings against other HP and non-HP organizations and across time. The figure has three regions that group industry responses into "ahead of norms," "industry norm," and "higher risk." The figure also has two lines on it that show the progress one HP division made between 1987 and 1990. [13]

Figure 2-3 SQPA assessments—quantitative/qualitative data categories

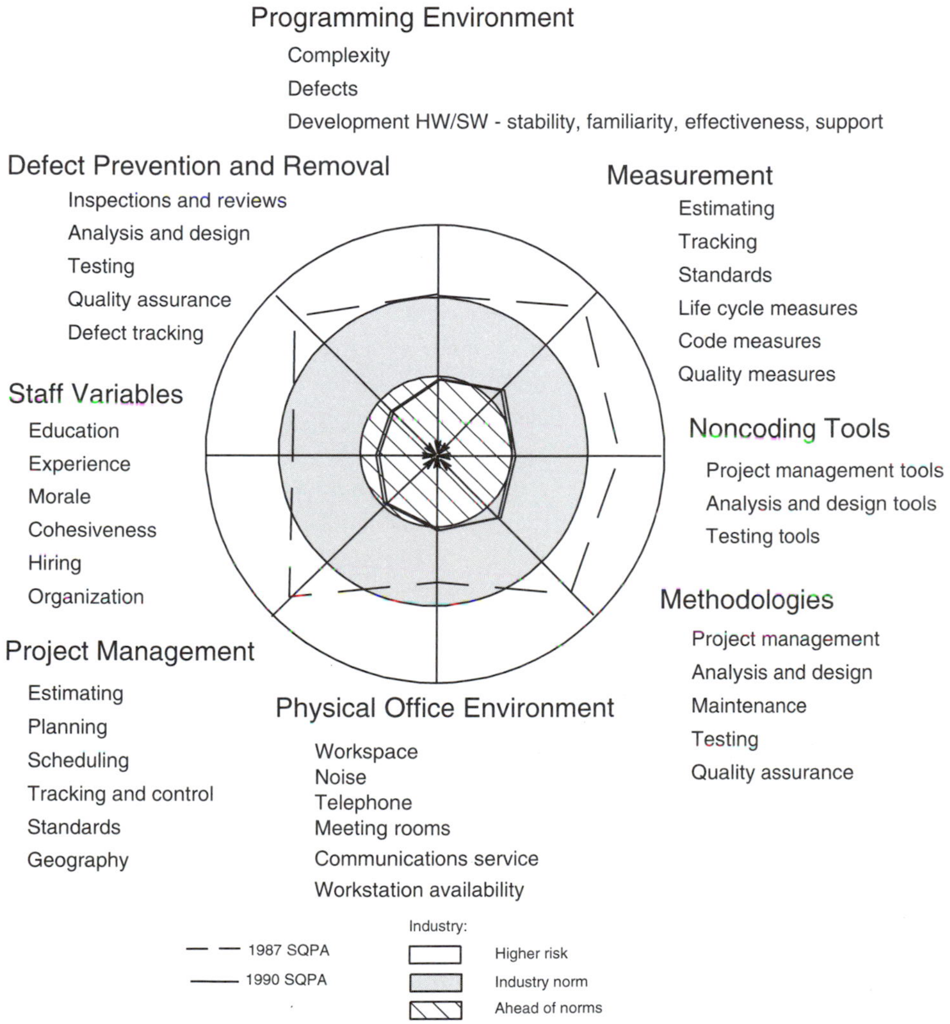

Programming Environment
Complexity
Defects
Development HW/SW - stability, familiarity, effectiveness, support

Defect Prevention and Removal
Inspections and reviews
Analysis and design
Testing
Quality assurance
Defect tracking

Measurement
Estimating
Tracking
Standards
Life cycle measures
Code measures
Quality measures

Staff Variables
Education
Experience
Morale
Cohesiveness
Hiring
Organization

Noncoding Tools
Project management tools
Analysis and design tools
Testing tools

Project Management
Estimating
Planning
Scheduling
Tracking and control
Standards
Geography

Physical Office Environment
Workspace
Noise
Telephone
Meeting rooms
Communications service
Workstation availability

Methodologies
Project management
Analysis and design
Maintenance
Testing
Quality assurance

— — 1987 SQPA
——— 1990 SQPA

Industry:
Higher risk
Industry norm
Ahead of norms

SQPA's goals were to

- analyze and compare software development processes,
- recommend improvements,
- communicate best practices, and
- provide links to other divisions facing similar challenges.

SQPA reviewers gave relatively standard suggestions to focus on the weakest areas from the model. Use of divisional data was carefully limited to minimize any impression that the assessments were audits.

Over 100 SQPA assessments were done. They played an important role in educating HP managers in basic software issues. They also helped motivate improvements in some organizations. Since 1991 HP has replaced SQPAs with a variety of methods, since other assessments seemed to have better potential for divisional follow-through. For example, we have used assessments focused on specific processes, CMM assessments, and QMS assessments.

Quality Maturity System (QMS)

HP has used a proprietary business-assessment process called QMS since 1988. Its objective is to "help build stronger and more competitive organizations through dedication to customers, continuous improvement, and the application of sound process management practices." [14] A team of two reviewers uses a combination of education and review processes that usually take 2 1/2 days in a division. Review questions are organized into the five areas shown in Figure 2-4.

Reviewers give results in scores against a five-point scale where 0 corresponds to no knowledge (in other words, ad hoc) in an area, and 5 means "world class." The scale allows an organization to track its progress over time and compare itself to other HP divisions. Reviewers also give improvement recommendations. QMS is not centered on software, but it is applied in software-focused organizations and can be used as a motivator for software process improvement.

Although the assessment questions and approach are based on good Total Quality Management (TQM) practices and intended to help guide a division to use best practices, the first phase of QMS's application also had an audit flavor. Initially, HP set a companywide goal for all divisions to reach a 3.5 level by 1994.

After the first four years of use, HP decided that it would strengthen TQM faster by eliminating the numeric companywide goal and by shifting the QMS categories and focus to better align with a basic model for running a business. The feeling was that an organization has limited time to spend.

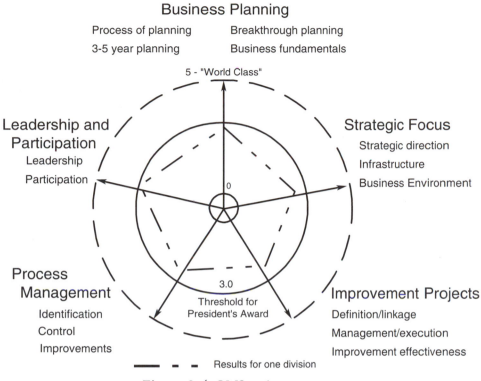

Figure 2-4 QMS review areas

Its management team would find this new business focus more directly relevant, and they would be more likely to act on the recommendations and information given by the reviewers. Thus, the review process entered a second phase that today more heavily emphasizes business needs and the actions that are most likely to help the reviewed organization achieve its business objectives. Some reviews are done without scores if the local management team prefers that method. Since 1993, a new motivation to have a scored review has been the possibility of winning an HP President's Quality Award that requires a QMS score of 3.0 or more as an initial qualifier.

Malcolm Baldrige National Quality Award

The Baldrige Award was created in 1987 and is promoted by the U.S. Department of Commerce. Up to two organizations per year are given the award in each of the categories of manufacturing, service, and small firms. Its goal is to "promote quality awareness, understand the requirements for quality excellence, and share information about successful quality strategies and the benefits." [15] Figure 2-5 shows a diagram of its seven major criteria and their percentage weights. [16]

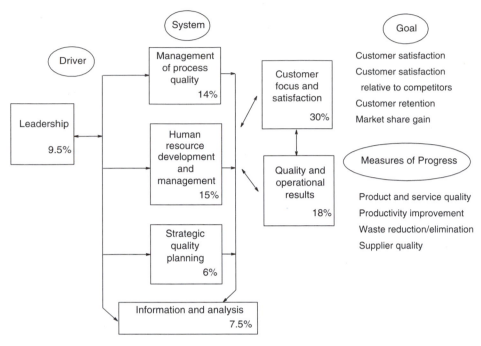

Figure 2-5 Baldrige Award criteria framework

The process is a third-party audit of quality and business practices done by judges from industry, academia, and consulting firms. Although its focus is not on software, it is included here because it emphasizes the influence of senior executive leadership in driving TQM, and it represents somewhat of a boundary case in terms of management aggressiveness. As with QMS, a high level of support can be a strong motivator for software process improvements as part of any quality program.

The audit requires a written application. If a company qualifies, this is followed by interviews with a team of examiners that take several days or more. The examiners look for both coverage of all the major categories and deployment of these qualities throughout the organization. Since it is a competition, the commitment to winning the award must be high and the cost to participate seriously will be large. An article by David Garvin describes "both Xerox, a 1989 winner, and Corning, a 1989 finalist, admit to having spent, respectively, $800,000 and 14,000 labor hours preparing applications and readying employees for site visits by Baldrige examiners," although it goes on to suggest that such expenses are not necessary: "Globe Metallurgical and Milliken & Co., 1988 and 1989 Baldrige winners spent far less on the application process." [17]

CHOOSING AN ASSESSMENT

The preceding five assessments show a range of some excellent available processes you can use. All of them have three purposes in common:

- They give a reference point of current strengths and opportunities.
- They motivate people to change.
- They model how to think about improvements.

Table 2-1 summarizes some of their attributes. The table certainly isn't exhaustive. For example, there is a European version of a CMM-extended assessment called Bootstrap. Another audit is the Japanese Deming Prize. ISO representatives are currently developing an assessment process, called SPICE, that may become important.

You can change some of the table's suggested strengths and weaknesses by adapting any of the processes. They all have various degrees of rigor in their "official" forms. The simplest variation is a self-assessment done by one or more people. Some assessments also have "intermediate" versions. For example, HP helped to create an "Instant Profile" approach to the CMM. [18] It is a short version of the more formal SEI assessment. You can also control costs and emphases by choosing to do an assessment using internal people rather than external ones. You can also adapt auditlike processes to be merely assessments if you care more about the change process than meeting the numeric criteria.

Another difference between the first three rows of the table and the last two is the one of assessing software only versus assessing your business quality practices. This difference is just one of the more obvious differences of scope and area emphasis.

So many differences are enough to make your head spin. How do you narrow the choices? Table 2-1 can help. Looking at when each assessment method is most effective (column 3) will give you a good sense for its potential use in your organization. The strengths and weaknesses add useful information. Note that many of the weaknesses can apply to other assessments besides the ones they are listed by, depending on how the assessment is run. The following questions will also help.

What makes you want to change? All changes are motivated by what is happening in your environment that makes someone uncomfortable. Such motivations can range all the way from two people having trouble working together up to a major threat in your business's market. So, first you need to identify your business need for change.

Who wants the changes to happen and how much do they want them? This question is the first test for organizational commitment to change. Sponsorship is a fundamental prerequisite for change or even for the type of

Table 2-1 Comparison of various assessments' potential to motivate and model software improvements

Assessment	What It does	When Most Effective	Strengths	Weaknesses
ISO9001 (with ISO9000-3)	Third-party audit against an international standard; seeks evidence of quality management and assurance	When required to sell products in specific markets; as a way of assuring definition of a consistent quality process	Gives buyers higher confidence in suppliers	Can encourage compliance with "letter of the law" rather than the "spirit"
CMM	Third-party or internal assessment of software processes against a maturity model	When an independent model will help open talks among groups who need to agree on a common approach; when used to guide choices, not judge organization	Helps break down artificial boundaries; generates widespread awareness and motivation; industry support and understanding	May be seen as bureaucratic; amount of time to do assessment can create resistance to even more time to do improvements
SQPA	Third-party assessment of software quality and business practices against a functional model	Small, young or dynamic organization; strong known organizational sponsor and champion(s)	Good mix of involving many people while finishing quickly to begin improvements; allows numeric benchmarks	No structured follow-through from assessors; answers somewhat "one size fits all"
QMS	Third-party assessment of quality and business practices against a business model	When audit aspects are minimized; organization isn't too new; strong management belief in quality	Integrates business and quality focus; emphasis on improvement plans and measuring improvements	Can be demotivating if management only pays lip service to process or quality/customer satisfaction
Baldrige Award	Third-party audit of quality and business practices against a weighted criteria model	Mature organization with excellent practices resisting complacency or wanting award as marketing advantage	Helps reinforce organization's quality vision and commitment; marketing benefit, if won	Can be demotivating if potential for achieving is too remote

assessment you use to trigger change.

What is the scope of needed changes? Most changes can be phased in some-how, but it is still desirable to match your assessment choice so that expectations for change are well and widely set. The scope includes how much of an organization will be affected and how complex the changes are.

How ready is your organization for change? If your organization has been successful when making past improvements, then an assessment that motivates a lot of people may not be necessary. If there is a track record of starting improvements and moving on to something else before they're done, then people will need stronger convincing that they should get excited and involved.

Make yourself a simple table of choices like the case in Figure 2-6. Note your evaluations or simply circle choices as in the figure. What do they tell you? How does this information match the alternatives in Table 2-1? In the example shown, the high-level support (high sponsorship) and almost strategic business need (prerequisite for long term) suggest that whatever assessment you choose doesn't need to motivate the management team as much as the "troops" (low organizational readiness).

A good strategy to improve low organizational readiness is to involve a large number of people involved at the assessment stage. Then they see that management is seriously investing and they also feel they might have some influence over what happens. It helps if you use a model that is close to their immediate concerns, which, in this case, is getting software products out. QMS and Baldrige are both more business related. ISO 9001 isn't designed to build engineering enthusiasm. Both the CMM and SQPA fit this case better. Whether either is ideal here or not, these questions have helped you better understand some of the things you need to consider. Keep your process for choosing an assessment simple. Be prepared either to strengthen visible sponsorship or to change models if early reactions suggest that the one you are using won't motivate people to change.

Figure 2-6 Examples of assessment choices

	Question to ask	"Low"	"Medium"	"High"
Business need	Why do you want to change things?	Short-term need	Prequisite for long term	Long-term need
Sponsorship	Who wants the changes to happen and how much do they want them?	Project teams	Middle management	High-level management
Scope	What is the scope of needed changes?	Small	Medium	Large
Organizational readiness	How ready is your organization for change?	Uncertain	Confident	Aggessive

All assessments encapsulate someone's model of an ideal process. Does the model you are considering match your organization's idea of an ideal process that produces exceptional products for your customers? Be sure that the model suggested by the assessment you choose is consistent with your business culture and that it is not so far away from your current practices that your people will still believe its proposed improvements possible. Use your choice to put *your* stake into the ground. Remember that your foremost concern in choosing is that it motivate your organization to change.

WHAT MAKES AN ASSESSMENT SUCCESSFUL?

All assessments are a means to an end. In spiral model terms, that end is "Do." As such, they can only be considered a success if we achieve the desired end. The assessments discussed here are all designed for an endpoint of successful process improvements. One way to learn about what these look like is to "assess" past failures.

From the SEI's experience with hundreds of CMM-based assessments, Bill Curtis gives eight reasons for failed software process improvements. [19]

- Executive disinterest
- Assess before improvement group is in place
- Mismatched findings (assessment scope driven by political boundaries rather than business needs)
- Assess everyone immediately (focus on assessment instead of improvement program)
- Ill-trained assessors
- Validate next level (success tied to CMM level rather than completing needed improvements)
- Over-rigidity with CMM (emphasis on yes/no with explicit practices rather than needed improvements)
- No action planning for accomplishing improvements

The most effective way for you to use an assessment process to avoid these roadblocks is to

- secure organizational commitment to well-defined improvements with measurable goals,
- clearly assign responsibilities for achieving the goals, and
- carefully define plans that are linked to business needs and that include ways to see and sustain measurable progress.

The success of any assessment is a function of its goals and whether people share those goals widely. You must clearly differentiate what the goals for your assessment are from the goals of later expected improvements. When you do that, you will be able to scope the assessment more appropriately to motivate, model, and plan to meet your organization's needs.

CONCLUSION _____

Assessments give us a different view of Deming's plan/do/check/act (PDCA). They suggest you start with "check," instead of "plan." The reality is that few software development organizations operate in the continuous process improvement loop required by PDCA. An assessment is a way of jump-starting PDCA. Perhaps we should relabel the process CAPD for software.

As the opening Monopoly story showed, the word "assess" can have positive or negative associations. The same is true for different types of assessments and the ways they are applied. They will strongly affect how well a process-improvement program may start and its chances for success. This is the message you must internalize.

Decide how much support there might be for an assessment and turn that support into an appropriately formal or informal one. The more time and effort everyone is willing to spend, the more accurate the results will be and the greater the commitment to change. Be careful not to confuse the completion of an assessment with an actual process improvement. It can be an important input to a process-improvement plan, though, so use your results to set measurable goals for specific, targeted improvements.

Assessments are done in many ways for many reasons. The most important aspect of a process-improvement assessment is your motivation for process improvement. The clearer your goal, the stronger your need, and the wider your support for change, the more likely that your assessment will provide a strong start for a series of improvements that will help keep your business healthy. There are some excellent available assessment processes to select from. Decide which of these best fits your needs and use it to put *your* stake into the ground.

BIBLIOGRAPHY

1. Cassafer, D., "Implementing KAIZEN (Continuous Improvement) through Retrospectives," *HP 1992 Software Engineering Productivity Conference Proceedings*, (Aug. 1992), pp. 13-21. (Not available outside HP.)
2. *ISO 9001, Quality Systems - Model for Quality Assurance in Design/Development, Production, Installation, and Servicing*, Int'l Organization for Standardization, Geneva, 1987.
3. *ISO 9000-3, Guidelines for the Application of ISO 9001 to the Development, Supply, and Maintenance of Software*, Int'l Organization for Standardization, Geneva, (June 1, 1991). *Figure 2-1 is taken from ISO 9000-3:1994 Table of Contents and is reproduced with the permission of the International Organization for Standardization, ISO. This standard can be obtained from any ISO member or from the ISO Central Secretariat, Case postale 56,1211 Geneva 20, Switzerland. Copyright remains with ISO.*
4. Lofgren, G., "Quality System Registration," *Quality Progress*, (May 1991), pp. 35-37.

5. Paulk, M., C. Weber, B. Curtis, and M. Chrissis, *The Capability Maturity Model: Guidelines for Improving the Software Process*, Reading, MA: Addison-Wesley, 1995, p. 5, 33.
6. Curtis, B., and M. Paulk, "Creating a Software Process Improvement Program," *Information and Software Technology*, Vol.35, No.6-7, (June-July 1993), pp.381-386.
7. Bollinger, T., and C. McGowan, "A Critical Look at Software Capability Evaluations," *IEEE Software*, (July 1991), pp. 25-41.
8. Curtis, B., and J. Statz, "Building the Cost-Benefit Case for Software Process Improvement," TeraQuest Metrics, Inc., Austin, Texas, 1995.
9. Herbsleb, J., A. Carleton, J. Rozum, J. Siegel, and D. Zubrow, "Benefits of CMM-Based Software Process Improvement: Initial Results," *Technical Report, CMU/SEI-94-TR-13*, (Aug. 1994).
10. Lawlis, P., R. Flowe, and J. Thordahl, "A Correlational Study of the CMM and Software Development Performance," *Crosstalk*, (Sept. 1995), pp. 21-25.
11. Dion, R., "Process Improvement and the Corporate Balance Sheet," *IEEE Software*, (July 1993), pp. 28-35.
12. Humphrey, W., T. Snyder, and R. Willis, "Software Process Improvement at Hughes Aircraft," *IEEE Software*, (July 1991), pp.11-23.
13. Zimmer, B., "A Case Study in Process Improvement," *Profile: Software Quality and Productivity at Hewlett-Packard*, (Dec. 1990). (Not available outside HP.)
14. *Quality Maturity System Review Process Handbook*, Hewlett-Packard Part No. 5959-1663, Sept. 1994, p. 3. (Not available outside HP.)
15. National Institute of Standards and Technology, *1993 Application Guidelines for the Malcolm Baldrige National Quality Award*, Washington DC: U.S. Dept. of Commerce, 1993.
16. Nakhai, B., and J. Neves, "The Deming, Baldrige, and European Quality Awards," *Quality Progress*, (April 1994), pp. 33-37.
17. *The quote included in this chapter is reprinted by permission of Harvard Business Review.* David A. Garvin, "How the Baldrige Award Really Works," *Harvard Business Review*, (November-December 1991), pp. 80-93. *Copyright ©1991 by the President and Fellows of Harvard College; all rights reserved.*
18. Whitney, R., E. Nawrocki, W. Hayes, and J. Siegel, "Interim Profile Development and Trial of a Method to Rapidly Measure Software Engineering Maturity Status," *Technical Report CMU/SEI-94-TR-4*, Pittsburgh: Carnegie-Mellon Univ., (March 1994).
19. Curtis, B., "A Mature Look at Maturity Assessment," *Conference on the Application of Software Measurement 1995*, Orlando, FL, (Nov. 1995).

3

Planning for Software Core Competence

New businesses are started daily. Their survival rate is not impressive, though. Even for the ones that prosper initially, there is often a fatal transition period after their first product success. What enables businesses to survive such transitions and prosper? Let's look at an example.

In the 1960s, customers increasingly wanted multiple instruments to function more easily and powerfully together. Seeing this as an opportunity, Hewlett-Packard set out to build its first computer. At the time, this wasn't visualized as building an entirely new business. It was seen as expanding existing businesses into instrument automation. [1] HP's existing know-how in building highly reliable instruments resulted in a computer that worked as reliably in poor physical environments as instruments did. These characteristics satisfied the needs of many customers far beyond the original instrument community. A recent article has labelled such powerful know-how a "core competence." [2] HP's definition is:

> A core competence is the collective know-how of an organization that gives it a competitive advantage. This know-how is a result of learning that is driven by business strategy and built through a process of continuous improvement and enhancement that may span a decade or longer.

For several years, we have explicitly identified existing and desired core competencies with a variety of HP divisions, and we have found that this new way of looking at business needs is very powerful. By thinking about those needs strategically, it is easier for managers to directly tie improvement objectives to business needs. Such objectives are compelling and more likely to sustain management commitment than ones justified solely around some methodology or technology that is poorly understood by decision-making managers.

Figure 3-1 is a model for how business and core-competence strategies parallel and complement each other. It particularly depicts software core competence. The figure's left side focuses on business strategy, which defines what you want to achieve. The figure's right side focuses on the core competencies required to achieve your business strategy. These are the processes, skills, technologies, and know-how that will make *your* business strategy a winner.

Figure 3-1 Core-competence framework
(highest level, software emphasis)

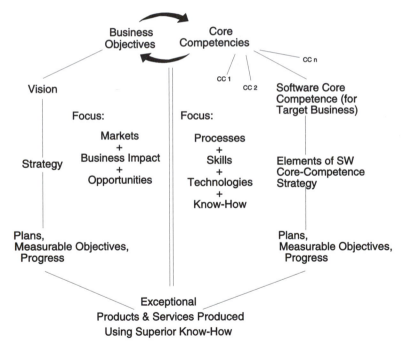

The opening story about HP's entry into computing shows how our core competence for producing highly reliable instruments led to significant new markets. It also spawned a core competence in technical computation systems. Just as customer needs pushed HP to this new core competence, meeting new customer needs with software is having an increasing influence on virtually every HP business today. What software abilities will form a sustainable basis for your organization's future business, and how can you be sure you develop those abilities before competitors?

Chapter 2 discussed various recent attempts to classify and evaluate software practices to identify strengths and weaknesses. Each of these approaches raises awareness of existing methods, both good and poor. Unfortunately, some assessments haven't successfully shown the necessary links between software practices and the long-term abilities needed for business success in a persuasive enough form. The key message of this chapter is that *core-competence planning is just as important as business planning in setting the long-term strategy of an organization.* The key results of the core-competence planning process are a set of clearly stated goals and action plans with clear links to business needs. More than any other method or process in the book, you will need help from your organization's management team to create these.

The good news is that our experience with core-competence planning says they will be eager to help create these goals and action plans. Even if your immediate improvement doesn't require a full plan like one created from the process described here, I encourage you to think through what your organization's plan would look like and plant ideas with your management to consider doing one.

CREATING A SOFTWARE CORE-COMPETENCE PLAN

Available planning time is precious. When you create a plan for core competence, you must effectively use materials and discussions already created for other planning processes. The most important source in HP is the 10-step business plan. [3] While other organization's business plans may differ in form, they will generally contain similar content. Figure 3-2 shows outlines for both a core-competence plan and HP's 10-step business plan. The many arrows from the business plan suggest that many parts of a core-competence plan can be leveraged from existing business plans. This section defines the core-competence terms used in Figure 3-2 and describes how to create a plan for your organization.

The primary difference between a business plan and a core-competence plan is focus. A core-competence plan focuses on processes, skills, technologies, and know-how. A business plan focuses on products and markets. The central theme for both derives from the business vision, purpose, and direction. Like an organization's business plan, creation of a core-competence plan must be driven by high-level management. While much of the content may be spearheaded by key leaders and chief technical contributors, final decisions and motivation must come from a high-level manager.

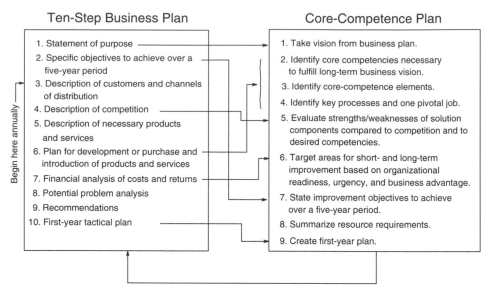

Figure 3-2 Relationships between business and core-competence plans

Management Leadership: Preplanning

i. Enlist a high-level manager to demonstrate ownership of the plan. While they can assign responsibility for producing a plan to their key people, they must own it. They must stay closely involved to provide leadership and consistency to their long-term business vision. Emphasize that the purpose of the plan is to *ensure that critical processes, skills, and technologies survive and evolve despite future organizational growth and change.*

Get them to decide which steps require their direct participation. It is most important for them to be directly involved in core-competence steps 1–3 shown in Figure 3-2. They should strongly consider at least some involvement in steps 4–6, and they can probably delegate steps 7–9, subject to their review.

ii. Work with them to set a clear objective for doing the plan. For example, "gain agreement by July 30 to a core-competence plan that will define, guide, and measure evolution in our key processes, skills, and know-how in order to accomplish our business vision and objectives."

iii. Agree on the scope of the planning activity. Include both the length of the document expected and the amount of time it should take to create. Like a business plan, a core-competence plan is a way to show direction and achieve consensus. Take the time necessary to do it well. Also be sure to fit the creation and updating of a core-competence plan into the strategic part of your yearly business-planning cycle. If you try to create a plan simultaneously with yearly financial targeting or heavy tactical planning pressures, it will be difficult to get the management attention necessary for a good plan.

Experiences with business plans suggest that:

- If your organization is new and its business plan is fresh in people's minds, there may be fewer people involved. Consensus may be easier than in a mature organization. On the other hand, the idea of core competence is likely to be less mature. It will not necessarily be well understood, yet. Your plan should be 5 to 10 pages long, and it should take less than a month to do.
- If your organization is mature, its business plan may be out-of-date. Remember, the business plan comes first. If necessary, get the management team to update the business plan. You also will face more complicated people issues. Your core-competence plan will probably be 10 to 20 pages long, and it will likely take you 1 to 3 months to do.

The Nine Steps of a Core-Competence Plan

The process for doing these nine steps varies with different businesses and needs. While the steps are described sequentially here, some will probably be done in parallel or iteratively. You also will probably revisit some steps after doing later ones. The order below is suggested for your *written plan.*

1. *Restate vision taken from business plan.* Make sure the planning team knows the vision and are excited by it. A vision of the future that is shared among the people of an organization is a powerful strategic component. It is a key to long-term survival. A good vision is exciting, is easy to visualize and remember, and is something that people in an organization will naturally use in their daily communications. The first section in HP's 10-step business plans also includes discussions of a value proposition and the basis for sustainable competitive advantage (derived during value-chain analysis).

- Copy your organization's vision statement from your business plan.
- Restate any parts of the value proposition that you expect to expand upon in later core-competence plan sections.
- Summarize your organization's basis for sustainable competitive advantage from your business plan. The basis for competitive advantage is strategically important activities that you do better than your competitors.
- List any other documents besides the business plan that your core-competence plan used as valuable sources.

- State who this plan is written for and how it will be used.

The first section in a core-competence plan provides a framework for the reader to understand the reason for the plan and the thinking that went into its creation. The staff discussion of this first part serves the valuable purpose of starting participants out with a common frame of reference—the business plan.

2. *Identify the core competencies necessary to fulfill your long-term business vision.* Use the definition from the start of this chapter. Core competencies by themselves are difficult to define precisely. For example, the Prahalad and Hamel article calls out fine optics, precision mechanics, and microelectronics as Canon's business core competencies. [2] A software core competence might be the ability to create software for real-time systems or the ability to create distributed object-oriented software. You will usually find that core competencies represent some aspect of an organization's ability. It may be helpful to separate these competencies into "fundamental" (necessary for business survival) and "leadership" or "core" (those that are long-term, key organizational differentiators).

- Define your organization's business core competencies (existing and desired). A core competence must satisfy *all* the following tests. It helps to start each core competence with "the ability to . . ."
  - It represents collective know-how.
  - It provides potential access to a wide variety of markets. [2]
  - It will make a significant contribution to the perceived customer benefits of the end product. [2]
  - It is difficult for competitors to imitate. [2]
  - It contributes to realizing the business vision and objectives.
- Apply the following exclusion tests. [4] You should *not* be able to call your core competencies any of these. If you can, ask "What is the core competence that gave me this (asset, attribute, . . .)?"
  - Asset (for example, installed base, a body of software)
  - Attribute (for example, a bold vision, your company culture)
  - Characteristic (for example, user-friendly products)
  - Organizational function (for example, great engineering, top marketing)
  - Product (for example, notebook computer, laser printer)
  - Business (for example, market share, profitability)

Be careful not to create an exhaustive list of everything you want to do. There should be *no more than four or five competencies* here, and it is ok if there are only a couple. You may find it easier to brainstorm step 3 below before you pick your core competencies. If you do step 3 first, then your challenge is to aggregate the core-competence elements into a small number of core competencies. Be sure to do the exclusion tests in either case.

3. *For each core competence, refine your core competence definition by adding principal strategic elements.* For a multiyear plan, it makes sense to refine each core competence into meaningful chunks. Figure 3-3 shows a model that helps you to do this. It also shows the first of three examples that fit the model. This first example is for an HP division that produces electronic instruments. It's interesting to note how the core competence of creating software for real-time systems continues to build on the core competence described earlier of technical computation systems. Here we start to see a more complete picture of what gives a core competence hard-to-reproduce know-how. The figure also introduces the idea of a core-competence element. An element is the collective know-how of a part of an organization, or part of the collective know-how of the entire organization.

Figure 3-3 The core-competence structure (example for a division that produces electronic instruments)

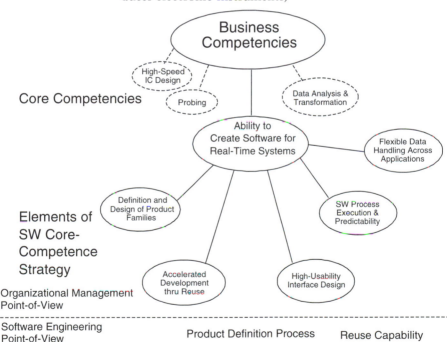

Solution Components - Combinations of These and Others Produce CC Elements	Product Definition Process	Reuse Capability
	SW Front-End Process	SCM Foundation
	Design Process	Inspections
	Architecture Capability	Process Definition
	Defect Tracking	Process Architecture

While this example suggests that the model is hierarchical, some HP divisions have created networked models. These have multiple business competencies linked to some specific software core competence. Other variations have linked individual elements upward to multiple core competencies. The model is thus a tool. *Use it to establish common language, shared values, and the scope of your plan.*

- Isolate from each core competence a small number of core-competence elements. There should be no more than 25–30 elements across all your existing and desired business core competencies. Do not let solution-specific ideas influence the choice of elements too much. If you do, you may later find that your competition was easily able to duplicate your results. For example, installing a defect-tracking system may be part of a core-competence element, but it cannot be an entire element. It could easily be a key part of a strategy to achieve software process execution and predictability (from Figure 3-3), though.
- Define each element carefully. Too general a definition will be heard as "motherhood and apple pie." A good definition will be specific enough that people gain a common understanding. An example is this definition: *Software process execution and predictability - A well-defined, ISO-compliant process definition is understood and used by firmware (and hardware) developers. It includes documented project plans, product architecture and designs, inspections, defect tracking, SCM, and a standard release-decision process. As a result, all project teams view the creation of product firmware as a low-risk part of bringing powerful products to market.*
- After defining the elements, test the completeness and validity of each core competence. Ask "Will subcontracting work requiring this core-competence ability lead to the loss of a long-term competitive advantage?"

4. *Identify key processes and one pivotal job.* Now that you have defined your existing and desired core competencies, it is time to look at available processes, methods, tools, and training to fill your needs. It is likely that key technical people in your organization already have plans and suggestions.

- Write down one "pivotal job" that you want to keep in mind as you create your plan. An article by Irvin and Michaels defines a pivotal job as one whose execution determines whether customers think the company is good at what you want to excel in. [5] Think about how you might build an organization around optimizing the success of the pivotal job function. By thinking in these terms, you can shape your plans to include what kind of people you need, what skill development they need, and how the organization will support them. For example, many HP instrument divisions traditionally view project managers as pivotal. For them, a project manager leads a team from project proposal all the way through realization, transfer to manufacturing, and introduction to the marketplace. Customers see the results of this consistency of purpose in powerful, coherently evolving product lines.

Alternatively, HP's computer businesses today seldom view project managers as pivotal. For them, the program-management function is now more pivotal, because cross-project coordination issues have driven them to organize differently. If your core-competence plan covers several separate business areas, you may have to consider more than one pivotal job. If you do, ask yourself "Will an increased focus on just one pivotal job help you to organize your processes to better meet your customer's needs?"

- Brainstorm a list of key processes (existing and desired).
- Combine and collapse your core-competence element list from step 3 and your brainstormed key process list into no more than 30 items. Enter them into the first two columns of a table like the one shown in Table 3-1. You may decide that some of your earlier core-competence elements should be solution components for items from your key-process list. Most key processes are solution-component candidates, though. A solution component can be a process, skill, technology, or some combination of them. Table 3-1 is for a different organization than the Figure 3-3 example. This example is for an organization that produces software systems that integrate software packages and applications.

5. Evaluate strengths and weaknesses of solution components compared to competition and to existing and desired competencies.

- For each core-competence element in your table, enter your assessment relative to your competitors. It also may be useful to enter similar assessments of the solution components. To avoid overanalyzing, use a simple --, -, 0, +, + + scale with "+" meaning better or higher. To optimize table readability, assume that your competitors are at "0" in each case. Note that not all entries are given in the example. You won't always know competitor's competencies to the same extent as you know your own.

Table 3-1 Competitive analysis of core-competence elements (partial example for a division that produces software systems that integrate software packages and applications)

Core-Competence Elements	Solution Components	Your Competence Relative to Competition	Business Advantage (Improvement Needed)	Organizational Readiness	Urgency	Business Advantage	Priority
Quality control (have)	Quality planning	++	Maintain quality competitive advantage				
	Defect tracking	++					
	Inspections	++	(Inspect all specifications and designs)	+	+	+	1
	Reliability modeling	+	(Tune model to different applications)	0	-	0	3
	Regression testing	0	(Reduce time to do)				
Process execution and predicability (needed)	Process definition	-	Shorter, more predictable time to market				
	Project planning	-	(ISO certify)	+	++	0	2
	Product arch./design		(Create recommended model, require, review)	0	++	++	1
	Defect tracking	++	(Create better design doc./update process)	+	++	+	1
	Failure analysis	+	(Assign ownership for acting on results)	+	0	+	2
	Inspections	+	(Inspect all specifications and designs)	+	+	+	1
	SCM	0	(Upgrade to supported model)	-	-	0	3
	Release process	-	(Document and standardize)	-	0	+	2
Product enhancing, updates, and delivery (needed)	Defect tracking	++	Superior ability to "walk in customer's shoes"				
	SCM	0	(Upgrade to supported model)	-	-	0	3
	On-line support	--	(Use full response-center resources)	-	0	++	2
	Customer feedback capture	-	(Create portfolio of surveys and customer contact report forms)	+	+	++	1
	Installation automation		(Eliminate all need for handholding; minimize installation instruction complexity)	++	0	+	2

- In addition to the table, state the sources for your competitive assessments. This is important because you should reevaluate your competitive position every year, and you need to leverage from previous years' work. Some potential sources of information include section 4 of your business plan, trade journal product assessments, technical articles written by your competition's staff, personnel who used to work for your competitors, studies done by consultants, and your direct evaluation of competitors' products.

6. *Target areas for short- and long-term improvement, based on organizational readiness, urgency, and business advantage.* Organizational readiness reflects your assessment of your people's ability to adapt to a given change, or the human element. Urgency is your management team's short-term assessment of each solution component. It will particularly reflect areas where you are playing catch-up or areas where your competitors are rapidly gaining on you. Business advantage is your long-term assessment of the gain you expect compared to your competition. There is a delicate balance among these. You need to decide which should drive your priorities. Continue to complete your version of Table 3-1 for all the following steps.

- Briefly define what improvements are needed. How will they improve business results? How will they help people doing pivotal-job functions?
- Discuss the organizational readiness for various solution components with key staff. This is probably best done before you analyze the urgency or the business advantages. The objective of this discussion is to assess organizational enthusiasm for some changes versus potential resistance. Continue using a simple - -, -, 0, +, + + scale.
- Discuss and gain consensus on the urgency of improvements.
- Discuss and gain consensus on the business advantage of improvements. Think in terms of both improved product competitiveness and cost savings.
- Decide your priorities. Use a simple 1,2,3 scale with 1 being highest.
- Write down the long-term infrastructure you need to support people in pivotal jobs and to sustain these processes *(be sure to include existing strengths)*.
- Take a step back and look at the big picture of overall core competence again. Will doing the top-priority items move you quickly toward your business goals and vision? Are any major pieces missing?

7. *State improvement objectives to achieve over a five-year period.* All the preceding steps are designed to efficiently move you toward the best decisions neces-

sary to achieve and sustain core competence. Most of the work done in the first six steps will not significantly change in later core-competence planning updates. Steps 7 through 9 are the all-important execution plans.

- Define your improvement goals. For example, *Transform customer understanding into a superior, sustainable competitive advantage* (for the third Table 3-1 core-competence element).
- State yearly, clear, measurable objectives for each goal. (The next section has a detailed discussion of measurements.) For example, *Design and implement a portfolio of customer-contact report forms that are used by product management, response center, support, field service, and the lab. Process performance measure (PPM) - number of forms turned in by different areas (set targets for the next three years). Improve customer use of response center. PPM - number and percentage of field issues handled by response center versus factory (set targets for the next five years). Reevaluate core-competence status at the end of the second year.* In HP, these objectives should move directly into Hoshin plans for each appropriate year. Assign appropriate responsibility when they do. (Hoshin planning is an annual HP business planning process. [6] The plans have two focuses. The first focus is to set breakthrough objectives to significantly improve business results. The second focus is to identify and measure key business processes—fundamentals—to achieve steady incremental improvements.)

These goals and objectives are the most important aspects of the execution part of the core-competence plan. They represent a transformation of the vision in step 1 into all the major pieces of how you expect to achieve the vision.

8. *Summarize resource requirements.* Create ballpark (+/- 33 percent) long-range planning estimates for resources. Don't overanalyze these requirements. You don't have a detailed design for how you will achieve your objectives yet, so you can't make very accurate estimates yet. This step is important because you record management staff assumptions that will greatly affect what is done when. You can view these assumptions as the first inputs into requirements setting and a request for an estimate to do the job.

9. *Create first-year plan.* In contrast to step 8, the first-year plan must be more accurate.

- Assign the responsibility for projects that will be worked on in the first year.
- Have managers for those projects create separate, detailed plans that include effort and time estimates, milestones, tactics, and so forth.

- Create a management-review process for the projects.
- Summarize the key points from these plans in the core-competence plan.

These are nine steps to create a core-competence plan. They are not rigid. They are a guide for creating a plan as quickly and efficiently as possible. They can be done sequentially, or some can be done in parallel. Like a good business plan, a good core-competence plan should be as brief as possible. It also must clearly signal direction and be flexible enough to survive management and organizational changes.

IMPLEMENTING THE CORE-COMPETENCE PLAN

Just as a high-level manager must own the business plan, there must be a high-level owner for the core-competence plan. For example, the Prahalad and Hamel article discusses how divisional managers at NEC "came together to identify next-generation competencies." [2] The software core-competence owner in HP will usually be an R&D manager. This is not a passive role. The owner must be committed enough to the plan to inspire and motivate others. The owner must be available to show unshakeable support, to make timely decisions, and to be accountable for success or failure.

Several other people or groups of people must be actively involved in the core-competence plan implementation.

- Your lab's key technical leaders must be involved in both planning and implementation stages.
- Sometimes there are also less obvious technical leaders. These "opinion leaders" were described in Chapter 1.
- There needs to be a group (probably cross-functional and part-time) that coordinates the work that must be done. The SEI calls such a group a "Software Engineering Process Group (SEPG)."
- Finally, we come to the doers. The project managers and technical people chosen to implement core-competence solution components give an important signal to the organization. Their assignments show your seriousness about achieving core competence. Top management's consistency in keeping them committed to their assignment in the face of emergencies and critical product releases gives a second important signal. A third signal is management's personal interest and enthusiasm in regular (quarterly) core-competence project reviews.

Measuring Progress Toward Core Competence

Core competence represents the attainment of an organizationwide ability. This will take time, and you need ways to gauge your progress. Figure 3-4 shows a model that will help you to understand what to measure and how those measurements relate to more familiar ones.

Figure 3-4 Measurement linkages between business and core-competence plans

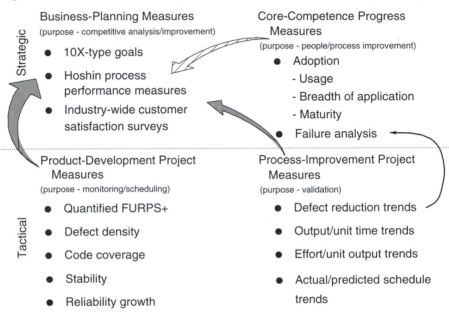

The upper-left quadrant shows three types of strategic high-level measures that HP uses. The first of these can be called "10X" measures. For example, HP's CEO set a goal in 1980 to improve our hardware quality by 10X. 10X goals were later set for software in 1986. HP's annual Hoshin planning process provides a second mechanism for setting high-level measures. Finally, each HP business uses industrywide customer satisfaction surveys to gauge direct customer reactions to products and services.

The lower-left quadrant shows examples of typical project measures. These include quantified FURPS (Functionality, Usability, Reliability, Performance, Supportability), defect density, code coverage, stability, and reliability growth models. [7] The arrow on the left side of Figure 3-4 shows that these metrics are also linked to strategic goals.

The lower-right quadrant shows process-improvement measures. These have been used to validate the results of process-improvement projects. They are typically tied to Hoshin or 10X goals and are focused on specific quality, cost, or schedule improvements. People who do revolutionary technological changes (for example, moving from traditional programming to the Ada language or to object-oriented programming) sometimes find these measures difficult to apply. The main problem in those cases is that the time constant for seeing a measurable return is long. The measures are still desirable in order to keep an organization focused on the reasons for improvement.

The upper-right quadrant shows two, high-level measures for measuring core-competence progress. The first of these is adoption. HP's Inspections Program has shown that metrics for training, usage, and adoption yield increasingly better indicators of progress toward final desired results—reduced time spent on rework, improved schedules, and so forth. These are soft links (represented by the striped arrow) back to business goals. Chapter 13 describes an HP adoption measure that includes the three components of usage, breadth of application, and maturity. Progress towards any core-competence solution component or element should be similarly measured.

The second core-competence progress measure is failure analysis. Failure analysis is a process for categorizing defect causes and using the information to target removal of costly or frequently occurring defects (this is discussed in detail in Chapter 11). By understanding your organization's defect patterns, you can see the results of improved organizational know-how as targeted defects are eliminated (represented by the arrow between the two right quadrants.). Depending on your business goals, later savings are then validated as improved quality, reduced time to market, higher productivity, and so forth.

A third major example illustrates the use of these measures. The core competencies for this example are shown in Figure 3-5. The business goal for this division might be to *optimize engineering effort to do defect repairs and minor enhancements*. Figure 3-5 suggests that a core competence in *maintaining software* is one essential ability to develop. (Chapter 8 also extends this example by showing a complete storyboard for a related process-improvement project.)

The core-competence plan would describe the strategy for gaining this core competence. Step 7 of that core-competence plan would state the objectives and the year-by-year goals to be sought. Assume that one of these might be: *Increase the effective usage of knowledge recovery know-how to reduce the division average time to fix defects by 75 percent by 1998 while keeping the average number of defects introduced at or below current averages*. Figure 3-6 summarizes a complete metric set for this abbreviated example.

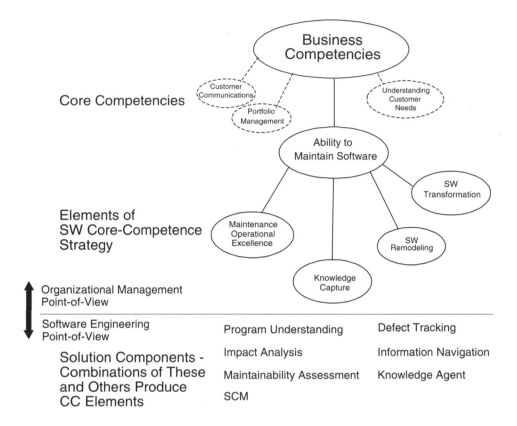

Figure 3-5 Core-competence in maintaining software (example for a division that maintains and enhances many software products)

Several important points can be drawn from this example. First, the business-planning (upper-left quadrant), product-development (lower-left quadrant), and process-improvement (lower-right quadrant) metrics are virtually identical. This represents an alignment of measures that is seldom totally achieved. Business metrics always include other financial measures that aren't shown here (like profit). Product-development metrics usually include other project-specific measures related to team dynamics or project risk. Process-improvement metrics are likely to require some additional environment-specific information to help ensure that other influencing effects are well understood.

The second point is that the core-competence metrics are truly different from the other metrics. Unless you make the effort to measure your progress in this way, you won't be able to see progress, and it is doubtful that you will get the results that we saw characterized in Chapter 1's spiral model.

Business Goal: Optimize engineering effort to do defect repairs and minor enhancements.

Strategic

Business-Planning Measures

Trend of average engineering time/defect by activity

Trend of number of defects introduced/total defects in a release

Trend of average time to respond to customer requests

Core-Competence Progress Measures

Adoption metric for each new technique or process change (e.g. program understanding)

Defect patterns before and after changes (e.g. reduced defects caused by incorrect program understanding)

Tactical

Product-Development Project Measures

Engineering time/defect by activity

Number of defects introduced while fixing defects and doing enhancements

Total defects per release

Time to respond to a customer request

Process-Improvement Project Measures

Before and after comparisons of:

- Engineering time/defect by activity
- Number of defects introduced while fixing defects and doing enhancements
- Total defects per release
- Time to respond to a customer request

Figure 3-6 Examples of business and core-competence metrics

Third, well-stated, business-planning metrics are very important. They are the anchor for all the metrics. If these are missing, progress will be weak and randomly directed. For this example, the Hoshin objective sets a quantified common target for product development, process improvements, and core-competence development.

It is both possible and desirable to measure progress toward core competence. It takes effort and time. Like measuring progress toward high-level business goals, though, the return will be well worth the investment. Remember that successfully implementing a core-competence plan requires

- clear responsibility for the plan,
- a mechanism for regularly updating the plan, and
- solidly integrated metrics for tracking progress and validating results.

The combination of these will help you to achieve long-term business success.

REMOVING BARRICADES THAT BLOCK THE ROAD TO CORE COMPETENCE

The road to core competence will not always be clear. Many of the barriers are ones that you have seen before, though. Table 3-2 groups them into planning and implementing. Instead of going into great detail, some possible actions are simply listed. The table is not all-inclusive. The assumption is that most barriers are not new. They almost always arise when you ask people to change. Only their context might be new.

Table 3-2 Actions for reducing barriers to the creation and use of core-competence plans

	Barriers	Possible Actions
Planning-Stage Barriers	Vision statement is missing or unclear.	Work with key staff to clarify and achieve organizational understanding.
	Strong competition is forcing heavy tactical emphasis.	Create prototype plan with small group in several one-day offsite meetings. Use to help make tactical decisions, and follow up six months later by creating better plan.
	Organization has little SW experience.	Hire experienced SW people. Use consultants to help create plan.
	Managers view new competence as foreign to their careers.	Don't back down on necessity of long-term changes. Describe a sequence of changes to minimize perceived career impacts.
Implementing-Stage Barriers	Customer emergencies threaten to pull key people away.	Keep key assignments in place to show the importance of core competence.
	Stagnant organization resists change.	Carefully plan pilot changes in respected organizational groups that are open to change.
	Your management changes.	Work with new management to understand their views and to gradually create their understanding of the plan.
	Engineers view new competence as foreign to their careers.	Don't try to move too fast. Use training to sell staff on long-term value and business situations as a point to start changes.

CONCLUSION

All organizations are driven to change and renew themselves by evolving business conditions. A company's survival depends on its ability to adapt to changing markets quickly, and the essence of survival is to be prepared. This is why you do strategic planning. Just as a good business plan optimizes product success, a good core-competence plan optimizes your long-term organizational know-how. Together, these plans work to give you long-term business and market leadership.

A core-competence plan is a powerful management tool that looks ahead in four essential ways.

- It spells out *strategic collective know-how* that is key to your organization's survival and evolution.
- It explicitly evaluates your strategic *competitive advantage* based on this know-how.
- It defines how your organization's know-how *links to your business strategy*.
- It provides a compelling *basis for long-term, continuous process improvement.*

The exciting things this provides for your process-improvement proposals and initiatives are hope and enthusiasm. Whether you can get your organization to make a complete transition to preparing a core-competence plan initially or you just get them to better think in these terms, you will discover that your improvement goals will be clearer, more exciting, and more likely to be achieved. This will definitely increase your probability of success, and it may play a significant role in helping your organization to survive and prosper when critical market transitions like the ones discussed at the start of this chapter occur.

BIBLIOGRAPHY

1. *Inventions of Opportunity: Matching Technology with Market Needs*, Selections from the pages of the HP Journal/Introduction by William R. Hewlett, Palo Alto, CA: Hewlett-Packard Co., 1983, p. xii.
2. Prahalad, C., and G. Hamel, "The Core Competence of the Corporation," *Harvard Business Review*, (May-June 1990), pp. 79-91.
3. *Business Planning for Competitive Advantage: The Ten-Step Approach*, Hewlett-Packard Corporate Development, Part Number 5955-4877, July, 1990. (Not available outside HP.)
4. "Core Competence," Competitive Manufacturing Institute Executive Development Center, Santa Clara University, Roberts Information Services, 1993.
5. Irvin, R.,and E. Michaels, "Core Skills: Doing the Right Things Right," *McKinsey Quarterly*, (Summer 1989), pp. 4-19.
6. Feurer, R., K. Chaharbaghi, and J. Wargin, "Analysis of Strategy Formulation and Implementation at Hewlett-Packard," *Management Decision*, Vol. 33 No. 10, (1995), pp. 4-16.
7. Grady, R., *Practical Software Metrics for Project Management and Process Improvement*, Englewood Cliffs, N. J.: Prentice-Hall, Inc., 1992, pp. 130, 180-181, 190-194.

4

An Investment Model for Software Process ══ *Improvement* ══

What do you think of when you hear the word "investment?" Some of us think of our house or a college fund or the stock market. Over the years, it seems that the increasing number of alternatives has made investing complicated. After the stock market crash of 1929, people became conservative. Savings accounts, a house, and savings bonds were the main choices. Then the stock market became attractive again, followed by mutual funds, a booming real estate market, and most recently, foreign markets.

Few of us have the time to understand these alternatives well. The same is true in business. Markets and technologies change, and it's hard to keep up. One business challenge today is an increasing dependence on software, both in product creation and in business infrastructures. Senior-level managers haven't had time to develop a context within which to understand the nature of this dependence or how to better manage to take advantage of it. None of the manufacturing, financial, marketing, or hardware development models seem to work here. It would be useful to have a management model for understanding software aspects better. This would complement the strategic thinking that a core-competence plan gives.

A high-level software management model would provide both intuitive understanding of problems and direction for how investments should be made in improvements. Then, depending on how much money and resources you can invest, you could better understand whether 5, 10, or 50 percent improvements are feasible for your organization and how long they might take. Once you have a model, it will help you to better decide which potential projects to select, either from your core-competence framework or from other improvements that become opportunistically available.

DESCRIPTION OF A SOFTWARE MANAGEMENT COST MODEL

All models simulate reality. Their accuracy depends on the amount of experience on which they are based, the detail they represent, the consistency and stability of the modeled process, and the modeler's skill. We want a high-level model here, so we will sacrifice detail for clarity. We plan to use it to educate managers and to make rough process-improvement estimates. Thus, even if our software processes are unstable, a model will still provide high-level understanding. The basis for the example model is measured HP data and other published results. Let's look at the major components of the model first.

New Development Components of the Model

The simplest view of software costs is that there are two categories: new development and maintenance. New development costs can be further separated into various tasks. The way used here is similar to other engineering fields: requirements/specifications, design, implementation, and test. These tasks are reasonably well defined and have been measured for various projects.

Figure 4-1 shows such data from 132 Hewlett-Packard software projects. [1] The data is further separated into three categories that are generally accepted in HP: firmware, systems, and applications software. Firmware is software that runs in ROM (Read Only Memory) or RAM (Random Access Memory) under control of a microprocessor. Systems software executes from the memory of one or more networked computers. Applications software operates on top of systems software in one or more computers to solve specific user problems.

For the purposes of a high-level model, we will ignore the variations among these three types and combine their data. The resulting development activity percentages are

- *requirements/specifications - 18%,*
- *design - 19%,*
- *implementation - 34%, and*
- *test - 29%.*

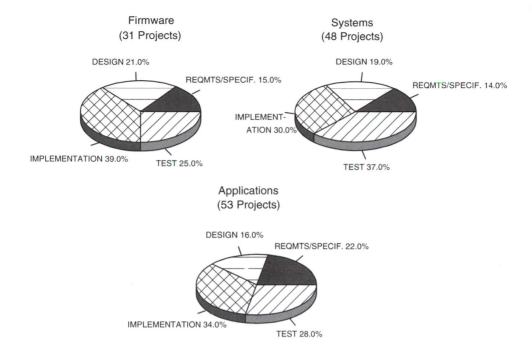

Firmware
(31 Projects)

DESIGN 21.0%

REQMTS/SPECIF. 15.0%

IMPLEMENTATION 39.0%

TEST 25.0%

Systems
(48 Projects)

DESIGN 19.0%

REQMTS/SPECIF. 14.0%

IMPLEMENT-
ATION 30.0%

TEST 37.0%

Applications
(53 Projects)

DESIGN 16.0%

REQMTS/SPECIF. 22.0%

IMPLEMENTATION 34.0%

TEST 28.0%

Figure 4-1 Percent engineering hours by phase

Maintenance Components of the Model

Maintenance is generally broken down into enhancing software (adaptive and perfective changes) and fixing software (corrective changes). These two major components of maintenance and their size compared with new development are different for different organizations. Figure 4-2 shows these from four industry studies. [2, 3, 4, 5]

Many respected sources have quoted higher ratios of maintenance to new development, so we can expect individual groups to vary. As with our new development assumptions, we will keep our model simple by ignoring variations caused by aspects such as types of business and organizational age. For the purposes of our model, we will also choose values that seem most reasonable for HP: new development—45%, enhancements—35%, defect fixing—20%.

Many of the same processes commonly used for maintenance are also used for new development. The major exception to this is termed "knowledge recovery" or "program understanding." This is the part of the job that takes place before a person can even start to fix a defect or create an enhancement. It is a problem that starts small after system release and con-

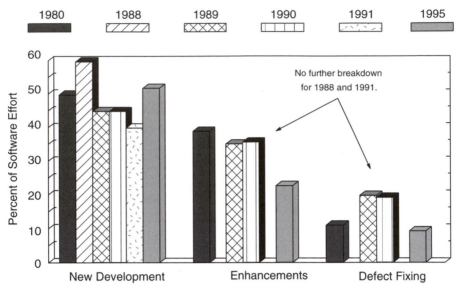

Figure 4-2 Software engineering resource workload (data for 1988-1991 copyright ©IEEE 1991; data for 1980 from ref. 2: B. Lientz/E. Swanson, SOFTWARE MAINTENANCE MANAGEMENT, (adapted from figures 3.5 and 5.2). ©1980 Addison-Wesley Publishing Company Inc. Reprinted by permission of Addison-Wesley Longman Inc.)

tinues to grow as changes are made and the rationale for early decisions is forgotten.*

Some studies have shown that knowledge recovery is 50 percent of maintenance costs. [6] This value is not as thoroughly researched as some of the others we will use, but it is believable, especially for aging systems.

For our high-level model then, we will combine these results into the components of maintenance.

- *Enhancements (35%) break down into 17.5% knowledge recovery and 17.5% that is treated as new development.*
- *Defect fixing (20%) breaks down into 10% knowledge recovery and another 10% rework that should be eliminated.*

Rework Components of the Model

The best opportunity for short-term software cost reduction today is to eliminate rework. Fixing defects consumes roughly 33 percent of new development today, [1] and we've already said that defect fixing from maintenance

---

*Knowledge recovery also can be a large development cost, especially when entering a new field. Some of this up-front knowledge recovery is already in the model's development parts. Cancelled projects and some separately counted investigation phase costs are excluded to simplify the model.

is also large. How can we characterize defect fixing so that we better understand the costs?

First, it is important to understand that not all defects are equal. The relative cost to fix defects depends heavily on their original cause and when they are found. Figure 4-3 shows the relative costs to fix defects after products are released to customers. These costs vary considerably from organization to organization. The figure is derived from five studies summarized in Boehm's *Software Engineering Economics* [7], and several more recent studies. [1, 8]

Figure 4-3 Relative costs to fix defects

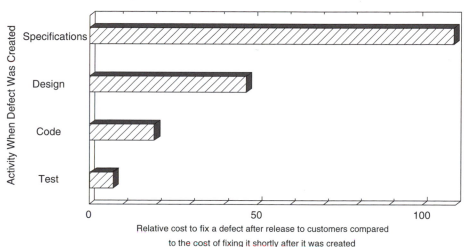

Relative cost to fix a defect after release to customers compared
to the cost of fixing it shortly after it was created

Second, the relative number of each defect type affects total defect costs. The HP data we will use here for our high-level model has a large standard deviation. We have analyzed HP software defects for some years now and have seen that defect origins vary considerably from division to division. [1] Our model uses average data from seven divisions. The left side of Figure 4-4 shows the average number of defects for five major classified categories. The right side of Figure 4-4 shows this data weighted with the relative costs shown in Figure 4-3.

The high-level model will then reflect rework as cost components for each of the four development activities: requirements/specifications, design, implementation, and test. Included are:

- *Total rework = 31%. One-third of both new development (45%/3 = 15%) and enhancements (17.5%/3 = 6%) are assumed rework. All of the maintenance defect fixing is rework (10%).*

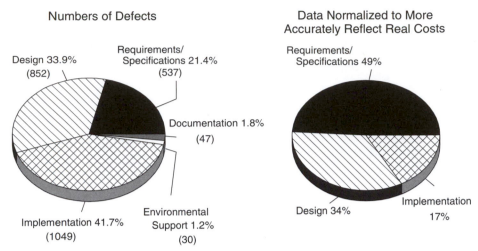

Figure 4-4 Software failure analysis summary for seven divisions
(data collected during test or maintenance)

- *Rework components are normalized to reflect the percentages shown in the right pie of Figure 4-4 (see Appendix A for how the rework for each phase is calculated and separately proportioned).*
- *After normalizations, all rework is attributed to the development activity where defects were created.*

The Complete Software Management Cost Model

Each of the first four figures in isolation provides valuable insight into software. Our goal, though, has been to combine them into a single model. Figure 4-5 shows this model. (Appendix A shows two of the many possible variations for this model. It also includes the spreadsheet used to create all three versions, so if none feel like *your* environment, you can use the spreadsheet's ideas to start to model your own.) As with most models, this one does not include everything. It is a cost-based model that primarily includes R&D costs. *It excludes cancelled projects and some benefits you can gain from reduced costs, such as improved time to market and potential increased customer satisfaction.*

There are three sets of arrows. The top set illustrates that maintenance work is preceded by knowledge recovery efforts. This work reconstructs earlier thinking that was not adequately captured. It can flow either into the work portions of the bars for enhancements or into the rework portions for defect fixes. The middle set of arrows suggests the normal flow of work products and documentation from development activity to activity. The bottom set flows from each development activity back to reenter as rework. This set emphasizes the many times that developers must go back and redo work products created earlier.

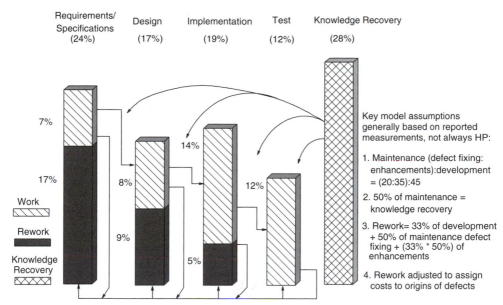

Figure 4-5 A management model of major software development/
maintenance cost components

Thus, the model graphically represents the key challenges faced by software developers. While doing so, it helps provide an intuitive understanding of issues, and it also gives some insight for how investments should be made in improvements. For example, we can imagine trade-offs between the work and rework portions of individual bars or between the work portions of the first four bars versus the knowledge recovery bar.

With this model in mind, we can now consider a variety of potential changes.

APPLICATION OF THE MODEL

The model divides total software costs into three major parts: work, rework, and knowledge recovery. What you choose to invest in improving will be driven by business and organizational pressures. For example, many information technology groups have a large maintenance backlog and are driven to be very responsive to change requests. They might choose to invest in knowledge recovery. Indeed, there is a large evolving industry that specializes in program understanding and reverse engineering tools for just such groups.

Another example is the rapidly changing computer and peripheral market. Companies that produce these new products are under strong pressure to beat their competitors to market. They might invest in better development technology.

A third example comes from virtually any business. There is a world-wide market demand for higher quality. Company survival often depends on producing software with fewer defects and less rework than the competition.

Of course, each of these problems can be approached in either a tactical or strategic way. The short-term approach is to work overtime or to test longer. While this might relieve immediate pressures, the problems will soon return, because no fundamental process change was made. The remainder of this chapter focuses on investments that you can expect to provide long-term paybacks.

Setting Expectations for Improvements—The Case for Inspections

A business must be run with a long-term strategy and realistic plans that support the strategy. In the previous examples, it's easy to look at the model and evaluate the context of various improvement proposals. Thus, it is already useful in helping us to decide which proposals to endorse. Does it also help us to estimate how our resource loading will change?

It gives us some insights. Let's look at an example. The savings from software inspections have been described probably more often than any other software improvement. Virtually all disciplines use reviews of various kinds. How much improvement does our model suggest we might see?

Let's assume our model represents organizations that use small numbers of inspections (a reasonable assumption, based on the sources for this model's data). If we augment such use, we would expect that some additional up-front investment would be necessarily followed by some additional ongoing costs (mostly increased engineering time in inspections). So, the top part of the first three bars in Figure 4-5 might get somewhat larger. In return, the rework portions of the bars should decrease even more.

It is unlikely that inspections will eliminate all rework. The greatest benefit will be in doing rework earlier, and therefore less expensively, than before. In addition, it takes time for change to occur. Inspections are a good example of a process change that has taken many years to spread through organizations.

So, realistically, even a proven good practice like inspections can have only a limited affect on a third of our costs at the expense of increasing the development portion. We could expect a short-term savings of possibly 10 percent. Long-term savings of maybe another 10 percent would appear later. These would result from fewer postrelease defects and decreased knowledge-recovery time.

However, note what the model suggests about inspections. Since the savings will come from the rework portions of the first three bars, it's crucial that you emphasize doing requirements and design inspections, since their rework portions are the largest. If you focus all your early efforts on code inspections and your model resembles Figure 4-5, the best early savings you could expect is only 3 to 4 percent! This might explain some of the early management disillusionment felt for some inspections programs that focused solely on code.

This example again suggests that the model provides valuable insights and can build confidence. If other organizational conditions supported choosing inspections, we might use this analysis to set the following improvement goal:

> *Reduce total project time in the next project by 10 percent and achieve a shorter, more stable testing phase by training the project team before the project begins and by inspecting all requirements, designs, and key code modules.* (Chapters 10 and 11 discuss results for projects with similar goals.)

More Aggressive Expectations—The Case for Reuse

Let's look at another popular proposed improvement that holds promise for good savings. Data shows that projects that reuse substantial amounts of software cost one-fourth as much as other software projects and have one-third the defect density. [9] These are exciting numbers that set high expectations. How can we propagate such techniques throughout an organization, and what does our model suggest about expected returns?

Total work costs in our model are 41 percent and rework costs are 31 percent. Suppose that our current level of reuse is 10 percent without doing anything special and that we can increase this amount to a new level of 50 percent with focused investments. The result would be

> (50% new level - 10% current level) × ((75% reuse savings × 41% model work cost) + (67% reuse savings × 31% model rework cost)) = 20.6% total software cost savings.

This simple analysis needs to be further explored. Most industrial reuse data comes from "fortuitous" reuse. This means that the costs of such reuse are small, because projects took advantage of designs and code that already existed. In contrast, design for reuse requires a separate group to produce and maintain components. These components also cost more to produce than they would normally, although the potential levels of reuse are higher and the benefits more repeatable.

Such components must be more broadly applicable than code that is fortuitously reused. Fortuitous reuse is effective even when code is only reused once, but code that is designed for reuse will be economically useful only when used multiple times. Such reuse requires a mental shift. Unlike some other process changes that can be done in shorter times, this reuse requires organizational changes that need management commitment and support for several years. Few organizations have made these changes easily.

Once made, these changes lead to other long-term savings reflected by the model. All maintenance components (except for existing code) would also be reduced, because the additional work to do design for reuse would produce better-documented and more defect-free work products. While the near-term savings would be less than the promise held out by data collected for fortuitously reused code, reuse still represents the largest single opportunity for cost improvement.

Again, this thinking should help you to more confidently set an improvement goal. This time, let's state one that focuses on time to market. We can do this by assuming that the cost savings directly translates to time. (Depending on your current development methods, the cost savings could be either more or less.)

> *Reduce project time to market by 20 percent by creating a reuse team that will increase the percentage of design and code reuse to 50 percent by three years from now.*

For an improvement like this one, it would be highly desirable to set one or two intermediate objectives, also. When you do, the project focus remains clear, and the organization has a way of seeing that the three-year goal will happen, despite other short-term indicators. For example,

> *Year 1: Create at least 20 new, reusable components that are used in the first year.*
> *Year 2: At least 35 percent of all released projects consists of reused code.* (Chapter 10 discusses results for projects with similar goals.)

A Portfolio of Investment Choices

Table 4-1 complements our software cost model by summarizing the potential impacts for various possible process changes, including the two just discussed. The savings shown for reuse reflect design for reuse. Some of the table entries are taken from detailed cost justifications given in *Practical Software Metrics for Project Management and Process Improvement.* [1] The others were calculated more recently as a part of HP improvement programs that are now in progress. Many other possible process changes are not shown.

Some generic applicable situations are given for each practice. Estimates on a relative scale are also given for the difficulty of change, cost of change, and approximate break-even time.

Table 4-1 Potential impact for various process changes

Changed Practice	Most Applicable Situation	Difficulty of Change	Cost of Change	Break-even Time of Change	% Expected Cost Improvement
Product Definition Improvement	Organizations that create new products				3-9
Detailed Design Methods (e.g., SA/SD)	Systems with many interfaces				3-12
Rapid Prototyping	Complex user interface, applications software				5-12
Systems Design Improvements	Chronic schedule slips due to design issues, follow-on backtracking				5-12
Inspections	All projects				8-20
Reuse	Stable environment with configuration management, applications domain				10-35
Complexity Analysis	Inspections done, systems software, firmware				2-5
Configuration Management	Large and/or complex software portfolio				3-10
Certification Process	All projects				3-6
SW Asset Management	Divisions with old existing code				3-6
Program Understanding	All maintenance and porting projects				3-7

Less / More / Most } Relative to other table entries; for break-even time, 0-1 year, 1-2 years, 2+ years

The cost improvements in Table 4-1 were calculated as if each practice were done by itself. The improvement percentages are the savings against our Figure 4-5 management model (which represents 100 percent of costs). The improvements include both the costs to make a change and the resulting savings. The smaller expected values generally represent short-term savings. Difficult to implement and costly practices will take longer to achieve savings.

Table 4-1 represents some of your investment opportunities. We already saw many of them listed as solution components in the core-competence examples in Chapter 3. This table gives you one more valuable way to evaluate and present alternatives. Think of them as the stocks and bonds of process improvement. Your financial position and business prospects will dictate how you should select an appropriate portfolio of investments.

Now we have a realistic high-level model of software development that shows key processes and their costs. We also have a list of potential improvements along with various parameters that help us to decide their potential for solving specific problems. The next step is to decide how much your organization is willing to invest in order to realize some of these returns.

HOW MUCH SHOULD YOU INVEST? _____

No investment discussion is complete without saying something about how much an organization should invest. I wish there were a simple answer to the question "How much?" but there isn't. Very few organizations have the same resources available as others, nor are they driven by the same business challenges. The core-competence process discussed in the last chapter showed some aspects that cause differences. The next chapter shows even more.

Having said that, it is still possible to make some suggestions. Let's start with another model, Figure 4-6. Like some financial investments, process improvements tie up money or resources for some time before returning more than you put in. Think of the area of the curve in the bottom of the figure as your cost of change, or the amount to invest. The time it takes for the top curve to offset the startup costs of the bottom curve is shown as the break-even time. Relative values for both the cost of change and the break-even time were suggested in Table 4-1. The slope of the positive curve is determined by your initial investment and by the difficulty of implementing and achieving effective usage. The asymptote (dashed line) above the top curve is the upper bound of the expected return on your investment. Like many investments, returns on process improvements can continue for years, until they are replaced by newer, better processes.

Figure 4-6 Simplified view of process-improvement investment

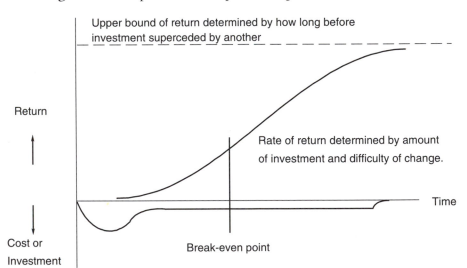

Your organization's portfolio of investments will be the sum of various similar curves. So, what should such a sum amount to? Herbsleb and others did a study of organizations that did process improvements well. The study suggested that those companies invested between 3 1/3 percent and 13 percent as a percentage of dollars per software engineer per year. [10] Are such amounts right for you? As I said at the start of this section, I wish there were a simple answer. Only your management team can decide whether such amounts are appropriate for your challenges and how you might allocate various portions among the best alternatives.

CONCLUSION

Despite software's youth, it's exciting that there has been enough data collected to create a useful investment model. The one here is based on past industry measurements, and we've seen that improvements projected from its components are consistent with those we might believe we could get from various processes, methods, and tools. At the start, the chapter suggested several key attributes for our investment model. These included:

- *Encourage an intuitive understanding of issues* - Modeling the three major development and maintenance components helps managers to better understand both software development issues and trade-offs.
- *Suggest a reasonable direction for how investments should be made* - By itself, our model can't set direction. By providing a common model for comparing proposed improvement returns (as in Table 4-1), a model does show how it can play a key role in framing decisions.
- *Help set realistic expectations for potential returns on investment* - The inspections and reuse examples suggest that the model also helps set good expectations.

Do all these positive attributes guarantee you and your managers will make the right choices to avoid "bankrupt savings and loans" and "market crashes"? Not entirely, but a model tuned to your processes should definitely help.

Even though you may not be responsible for making the final investment decisions in your organization, this chapter has given you a set of important models and approaches to prepare your decision makers to make more knowledgeable choices. No matter how much they end up investing, at least you should be more confident that software choices will have a better chance against other alternatives than before.

BIBLIOGRAPHY

1. Grady, R., *Practical Software Metrics for Project Management and Process Improvement*, Englewood Cliffs, N. J.: Prentice-Hall, Inc., 1992, pp. 42, 43, 49, 53, Chapter 12, Chapter 14.
2. Lientz, B., and E. Swanson, *Software Maintenance Management*, Reading, Mass.: Addison-Wesley, 1980 pp. 24,73.
3. Abran, A., and H. Nguyenkim, "Analysis of Maintenance Work Categories through Measurement," *Proceedings of the IEEE Conference on Software Maintenance*, Sorrento, Italy, (1991), pp. 104-113.
4. Foster, J., "Program Lifetime: A Vital Statistic for Maintenance," *Proceedings of the IEEE Conference on Software Maintenance*, Sorrento, Italy, (1991), pp. 98-103.
5. Rubin, H., E. Yourdon, and H. Battaglia, "Industry Canada Worldwide Benchmark Project," *Conf. on the Appl. Software Metrics*, Orlando, Fla., (Nov. 1995), pp. 51-52.
6. Corbi, T., "Program Understanding: Challenge for the 1990s," *IBM Systems Journal*, Vol. 28, No. 2, (1989), pp. 294-306.
7. Boehm, B., *Software Engineering Economics*. Englewood Cliffs, N. J.: Prentice-Hall, Inc., 1981, p. 40.
8. Moller, K. H., "Increasing of Software Quality by Objectives and Residual Fault Prognosis," *First E.O.Q.C. Seminar on Software Quality*, Brussels, Belgium, (April 1988), pp. 478-488.
9. Grady, R., and D. Caswell, *Software Metrics: Establishing a Company-Wide Program*, Englewood Cliffs, N. J.: Prentice-Hall, Inc., 1987, pp. 111, 112.
10. Herbsleb, J., A. Carleton, J. Rozum, J. Siegel, and D. Zubrow, "Benefits of CMM-Based Software Process Improvement: Initial Results," *Technical Report, CMU/SEI-94-TR-13*, (Aug. 1994), p. 10.

5

Gaining Management Commitment for Software Process Improvements

There's an old joke about the difference between the roles that a chicken and a pig play in getting you a ham-and-egg breakfast. The punch line is that the chicken is involved, but the pig is committed. Now, before you run off and accuse me of calling managers chickens and pigs, that isn't the connection that I'm trying to make with this story. The distinction between management involvement and true commitment is, though. How can you tell if your managers will support the software process improvements necessary for your organization's survival? And what can you do to strengthen their commitment?

This chapter discusses your manager's concerns, especially in the context of you leading a software process-improvement effort. Management concerns affect commitment. Thus, they will determine your process-improvement proposal's priority. This chapter gives suggestions and examples for ways to raise this priority. Some of the suggestions may cause you to consider doing things that don't seem directly related to your project. Even so, your acting on them may be the best way to sustain your project's momentum and future. The suggestions also provide useful ways to think about how you might adjust your project's scope to align it to your organization's readiness to adopt an improvement. This, too, will help you to succeed.

Figure 5-1 shows a high-level model for assessing management commitment, with arrows reflecting the commitment of a real organization. It has seven business aspects and five organizational aspects that influence gaining and sustaining commitment. The key word here is "influence." The aspects don't all have to be high for you to succeed, but *one or more can distract your managers enough to jeopardize a process-improvement project.* This means that you need to be aware of the status of the aspects and know what you can do to improve negative influences. In the extreme, you also need to be ready to walk away from a project that faces too many negatives.

Figure 5-1 A force-field model for summarizing aspects
of management commitment

			Positive	Neutral	Negative
Business	Strategic	Vision Business Strategic Focus Core Competence	← →		
	Tactical	Customer Perceptions Market Share Product Cycle Time Profitability			
Organizational	Strategic	Organizational Maturity Process Improvement Infrastructure		→	
	Tactical	Organizational Inertia Stability Cost/Time Alignment			

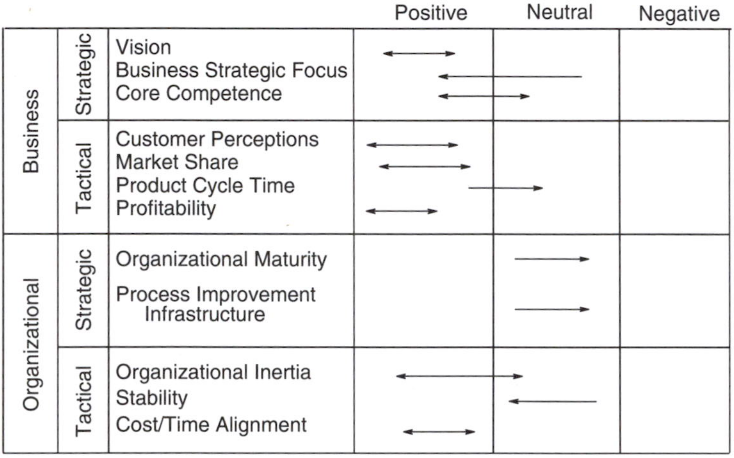

The figure is also a tool to summarize your assessment of management commitment. A force-field analysis is a simple way to visualize positive and negative influences. [1] The use of arrows shows these subjective results. This adapted form uses arrows to express added meaning. An arrow's length shows that the value for an item falls within a range. It is a band of uncertainty. An arrow's direction shows possible future movement. No anticipated movement is reflected by a line with arrows at both ends.

Figure 5-1 comes from a Hewlett-Packard division working to improve their processes. Rather than discuss their challenges first, this chapter generally explores the 12 aspects and offers suggestions and examples for how to evaluate and strengthen them. It then unites them in another example with approaches to gain *and* maintain management commitment more successfully.

Finally, the chapter ends with an addendum: "Advice to Managers Whose Business Depends on Software." It puts the 12 aspects into a more traditional leading/organizing/planning/controlling context. It also summarizes what top managers can do to help their people to improve their software processes.

BUSINESS ASPECTS INFLUENCE MANAGEMENT COMMITMENT

Most of you involved with software today spend a lot of your time with people, project-specific, and organizational issues. However, business aspects also affect you. By business aspects, I mean high-level management choices that are directly driven by the marketplace and competitors. Of course, your company's top-level managers usually make such decisions.

While they spend their time thinking about these decisions, you should do your job better by being able to focus your efforts. That's easy to say, but what about the negative consequences that their decisions might have on process-improvement momentum? You need to recognize the role these aspects play in management's commitment and use your knowledge of your organization to make the aspects work in your favor. Let's look at some examples.

Strategic Components—Is There a "Big Picture"?

Business aspects can be divided into those that are strategic and those that are tactical. There are three strategic aspects that control the "Big Picture":

- Vision
- Business strategic focus
- Core competence

Vision - A vision of the future that the people of an organization share is the most powerful strategic component. It is key to long-term survival. A good vision statement is exciting, is easy to visualize and remember, and is something people will naturally use in their daily communications. One memorable HP example was Bill Hewlett's vision of a shirt-pocket-sized calculator to replace a slide rule. That vision led to an entire business that still prospers for HP today.

If an organization has no clear vision, it's likely that activities will be primarily managed with short-term, tactical decisions. Process improvements will get low priorities. What can *you* do if there doesn't seem to be a vision for the group that you are in? After all, it isn't your responsibility to create one. Even so, your success will be limited unless you can help your management define one.

If you are part of a new business, the odds are high that there is a business plan. It should include a vision of some sort. Ask if you can see it. If your manager is reluctant to show you, use the opportunity to ask what the business is expected to evolve to in five years. That's your opening to learning what the vision is. Perhaps your manager will see the value of sharing that vision more widely.

Being in a well-established organization can be harder. Often it has been many years since a business plan was written. Management and the organization have changed and the vision has become blurred. It may be desirable to create a new one. Here you might suggest that your manager set aside some staff meeting time to brainstorm a shared vision. In one division I was in, we created a good vision statement after roughly three 10-minute staff meeting sessions plus some work between meetings. However, after that it took time and effort to raise it from just a statement to a shared concept.

Another tactic is for the group to create a new, shared vision at an off-site meeting. In either case, a vision will strengthen your organization.

Business strategic focus - A vision is an endpoint being sought. An organization's business strategy is the road it is taking. Table 5-1 shows three approaches that are often taken. [2] You can argue that your top management wants you to do all three. Lasting businesses are successful with all three at different times, but at any given time their primary focus is on one. Lack of focus creates problems.

Table 5-1 Major software business strategies (this table is a modified subset of a table called "Major Strategies of a Software Business" in ref. 2)

Major Characteristics	Maximize Customer Satisfaction	Minimize Engineering Effort & Schedule	Sustain Product Integrity & Market
Major Business Factor	Attempt to capture market share	Competitive pressures forcing new product development or cost control	Hold/increase market share; improve product faster than competitors
When Most Effective	When initially entering market	When there are several competitive products or you sell more profitable products	When features are competitive and adequate market share is held
Characteristic Features	Customer communications, quick responses	Focus on delivery dates and effort	Pressure to add/improve features; improving quality

So what can *you* do? As the person responsible for process improvements or simply someone who wants to start such a change, you must create a plan that assumes a strategic focus. Take your best guess at your organization's current focus. When you have your plan reviewed, use the opportunity to initiate discussion and, hopefully, improve clarity. Without a strong direction, your best approach is to focus on quick-return improvements.

Core competence - If the business strategy is the road your company is on, core competencies are its people's key abilities when traveling that road. Core competencies go beyond organizational boundaries. As discussed in Chapter 3, they are abilities that people excel in that set a company apart from its competition. For example, HP's core competencies would have to include its people's expertise in measurement technology and technical computation systems.

The need to gain and hold competitive advantage drives all process improvements. Without it, businesses struggle and management commitment to improvement fails because of cost cutting. So how can *you* use the idea of software core competence to strengthen commitment? Analyze your company's software strengths. Most modern companies integrate software into their products. What strengths has this brought your company? What other abilities are needed?

View process improvement as helping to build core competence. A core competence must include an infrastructure that sustains your people's strongly held beliefs and abilities. Your job includes building an infrastructure strong enough to support the long-term excellence of specific software abilities. To do this, create a process-improvement plan explaining which abilities are needed. If you can convince your management to extend your plan into a core-competence plan, even better.

Table 5-2 summarizes this section's suggestions related to the three strategic business aspects. Remember, strategic business aspects are visible or they can be discovered. They are the strongest available potentially *positive* influences on process improvements. Align your plans with them and you will increase your chances for success.

Table 5-2 Strategic business aspects that influence management commitment

Commitment Influencers	Forces For (Positive Influences)	Forces Against (Negative Influences)	Negative Symptoms	Action to Strengthen Aspect
Vision	Clear, exciting vision understood by many	No vision; vision not communicated	Short-term thinking, lack of organizational focus	Create business plan; organize strategy meetings to emphasize shared vision
Business Strategic Focus	New market or hold large market share, clear priorities	Multiple competitors with different product strengths; no clear priority	No clear focus; cost cutting	Appropriate metrics; quality/productivity improvement plan; focus on quick-return process improvements
Core Competence in Software	History of product successes using SW, management speaks of necessary software	Little organizational SW experience	Poor quality, large scheduling surprises due to SW	Create core-competence plan, hire experienced SW people, train, establish infrastructure

Tactical Components—Is There a Leak in the Roof?

Four tactical business components affect process-improvement projects:

- Customer perceptions
- Market share
- Product cycle time
- Profitability

Customer perceptions - This is the most important of the tactical aspects. However, if a business doesn't make a conscious effort to monitor customer perceptions, negative symptoms may first be interpreted as one of the other tactical aspects.

Customer perceptions come from service quality and product quality. One study suggests that service quality most influences perceptions. The study found the primary reason for switching to a competitive product was poor service quality almost 70 percent of the time. [3] Service quality includes many things, such as responsiveness to key accounts, to problems, and to product needs and changes.

On the other hand, everything designed and built into a product affects product quality. HP summarizes these attributes with the term "FURPS" (functionality, usability, reliability, performance, and supportability). [2] The FURPS model expands into many "ilities" that vary in importance among products.

Negative customer perceptions are quickly felt throughout an organization. They demand immediate attention, and they preempt and delay process improvements. What can *you* do to help prevent this? You can influence connections between developers, service people, and customers. The need is clear, but often organizational protocol can get in the way here.

As a minimum, you need to develop connections that bring you closer to your company's customers, formally or informally. Get invited to customer meetings. Talk with sales and support people. Read customer-reported defects and complaints. You can influence others by raising questions about what you've heard or examples of customer wants. Show others the value of these contacts by example. By doing these things, you open possibilities for improving your organization's customer perceptions, and you sensitize yourself and your team to *your* customer's (the development teams') needs.

Market share (or slow growth) - Sometimes market share is overemphasized and treated as if it were directly controllable. (Sometimes what is most desired is rapid sales growth.) Gaining it is the result of doing everything well. Losing it is a negative symptom that foretells changes to come. The bottom line is that true loss of market share suggests product definition problems. Not understanding customer needs will finally lead to lost market share.

People can also think low sales reflect lost market share. Whether low sales are real or are from poor economic factors, market saturation, or simply poor sales estimates, you must approach their negative symptoms in the same way. If you don't, management attention will be increasingly drawn away from process improvements, and the business can be thrown into a cost-cutting spiral.

What can *you* do? At best, you can influence projects in development or under consideration (including process improvements). Drive toward feature sets that emphasize key differentiators. Focus on particular customer needs in high-return market segments.

Product cycle time - Many markets that include computers and software are under great pressure to produce products more quickly. Yet such products are also becoming more complex. In the computer business especially, this has been accompanied by more complex organizations. Often, pieces of the same organization are physically separated. All these aspects create delays that lead to product cycle-time pressures. Resulting pressure on developers can increase their resistance to any changes that could delay their schedules.

What can *you* do to reduce cycle-time effects on process-improvement projects? The best short-term organizational action is to make products more target-market specific. Anything you can do to encourage this will help your business to focus only on those features required for its market.

This strategy has a down side, though. If the organization hasn't taken the extra time to create a good long-term product architecture with a good vision of its market's trends, follow-on products will be poorly designed and hard to maintain. This will finally increase product cycle time. A good architecture will also enable you to create reusable components for future products. Such components are the best way of achieving the desired reduced cycle times.

These are product-focused actions. While you need to remember them as you work on process improvements, there are other methods to consider with process-improvement customers.

With Information Technology (IT) software, product cycle-time pressures have led to methods like RAD (Rapid Application Development) and Accelerated Systems Development. [4] Their approach is to speed delivery of new or changed systems that are targeted for a single, well-defined customer. Such applications combine prototyping, Joint Application Development (JAD—a method for working closely with the customer throughout development), project management that limits time spent on various tasks, and specialized CASE (Computer Aided Software Engineering) tools to aid in design and documentation capture. Since process improvements are often made for a single, well-defined customer, it seems likely that many of these techniques will also work well for improvement projects.

Profitability - This is the last of the four tactical business aspects. It is the bottom line result of everything your company does. It is a strong negative influence on process improvement, though, when your management gets into a cost-cutting spiral to improve short-term profits.

Today's software development groups are especially vulnerable. Many high-level managers have successfully used strategies that included third-party or offshore manufacturing. These strategies often worked for hardware, because the key product values were well understood and kept as a business advantage. The values were contained in the designs, not in assembly or repair operations that were easy to learn and could be done almost anywhere.

It's not obvious yet which software activities can be contracted for and which ones are key for survival. For example, since software changes and evolves for many years, are maintenance and evolution activities critical core competencies?

It is also tempting to contract for testing. But good testing may turn out to be only a small part of total verification and validation practices. Having a third-party write tests might be safe. Contracting for combined test writing and execution might not be. Timely information fed back from testing (which may be hard to get with offsite, third-party testing) may be more valuable than less timely, cheaper testing.

Table 5-3 Tactical business aspects that influence management commitment

Commitment Influencers	Forces For (Positive Influences)	Forces Against (Negative Influences)	Negative Symptoms	Action to Strengthen Aspect
Customer Perceptions	Good FURPS; good customer service	Poor responsiveness or products; loss of confidence (by customers)	Loss of key customers; loss of market share	Focus on responsiveness; increase lab project manager and engineering customer contact
Market Share (or slow growth)	New market or hold large market share	Heavy competition	New products don't meet sales projections	Improve product definition; reduce TTM by focus on smaller feature set; concentrate on high-return market segments
Product Cycle Time	Good understanding of customer needs; young organization	Dependence on other organizations; complex products	Other companies announcing new, better products before you do	Reduce product complexity by defining reusable architecture components or making products more target-market specific; use JAD/RAD for process improvements
Profitability	Large market share, patents, excellent processes	Strong competition, overdependence on 3rd-party product content	Cost cutting	Get support through commitment to core competence; focus on product differentiators and on high-return market segments

So what can *you* do when your organization seeks more profit? The answers here start with the same ones given in the market share discussion. Help product developers maintain their focus on key product differentiators and on high-return market segments. The big difference here is that you must also keep the balance between short-term cuts and core competence visible. Your best weapon is an approved long-term productivity plan (or core-competence plan). It must define what software core competence is for your business, the necessary role it plays in achieving business goals, and how you plan to achieve it.

Table 5-3 summarizes the tactical business aspect suggestions. Remember, these aspects are easier to see than the strategic ones, and they often can be negative influences on your ability to improve processes. You must be alert for them and make conscious efforts to minimize their potential impacts.

Summary

This first section has discussed seven business aspects that influence management commitment. Perhaps our biggest weakness as project managers and engineers is in trusting that "management" can control these. When you are part of a process-improvement team, remember that these aspects are the main concerns of your "customers." They expect your improvements to affect not just their processes, but also their business. Tables 5-2 and 5-3 will help you to better frame your efforts to do this.

ORGANIZATIONAL ASPECTS INFLUENCE MANAGEMENT COMMITMENT ___

Next to competitive business aspects, organizational ones most influence management commitment. Project managers and engineers can feel more at home with these. You may not have a lot of control over them, but you probably understand them better because you are closer to them. You also are more likely to have been delegated authority to make decisions directly related to these aspects. Like business aspects, organizational ones can be divided into strategic and tactical groups.

Strategic Components—What League Are We In?

Two strategic aspects affect process-improvement success:

- Organizational maturity
- Process-improvement infrastructure

Organizational maturity - The SEI Capability Maturity Model described in Chapter 2 suggests that groups with more mature processes produce higher-quality software more effectively. [5] Their assessment process has a simple five-level scale that has captured managers' interest. HP helped to create an "Instant Profile" approach to the CMM. [6] It is a short version of the more formal SEI assessment. Figure 5-2 shows results for an HP division. Questions for each key process area are asked of typically 60 percent of a division's R&D people, and the extent that a practice is satisfied is computed. The practices are grouped into four of the five SEI CMM levels. None are given for level 1 (ad hoc), since a division at that level isn't considered to have any repeatable processes.

Figure 5-2 Instant profile assessment of an organization

Key Process Areas	Not Satisfied	Partially Satisfied	Fully Satisfied	
Process Change Mgmt.				Level 5 Optimizing
Tech. Change Mgmt.				
Defect Prevention				
SW Quality Mgmt.				Level 4 Managed
Quantitative Proc. Mgmt.				
Peer Reviews				Level 3 Defined
Intergroup Coordination				
SW Product Engineering				
Integrated SW Mgmt.				
Training Program				
Org. Process Definition				
Org. Process Focus				
Configuration Mgmt.				Level 2 Repeatable
Quality Assurance				
Subcontract Mgmt.	(Not applicable)			
Project Tracking				
Project Planning				
Requirements Mgmt.				

In an immature organization, the major thing that distracts management commitment is fragile processes that can fail at any time. When they do, fire-drill tactics consume management's attention, and process improvements are delayed or cancelled.

There are several good reasons to do some form of maturity assessment.

1. They yield a broad picture of a software organization.
2. A formal assessment can add to more sustained management commitment.
3. Results can be used as a useful source of information when creating a process-improvement plan.

If low maturity is interfering with improving processes, what can *you* do? A simple first step is to write down some of the organization's processes. Getting key engineers to review simple documents can lead to important clarifications. The results are then a basis for improvements. It is also critical to start tracking defects. This will expose the costs of immaturity. Start inspections. These will make poor documentation and incomplete processes visible more quickly.

The SEI model suggests that the first areas to focus on are project management and oversight (the level 2 areas in Figure 5-2). Persuading management to mandate brief, written project plans is one way to start this focus. Be sure to use these plans in a positive way to help motivate improving key risk areas.

Process-improvement infrastructure - Mature disciplines leverage specialized expertise. For example, in electronic designs creation, there may be groups that specialize in designing power supplies, or doing printed-circuit layouts, or technicians that build prototypes. Often some of these jobs are separately managed by an engineering services group. Since the software field is still immature, it isn't surprising that we don't yet know how to separate out infrastructure tasks efficiently.

The best recorded HP examples of the benefits of an infrastructure (and drawbacks of its absence) are in the history of HP's inspections (see Chapter 13). Elements that clearly accelerated adoption and improvements included local support groups, productivity managers, companywide productivity conferences, divisional chief moderators, and a company inspections program manager. In contrast, their absence or untimely removal reduced management visibility into improvements, often stopped progress, and sometimes eliminated gains already made.

What can *you* do to build a process-improvement infrastructure? You can target needed expertise and develop it on your process-improvement project. Alternatively, convince other project managers to develop it. Offer to develop some team expertise in exchange for other needed expertise.

Work with other project managers to justify the temporary use of people dedicated to specific improvements. Then, justify permanent resources based on their successes. Remember, building an *infrastructure* requires that you drop normal project-ownership boundaries and that you carefully monitor and justify in terms of company benefits versus costs.

Table 5-4 summarizes the strategic organizational suggestions. These especially control the penetration of improvements and must be carefully matched to overriding business aspects. Thus, they also can act as negative influences. For example, the Figure 5-1 force-field analysis has many positive

Table 5-4 Strategic organizational aspects that
influence management commitment

Commitment Influencers	Forces For (Positive Influences)	Forces Against (Negative Influences)	Negative Symptoms	Action to Strengthen Aspect
Organizational Maturity	Basic SW engineering practices in use	Young organization; past product successes due to exceptional individuals	Few processes written down; few or no metrics	Measure defects; create one-page process descriptions; start or improve inspections; do written project plans
Process-Improvement Infrastructure	Business requirements (e.g., ISO 9000, medical, pharmaceutical)	Young organization; cost controls	Resources dedicated to productivity or quality disappear	Justify a person temporarily dedicated to a specific improvement; then justify permanent resources based on success

forces, yet the organization's business success and rapid growth are self-limiting. They have aggressively created a reusable software framework. However, their success is limited by their maturity and the challenge of installing an infrastructure while staying ahead of their competitors.

Tactical Components—Now Is the Time . . . For What?

Just as business conditions change, organizations change. Understanding your organization and timing changes well can greatly enhance process-improvement success. There are three tactical aspects:

- Organizational inertia
- Stability
- Cost/time alignment

Organizational inertia - Let's face it. Some organizations have a lot of inertia. The symptom is clear: Too many people have to agree before a decision can be made. What can *you* do? Pick your improvement targets carefully. Seek success in a subset of the organization that is more adventurous, but respected. Don't always use the same group, either. If you do, you risk isolating them from everyone else as a special case, and they become less believable as a success reference.

Instead of asking permission of high management, make improvements at the project level. Then, use project-level success stories to justify wider adoption of the changes.

Stability - Organizational instability is one of the strongest demotivators you will face when improving processes. It is probably the largest source of both project and process-improvement setbacks. Even when organizational changes are the result of a fast-growing, successful business, they can erode management's commitment to process improvements. It simply takes too much energy and focus keeping pace with organizational needs. The best road to recovery from such reorganizations is for management to spend a lot of time on "hygiene" aspects. They (and you) must talk with people to clarify new roles. Make sure that people start spending productive time on the new emphases, and make sure that people feel valued.

What happens to process improvements and what can *you* do? First, well-selected improvements are based on long-term company needs. They should survive organizational changes. In an unstable environment, focus on quick-return improvements or ones that can be partially done in short increments. Temporarily avoid projects that will take more than 6 to 9 months to show measurable returns. This tactic may mean that you won't be able to work on changes that are the most exciting or that have the best potential long-term benefits, at least not right away.

Cost/time alignment - We all learned when we were growing up that there were optimum times to ask Mom or Dad for some money. Organizations are similar. If you don't understand the approval process and the current economic conditions, you can be stopped cold. The symptoms are familiar. Purchase orders or consulting contracts aren't approved. Sometimes they just disappear for weeks.

What can *you* do? First, create a strong economic case for your improvement. If it shows timely, good returns, that will help prevent thoughts that

Table 5-5 Tactical organizational aspects that influence management commitment

Commitment Influencers	Forces For (Positive Influences)	Forces Against (Negative Influences)	Negative Symptoms	Action to Strengthen Aspect
Organizational Inertia	Young (in mindset) organizations have less inertia	Old organizations often have bureaucracies and fiefdoms that impede improvements	Too many people have to agree before a decision is made; too many meetings	Seek success in a subset of the organization that is more adventuresome, but respected
Stability	Specialized business; geographic location with stable work force; respected management	Rapidly changing business; change of management	Poor morale; short-term mentality; high personnel turnover	Focus *only* on quick-return improvements or those that can be done incrementally
Cost/Time Alignment	Good quarterly or monthly results; targeted project is on schedule	Targeting time in tight economic times; major project is behind schedule	Purchase orders or consulting/ training contracts aren't approved; people's priorities aren't changed to support improvements	Create strong economic justification; make sure project manager of target project agrees; carefully time your process improvement proposals

it is just another short-term cost to avoid. Be sure to present your case in business terms consistent with your organization's strategic business focus. Second, make sure that the initial project teams who will benefit are strong allies. The more of you who can help convince the decision makers, the better. Third, center improvements on a strong quality/productivity plan and carefully time them.

Table 5-5 summarizes the tactical organizational suggestions. Remember, these aspects are sources of critical information. You can turn each of them into a positive influence for management commitment.

Summary

This second section described five organizational influences on management commitment. Draw on your project management strengths and techniques to use these aspects wisely to both gain commitment and plan for success. Tables 5-4 and 5-5 will help you to frame these efforts. Then, create an overall, strategic process-improvement plan plus tactical implementation plans for every improvement you do.

USING A FORCE-FIELD ANALYSIS OF MANAGEMENT COMMITMENT _____

Figure 5-3 shows a force-field analysis for another HP division early in its attempts to improve its software processes. The division was created to pursue a new software market for HP. It was staffed largely by people from divisions that were downsizing. Parts were geographically separated. The force field was created after having several meetings with a total of about 12 division people. They included engineers and two management levels. One of the people was responsible for quality improvements. Filling out a table like this only takes about 15 minutes once you have worked with division people in a few different settings. Remember that these tables don't reflect just an organization's manager. They reflect the net commitment of the management team. This reflection can be seen without even meeting the manager in charge.

Preparing a Force-Field Analysis

Some parts of the analysis were easier to do than others. For example, it was clear the vision was positive. It had been developed with the manager's staff, was well documented, and had been discussed at enough meetings that people were aware of it. Similarly, core competence was assessed as neutral and improving, because the staff had consciously defined what was needed and were taking steps to build it.

			Positive	Neutral	Negative
Business	**Strategic**	Vision	←		
		Business Strategic Focus		→	
		Core Competence		←	
	Tactical	Customer Perceptions	←		
		Market Share		←	
		Product Cycle Time		→	
		Profitability		←	
Organizational	**Strategic**	Organizational Maturity			→
		Process Improvement Infrastructure		←→	
	Tactical	Organizational Inertia			→
		Stability		←	
		Cost/Time Alignment		←→	

Figure 5-3 Force-field analysis of management commitment

Organizational maturity was assessed negatively, since the division was made up of former pieces of several different businesses. Their mutual processes were different and that created conflicts. It also led to a negative rating for organizational inertia. Several improvement meetings were characterized by different managers reflecting opposing positions. Their teams "couldn't change," because it would mean that they would have to do "everything" differently.

Process-improvement infrastructure was neutral, because there were dedicated resources, but the conflicting processes made it hard for people in the infrastructure to be effective.

The harder parts of the analysis included the business strategic focus. There was a lot of carryover thinking from the past businesses. That made it hard to tell if the division had a focused approach. Market share was neutral and improving, because the organization was new and prospects were good for increasing the customer base for a couple of years. Cycle-time pressures were already starting to emerge, though. There were stated goals to create and support more business with the same or fewer people.

Another tough guess was for profitability. Because it was a young organization, profitability could be interpreted differently by different people. Stability was assessed as neutral and improving, because new organizations usually don't restructure for a couple of years and their stated hiring controls would minimize rapid personnel growth issues. Finally, cost/time alignment was difficult to assess. As a new organization, they had some flexibility, but their separate histories and the headcount constraints led to inconsistent behaviors.

Acting on What the Force-Field Summary Tells You

This example gives you a good idea of how to do a force-field analysis. Now that you better understand the 12 aspects, how would you use this analysis if it was for your organization? There are four steps:

1. Look at the total table and its trends. What is your general impression?
2. Write down three or four negatives or neutrals with negative trends to anticipate potential resistance sources.
3. Summarize useful suggestions from Tables 5-2 through 5-5.
4. Write down positive trends to reinforce positive feelings about the organization and to frame progress toward a desired state.

General impression - The total picture in Figure 5-3 is neutral. There are definite signs of organizational issues, so you must approach changes with sensitivity to local feelings and politics. The business half of the picture is brighter. It's likely that there will be some management support for improvements and that it can probably be sustained long enough to achieve some results.

Potential sources of resistance - The two negative column arrows can't be ignored. Also, it is best to choose at least one arrow from the business half, since your sponsor is most likely to directly see and appreciate improvements there. Business strategic focus is the best choice to strengthen there, since it is a potential source of misaligned expectations.

Useful suggestions - Here are some of the suggestions from Tables 5-2 through 5-5 you should consider:

Organizational maturity - Measure defects. Create one-page process descriptions. Start or improve inspections. Do written project plans.

Organizational inertia - Seek success in a subset of the division that is more adventuresome, but respected.

Business strategic focus - Focus metrics and projects to align with the primary business aspect (if one is clearly emphasized). Create a quality/productivity improvement plan. Focus on quick-return process improvements.

Emphasize the positive - This division has a good reputation, is doing well in the marketplace, and management has shown very good vision and leadership. Link process improvements to these strengths to gain enthusiasm and support for well-defined, quick improvement projects. These can form the basis for later, more ambitious projects.

The advantage of doing this simple analysis is that you then have a realistic high-level picture of your challenges. Remember that *the analysis is not a judgment of the organization or of its management.* It's simply a way to summarize important aspects that you need to be aware of and sensitive to. Use your evaluations to optimize your plans and to create backup strategies. Focus on aligning the amount of change your project is attempting to the organization's ability to change and on changing the balance of forces to improve your chances of success. Once you've assessed your organization, you probably don't need to reassess and revisit your plans more than once a year.

The force-field analysis in Figure 5-3 was done two years before this chapter was written. Several modest process-improvement projects were attempted during the two years and some succeeded. Others stalled. The business continued to do well, and some previous organizational instabilities improved. The force-field areas of organizational maturity, process-improvement infrastructure, and organizational inertia improved. The profitability and vision forces decayed.

Their story continues and offers a more sympathetic view of the earlier chicken-and-pig story. All too often, "lack of management commitment" is blamed for process-improvement project failures. This sounds so simple. We can sagely nod our heads and say "Management did it again." The force-field model used here shows that process-improvement projects are fragile enterprises affected by many things, though. This last example emphasizes that, even with strong management leadership, care must be taken to pick, carefully time, and protect process-improvement projects. Many other business and organizational aspects affect their fates.

Also, despite "lack of management commitment," there are things that you can do to help restore and strengthen support. Tables 5-2 through 5-5 show many of them. Gaining management commitment won't always be easy, but the same question can be asked of you: "Are you committed or simply involved?"

ADDENDUM:
ADVICE TO MANAGERS WHOSE BUSINESS DEPENDS ON SOFTWARE

Most of the truly excellent managers I've known provide their best leadership by asking their people what they need them to do. Having described a model for gaining management commitment for people who are responsible for process improvements, it only seems fair to give high-level managers my views of how they can best help those people. While business and organizational conditions will change what your people might ask of you, here is a set of requests to prepare for.

Leadership

Vision - Describe an exciting future of which I'm a proud part.

Business strategic focus - I know competition requires constant improvements in customer satisfaction, engineering effectiveness, time to market, and reduced defects. Help me to focus on one of these as our primary approach.

Market share - If we are losing ground, lead us to improve our product definition process. This is not a natural area for engineers to understand.

Planning

Core competence - Acknowledge that software is a key component of our success. Show your commitment by asking key people to work with you to plan for and develop core competence in specific software areas.

Process-improvement infrastructure - Don't force us to make process improvements in our spare time. Don't overspend here, but also don't starve this long-term investment.

Cost/time alignment - Think about improvement savings in cumulative terms. Don't ask us to show huge paybacks for single process-improvement projects, and protect the momentum of making improvements in tight times.

Organization

Organizational maturity - Support steps that improve our organization's maturity. Challenge us to make measurable improvements in areas we target.

Organizational inertia - Streamline our decision-making processes. Delegate responsibilities within the framework of a written business plan.

Stability - If business conditions force us to reorganize or change major responsibilities, spend time with us. Listen to us. Go out of your way to help us to be productive in the new environment as soon as possible.

Control

Customer perceptions - We are engineers and we often think in different terms than our customers. Establish regular feedback paths from our customers. Foster a customer-focused mentality.

Product cycle times - Empower respected engineers in our organization to create a long-term technical architecture as a way to improve product cycle times.

Profitability - Focus our marketing people on learning from our customers what our key product differentiators are. Focus our engineers on effective delivery of these features to high-return market segments.

BIBLIOGRAPHY

1. Moran, J., R. Talbot, and R. Benson, *A Guide to Graphical Problem-Solving Processes*, Milwaukee, Wis.: ASQC Quality Press, 1990, pp. 51-53.
2. Grady, R., *Practical Software Metrics for Project Management and Process Improvement*, Englewood Cliffs, N. J.: Prentice-Hall, Inc., 1992, p. 24.
3. Whiteley, R., *The Customer-Driven Company*, Reading, Mass.: Addison-Wesley, 1991, pp. 9-10.
4. Folkes, S., and S. Stubenvoll, *Accelerated Systems Development*, Englewood Cliffs, N. J.: Prentice-Hall, Inc., 1992.
5. Paulk, M., B. Curtis, M. Chrissis, and C. Weber, "Capability Maturity Model, Version 1.1," *IEEE Software*, (July 1993), pp. 18-27.
6. Whitney, R., E. Nawrocki, W. Hayes, and J. Siegel, "Interim Profile Development and Trial of a Method to Rapidly Measure Software Engineering Maturity Status," *Technical Report CMU/SEI-94-TR-4*, Pittsburgh: Carnegie-Mellon Univ., (March 1994).

Part Two

DO
Train, Adapt, Consult, Remove Barriers

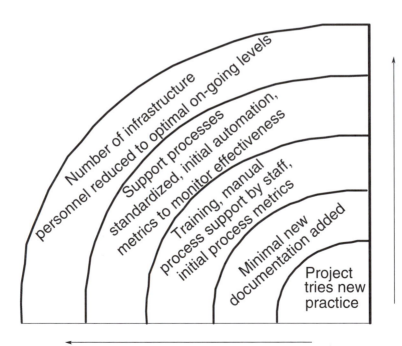

Number of infrastructure personnel reduced to optimal on-going levels

Support processes standardized, initial automation, metrics to monitor effectiveness

Training, manual process support by staff, initial process metrics

Minimal new documentation added

Project tries new practice

Increasing Adoption

T he PLAN section has given you some powerful tools for planning your process improvements. Such planning never stops, so many other ideas in this next section and in later ones will complement the initial set. The next three chapters switch the focus to evaluating and working with the organizational and people forces that control the success of your process-improvement project. This is in line with Chapter 1's DO label of "structuring for success."

"Moving Past Reasons Not to Succeed" first discusses symptoms of "stuck" behaviors and gives several useful models and examples for moving past reasons that you hear when improvement projects slow down. It also reinforces these models with a persuasive series of process-improvement success stories.

"Creating an Environment for Success" compares product projects to process-improvement projects to give a variety of useful ways to structure successful projects, including an outline for a process-improvement plan.

Finally, "Telling the Story of Software Process Improvements" shows a detailed example of how to storyboard a success story for your project. Like many of the other methods introduced in the DO section, a storyboard is something you will evolve and frequently use throughout a process-improvement implementation. It also provides a natural transition to CHECK, since it reinforces the groundwork you need to do before you get to the next phase.

6

Moving Past
Reasons Not
to Succeed

I've been fortunate to work for some excellent managers during my career. One of my early ones had a memorable way to get me to free my mind from an apparent dead end. At times, when I would say "we can't do that because . . . ," they would say "oh, that's standard reason number seven." They would then list several other "standard reasons," and we would start to talk about obvious exceptions that one or the other of us had seen. They were careful to do this so that I never felt that they were making fun of me. By approaching my problem in a semihumorous way, they showed me that I was the one who was stuck, and we got to solution-oriented thinking quickly.

We've all had the exhilaration of finding ways around seemingly insoluble problems. We have also felt totally stuck at other times. What can we learn from my former manager's technique that will help us to get ourselves and others unstuck at similar times? Also, are there other approaches that will help?

The theme of this chapter is success, not excuses not to succeed. By looking at these typical symptoms of stuck thinking in a process-improvement context, we can prepare to defuse similar future resistance. All the cases described here are real. While their resolutions may not all be optimum or described completely, the intent is to help you be more creative in addressing such standard answers, whether it is you who is giving the answer, or someone else.

REASON 1: "MANAGEMENT WILL NEVER GO ALONG WITH IT." _____

It seems that one of the most often heard reasons to delay process improvements is "management will never go along with it." It takes several forms. "They aren't committed." "They don't understand software." "It's against Corporate (or Government) policy." It's hard to challenge reasons that are both so authoritative and vague. Let's look at an example of how to move similar situations forward opportunely.

Years ago when I joined Hewlett-Packard, it was a much smaller company. There were only a few divisions, and they were small enough that you could get to know most people in your division. The company had a policy of few offices, and engineers worked in open areas with no walls. This encouraged open communications and team spirit. Unfortunately, such a setup was not good for uninterrupted thinking. It was particularly hard when we were trying to work through complex software logic.

The division I was part of grew rapidly. This led to crowded conditions as a move to a larger building was planned. We were HP's first business centered on building systems with computers, so software was very important. I was asked to manage a large project that involved a rapid buildup of software contract programmers. The only way to find space for them was to use a conference room until the move. We put nine people into a small room that barely had room for nine desks. This was an opportunity.

We used the lack of space to justify three-level, desk-top bookcases for the nine desks. These weren't noticed until we moved to the new building several months later. By then our project was running at full steam. In the new building, the bookcases stood out like a sore thumb. How dared we violate the long traditions of open spaces? There were quite a few challenges from various departments. We successfully defended keeping the bookcases, though, since hardware engineers traditionally had workbenches. While these were usually in separate areas, we were able to argue that our bookcases served an equivalent function in keeping our desks free to spread out listings. We even got bookcases for the rest of our team.

Gradually, people in other departments managed to also add bookcases, and as "management" saw that HP's teamwork and communications didn't suffer, desktop bookcases became common. It took several years more before sound-dampening partitions were accepted to better serve the functions that our original wooden bookcases had.

This improvement captures the essence of moving past "management will never go along with it." The original policy was based on reasonable intentions. When you do process improvements, you may find that yours conflicts with other, past, successful practices. It becomes your challenge to help evolve these previous practices when the time is right. We have seen many other similar changes: At one time it was unheard of that programmers should each have their own terminal. Later, workstations and personal computers were certainly something that should only be used by a few. And color displays—not for the masses! Ergonomics is an entire new scientific field that studies the very real physical conditions that interfere with effective work. Such conditions are just the most recent changes that "management would never have gone along with" in the past. In each case, opportunities appeared as cost structures changed.

What can we do to transform the belief "management will never go along with it" into "management is ready to support that"? It isn't necessarily "management" who isn't ready. It might be you or your colleagues who *think* management isn't ready. When you hear the reason "management will never go along with it," look for opportunities.

Probe for the origin of the belief.

> "Who in management won't go along with it?"
> "How do you *know* they won't?"

Probe for the boundaries of the belief.

> "They'll *never* go along with it?"
> "Are there any similar situations when they did?"
> "Under what conditions *would* they or *have* they?"

Restate what you've heard. Try to use the other person's words as directly as possible without adding your own opinions (unless asked for them and you clearly incorporate them into your restatement of their response). By trying to use the other person's own words, you will become a better listener. It will be easier to maintain rapport, and there is less risk that you will misinterpret their beliefs. You may disagree with what they seem to believe, but you need to assume that their beliefs make sense to them based on their personal experiences. When you focus on understanding someone else's views, two things happen: You enrich your ability to recognize and deal with similar future situations, and the other person becomes more creative in dealing with the present one.

Ask how this new information might be used to move the desired process improvement forward. You need to time this question carefully. If the other person is still in a "stuck" state, don't ask this yet. Continue to probe with some other questions and restate what you've heard again. You can recognize a "stuck" state by words like "can't, won't, or don't"; by facial signs like a negative head shake or a frown; or by body postures like crossed arms or legs.

Another Example

(Note: In all the examples, imagine playing a variety of roles as the person asking questions: project manager, process-improvement manager, consultant, colleague, friend, . . . Also imagine "you" becomes "we" and "your" becomes "our" as your role changes.)

Let's explore a hypothetical conversation for another real process-improvement roadblock. This time, the person you're talking with has proposed an improvement that would tie defect-fixing priorities to ongoing metrics to monitor average defect-fix response times.

"Who in management won't go along with spending some time reducing the defect backlog?"

"Our R&D manager."

"How do you __know__ they won't?"

"Well, at the offsite last year, they said that functionality comes first. We would never have any time to reduce the defect backlog."

"__Never?__"

"That's what they said."

"That sounds final, all right. Are there any situations when they have agreed to reduce the backlog?"

"I heard that they were pretty upset when they were given our customer satisfaction survey results two weeks ago. The survey showed that one of our most important customers is really upset with our defect rates and our responsiveness to them."

"How did the R&D manager respond to that?"

"They commented that maybe they would have to consider dedicating a couple of people's time to reducing that customer's defect list."

"So the R&D manager said last year at an offsite that the lab would never focus on reducing the software defect backlog, because it needed to work too hard adding new

functionality. However, when they heard the results of the customer satisfaction survey two weeks ago that showed how negatively defect rates were affecting your most important customer, your manager commented that they would consider dedicating a couple of people's time to reducing that customer's defect list."

Then, ask how this new attitude might help them tie their process-improvement suggestions for monitoring response time into the changes that will be made.

REASON 2: "WE TRIED IT BEFORE AND IT DIDN'T WORK." _____

When I hear this reason, I vividly see the Peanuts® comic-strip characters Charlie Brown and Lucy. Every year when football season starts, Lucy holds the football on the ground for Charlie to kick. Every year, she pulls it away at the last second, and Charlie falls flat on his back while trying to kick it. Charlie may have good reason to stop trying to kick a football, but I don't believe that process improvements fail so consistently.

I've worked with a lot of groups to help them implement software metrics. When I do, it's amazing how often I hear "we tried it before and it didn't work." Sometimes it's said as a generalization for all metrics. Sometimes it's said just for collecting the time people spend on various activities. Usually it's easy to trace such responses to one manager who has left people with the impression that data could be used against them. Such managers are seldom even a high-level manager. Understanding this goes a long way toward getting other managers to think more openly, since they don't identify with the insensitive actions of one particular manager in one situation.

HP has another particularly good example of overcoming "we tried it before and it didn't work" on a large scale. Customers have used our Precision Architecture computers for so long now that it's hard to imagine a time when we had several different computer architectures. Converging these all to a common architecture was a huge task. But that was just the beginning. Many of our customers had previously converted from one computer type to another at some point, and some of them had had bad experiences.

Anticipating potential issues when customers switched to HP's new computers, HP created a Migration Center to optimize the transition process. The center was an HP facility that had computers that were configured to match those that customers would use in their facilities. HP engineers worked with customer engineers to make sure that the customer's applications entirely worked before they did a cross-over in their own facility. This was a highly successful way to minimize our customer's risk.

The Migration Center existed for over three years. Their people and over 200 HP customers worked together to prove many times that "we tried it before and we know it worked." Just imagine the confidence of the HP team for their process by the time they had successfully done all these conversions. When you hear the reason "we tried it before and it didn't work," remember the skeptical customers helped by the Migration Center.

Probe for the origin of the belief.

> "What was tried before?"
> "Who tried it?"
> "What happened?"

Probe for the boundaries of the belief.

> "How is this situation the same?"
> "How is this situation different?"
> "What might you try this time?"

Restate what you've heard. For the remaining examples, imagine a conversation like the first example, with questions and answers. Only the restatements will be included here.

> "So the Driver Section bought a customized database system two years ago that they thought would help them to reuse code. After one year's use, they had catalogued 20 to 30 components but only reused half a dozen. They just didn't feel that the overhead to support the database was justified by so little reuse.
>
> "The proposed new approach will also need some way to archive and access reusable assets. This time, you think you can emphasize designed assets that you know will be used in multiple products that have a well-defined, sustainable architecture. You can also more clearly define responsibilities for who will create, use, and support the assets. Finally, you can define processes for tracking increasing usage and for early review of product designs to make sure reused assets are used and evolved."

Then, ask if there is anything else that can be done that will help ensure the new approach is successful.

EXPERIENCE MAPS

The first examples have illustrated several things. People with strong beliefs may be more flexible than they seem. To discover this, there are nonthreatening questions you can ask. Use these to seek more information from others about the origin of their beliefs and the boundaries of those beliefs. Questions oriented to information gathering don't challenge the knowledge of belief-holders. "Why" questions do. When you ask "why," it suggests that you might disagree with another person. "What," "who," and "how" questions are less likely to challenge, and they help *you* to be more open to learning.

Figure 6-1 symbolically shows a person's experience map. This is a way to visualize how your experiences may or may not coincide with someone else's. The box within the map suggests a set of a person's beliefs related to a reason you two are discussing. The overlapping small box suggests your beliefs related to the reason. The nonoverlapping areas of both small boxes represent opportunities for both of you to learn and consider new ideas.

We view and catalogue experiences into a personal framework or map. Every time we experience something new, we change, and our map also changes. By carefully listening to what other people say, we can learn what they feel the roadblocks are, and there are useful questions we can ask to help remove them.

Figure 6-1 Converging beliefs

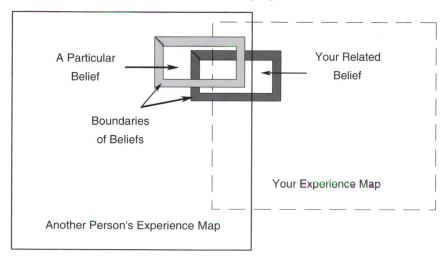

Sometimes, a person feels that roadblocks are so strong that it continues to be hard to find ways around them. The next examples show how to use a future desired state to overcome such a focus on roadblocks.

REASON 3:
"THE OTHER GROUP THAT MADE IT WORK IS DIFFERENT FROM US." ____

This reason is so popular that it has earned its own name: "Not Invented Here (NIH*)." NIH is so significant that its importance is probably right up there with Newton's laws of gravity and motion.

---

* You might think that a term like NIH dates back to Roman or Greek times, but Professor Ted Levitt of Harvard apparently was the first to coin the term in the 1960s to describe our all-too-human tendencies to reject other people's solutions so that we can create our own. [1]

I have a good friend who left HP to work with a company that sells software tools. One of their tools measures code coverage. It takes source code that you plan to test and adds other code that then keeps track of which of your code executes when you run your test cases. My friend has told me some true horror stories about some groups in major software-supplying companies. Groups in these companies complained about having significant testing problems and delayed products. However, they "knew" code coverage was high because they spent so much time testing. Evidence from other companies suggesting that their coverage might actually be low didn't apply, since "they were different."

My friend relates case after case where they have worked with these companies to test their coverage. When they do, many of them found their real coverage was around 30 percent, and occasionally as low as 15 percent. (HP groups have found that it is worthwhile to achieve at least 80 percent coverage. [2]) Even after learning they had these low coverages, someone *still* needed to convince most of these groups that working to get much better coverage would help reduce their testing and release problems. They really wanted to be different! When you hear "the other group that made it work is different from us,"

Probe for the origin of the belief.

> "What are some of the differences?"
> "Tell me some other things you know about the other organization."
> "Who else do you know who could tell us more about the other organization?"

Probe for the boundaries of the belief.

> "What are some ways that the two organizations are similar?"
> "Are there other, more similar organizations where this improvement has worked?"
> "Are there any situations when this solution could work for you?"

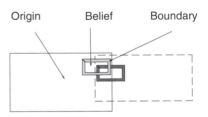

Restate what you've heard. (Again, a different real case.)

> "So you can't estimate when your team will finish adapting this order processing system for our division. The modification and

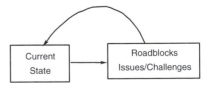

adoption of the system for those six other divisions was much simpler, because they don't sell systems. You've been over to talk with people at three of them and two of your programmers used to work in two of the others. One of the other divisions occasionally does systems, but they aren't nearly as complicated. Since the scope is so different, you can't estimate how long your programmers will take. You just can't see any way around the problem."

Reframe their challenge into a desired future state.

"Let's think about this system two years from now, when your project has been successful. What do you see? What do you hear? What does it feel like? What were some of the things you did that created your success?"

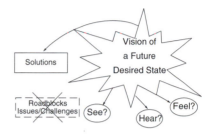

Getting someone to think from a future desired state is a powerful way to help them to think of other alternatives. When they make a shift to their desired state, they will use words like "can, might, should, or will." They will nod their head positively and might smile, and their gestures will be animated. Once you sense this, continue your questions until they have worked out what they want to do.

Restate what you've heard.

"So it's hard to estimate what it would take to adapt this order-processing system. Other division's challenges weren't the same, because they don't sell systems. You've certainly researched this well, and your scope is very different. When you think about it from a successful vantage point two years from now, you can see that your team *was* able to determine that there are 40 tasks to do, and 35 of those were comparable to the other divisions' tasks. Thus, you could base your estimates for those on past efforts. You also decided that large time estimates for the other five tasks combined with careful monitoring and risk management would allow you to make a decent estimate for the total job. This new way of thinking about estimates helped you and your team to finish the project on time with few emergencies."

Then, ask them what else they can think of that will help make this estimation process work even better for both this project and other, future projects.

It isn't easy for a group to estimate a major software job if they haven't done anything similar before. Both the managers responsible for doing the estimates and the ones asking for estimates can become very frustrated. Yet often, as here, there is a basis for an improved estimation process. This difficult, year-long project finished right on the schedule they based on their early estimates without excessive overtime or poor quality.

REASON 4: "ALL THESE OTHER THINGS HAVE TO BE DONE FIRST." _____

This reason is another classic. My same manager who had a standard list for not doing things called this one "delay is the deadliest form of denial." It's deadly because you tend to keep adjusting other tasks and responsibilities to each new date in good faith. So each unexpected delay ends up having a ripple effect on people who were scheduled to do critical tasks and, ultimately, on the timeliness and potential payback of any improvement. It's better to know up front if the perceived value of an improvement is so low that you have a low probability of success. At least you can walk away then without the bad feelings and waste that you might otherwise experience.

It's ironic that I started outlining this section of the chapter while waiting for an airplane to fly to San Diego. As the schedule changed from 4:55 to 6:10 to 7:00 to a final departure of 7:20, I thought of how I could have enjoyed a nice dinner instead of being cooped up in a stuffy waiting area with a group of increasingly grumpy people. Such repeated delays are a real danger signal for process improvements.

"All these other things have to be done first" is almost guaranteed to come up many times during long-term, process-improvement investments, such as reuse. There will be conflicts with product programs, particularly near product releases. Schedule pressures increase temptations to use "slightly modified" components instead of evolving them to best serve all projects. There are tough decisions needed to balance strategic and tactical needs. The more these projects diverge from strategic goals, the more they expose the organization to expensive future maintenance and customer dissatisfaction.

Organizations that have managed to avoid such delaying effects have been strongly motivated to widely reuse software assets. Their markets forced them to create more products to stay ahead of the competition. They realized that the overhead to support several simultaneous test and release efforts exponentially complicated processes initially set up for single products. They also realized they couldn't hire experienced resources fast enough to sustain historical quality, both in terms of understanding customer needs and in terms of doing products well.

To transition from the belief "all these other things have to be done first" to considering reuse activities as "first," these organizations assigned dedicated people to work flexibly with users, remove roadblocks, and follow through until reuse was an accepted part of their maps. When you hear the reason "all these other things have to be done first,"

Probe for the origin of the belief.

"Which other things need to be done first?"
"Who decided that all those things had to be done first?"

Probe for the boundaries of the belief.

"Who is involved in getting the other things done?"
"Would any of those things be easier to do if the process improvement was already in use?"
"What would happen if some of those things didn't get done first?"

Restate what you've heard. (Again, a different real case.)

"So you think the new defect-tracking system would be great, but your team has too many other things it has to do first. They still have to develop 50K lines of code, and other projects you've managed have taken longer to do this than you've targeted time for. There may be some differences between this project and the others, but your team still also has to integrate and test the entire system. You need everyone to do these and you're under huge pressure to finish on time.

"Looking back at your successful project a year from now, you see that your team's use of the new tracking system definitely saved time over the previous approach. The new system gave you much better rollup information which led to better, more timely decisions. A key breakthrough was when we figured out a way to parallel the new system with the old one and gradually trained the team one or two at a time."

Then, ask who else should be involved to plan the system paralleling and individual training.

A VISION OF A FUTURE DESIRED STATE

The last two examples complemented the first two to show how a vision of a future desired state is a powerful tool to stimulate discussion. We can graphically think of what's happening in all these cases as moving from the current state shown in Figure 6-2 to the starburst labeled "vision of a future desired state." Some paths are blocked. Solutions open others. The leftmost arrow in the figure also shows how a person's experience map influences their current state. Learning more about their belief origins and boundaries is a good way to better understand both the person and situation.

The figure also shows how the vision of a future desired state can be clarified by asking what someone sees, hears, or feels in that state. Finally, the figure shows various comments below the boxes that we heard from Reason 4 (the defect-tracking example) about the current situation and future desired state. Use a visual model like this to help you both gather useful information and organize it in a way to effectively reflect it back to someone else.

REASON 5: "WE DON'T HAVE TIME." ("WE'LL MISS OUR SCHEDULE.") _____

This reason conjures up the image of a group furiously bailing out a boat, while no one tries to fix the leak. It is one of the hardest reasons to challenge. Its origin is based on unknowns similar to the unknowns in the previous example. The project team is probably doing things they have never done before, and they don't know how much or even whether a proposed process improvement will help them.

We have repeatedly heard this reason as we've worked with HP organizations to start inspections. A good way to think about this reason is to imagine an experience map that ignores or masks out sections of experience due to an overemphasis on time. The key thing to do is to reexpand the map to include other risks besides missing a schedule. You can do this by probing for the belief origins and boundaries, using many of the same questions from the earlier examples.

Our experience suggests several things we must do. We need to explore what other risks exist. Which of these will inspections help minimize? Then, we need to translate these risks to the time framework, since this is the emphasis of most concern. Usually these steps will help resistant teams to try inspections on some critical work products. We then explore ways to help them to minimize any time impacts on their project schedule, such as customized training, non-team-member facilitators, and meeting follow-up support.

Even with this help, success is fragile. It is important to make sure that people prepare well for the inspection meetings and that they follow a good meeting process. We make sure they measure meeting results and acknowledge successes. We also make sure they review results with the responsible manager to make sure that the manager also acknowledges success and shows support. It is important throughout the inspection introduction process to be flexible, to remove roadblocks, and to follow through

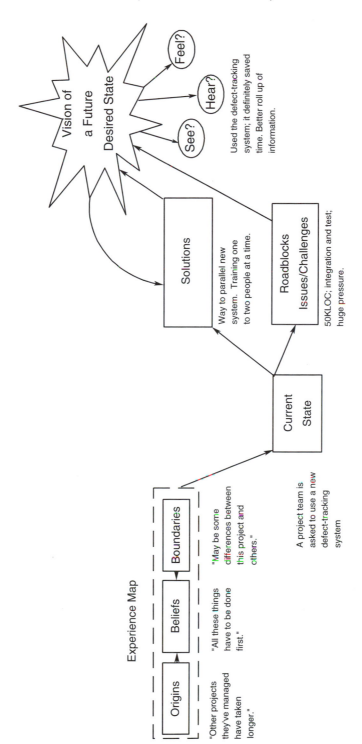

Figure 6-2 A vision of a future desired state

until both the manager and the team have enough experience with inspections that their experience is an accepted part of their maps. When you hear "we don't have time,"

Probe for the origin of the belief.

> "What are your schedule constraints?"
> "Who set your schedule and when was it set?"
> "What will happen if you miss your schedule?"

Probe for the boundaries of the belief.

> "Besides your schedule constraints, are there other project risks?"
> "Have you or your team used this process improvement before?"
> "What other teams have used this process improvement and
>   what were their results?"
> "Are there any alternatives that you could try that would help
>   you to get similar, successful results?"

Restate what you've heard. (Again, a different real case.)

> "So you have a project team of 15 engineers to do your system and a drop-dead date of 15 months from now. You and your team drew up the schedule, but you are keenly aware of how urgently your division needs this new product. You're afraid that if you don't create and review better design documents than in the past, you will run into problems during test as you did with the previous project. You heard a persuasive presentation at last year's Productivity Conference about one team who did structured design documents, but no automated tools are available. You are tempted to try an approach where a technician would use a drawing tool to do the drawings, make changes, and control revisions. Such a solution wouldn't provide automated checks, but it would give you better design documents and much better artifacts to inspect."

Then, ask how such a solution would help the lab to evolve to better automated solutions as they become available.

This team did use a technician in the way suggested above. Their process worked well with little or no schedule effects. They created much better design documents than they had in the past, and their lab today uses advanced design methods.

REASON 6: "WE NEED EXTRA RESOURCES." _____

I was fortunate early in my project-management career. Several excellent books, including *The Mythical Man Month*, were published. I believe that a famous quote from it still applies: "Adding manpower to a late software project makes it later." [3]

One of the largest early projects that I managed was to create the HP ATLAS Compiler. This was a large compilation system consisting of three interacting compilers. [4] Processing the large source programs these compilers used as input (sometimes over 100 pages of English-like text) was a challenge, especially since the computers we used only had 32K words of memory. As with most things that have never been done before, this project was difficult to estimate. To complicate things even more, we had made contractual delivery commitments early in the project.

As the project proceeded, I felt increasing pressure to add more people. Fortunately, "Brooks' Law" was fresh in my mind, so I resisted adding more programmers. Looking back, I realize that this never stopped us from making process improvements as we moved through the project. We decided to do design inspections. We created several compiler tools. We created a special debug capability. We implemented configuration management procedures that saved us twice after widespread disk failures.

It's hard to say whether we wouldn't have finished sooner if we had added more people or hadn't spent time on those process improvements. Because we did successfully complete the project on time, my beliefs about exploring alternatives to adding more people were strengthened. When you hear the reason "we need extra resources,"

Probe for the origin of the belief.

> "How much effort will it take to make this improvement, and
> how much will be returned to you if you do it?"
> "Can the project schedule be changed?"
> "Can the project content be changed?"

Probe for the boundaries of the belief.

> "Are there any ways to do the improvement that might involve
> less of your team's time?"
> "What trade-offs among schedule and content might allow you
> to do the improvement?"
> "Are there any other project risks that this improvement might
> minimize?"

Restate what you've heard. (Again, a different real case.)

"So you've got a huge backlog of defects, and you think that it will take your engineers too much time to enter defect origin and type information into your defect-tracking system. Your next release deadline is fixed and rapidly approaching. You're open to having someone from outside the team look at past logged defects to reconstruct causal information. However, you doubt if what they find will be valuable enough to justify the time necessary for future causal-data logging by your team.

"Imagining a year from now that your team did do the logging, you are feeling much more confident about your next release. You now know what your most common defect sources are and their effect on your customers. Because of this, you have made changes that have already significantly reduced the incoming defect rate. This more than offset the 3 to 4 minutes per defect that it took to regularly capture the data. This was a significant improvement!"

Then, ask who, besides themself, should review the causal results after you have some-one reconstruct the information. Also, what other steps should be planned, assuming their results appear as promising as other divisions' results have?

After having an outside engineer do such an analysis, this division went on to train all their engineers in causal-data logging. This data helped them to identify high-leverage opportunities, and it motivated them to make resulting improvements.

Of the first eight similar efforts in HP divisions, four so far have been motivated to adopt logging and failure analysis as an ongoing process.

THE LADDER OF INFERENCE

The openness of a group to undergo change depends upon how they view the change. This, in turn, depends on individual and shared experiences that influence how the change appears.

Rick Ross has created a model of the way people develop beliefs in *The Fifth Discipline Fieldbook*, based on Chris Argyris's concept of the ladder of inference. [5,6,7] Figure 6-3 shows this model. It starts with *data* you direct-ly see and experience in your environment. You *filter* out some data and add *meanings* to the remaining data. From these, you make *assumptions* which lead to *conclusions*. You integrate these with your past experiences to form *beliefs*. Your beliefs are the basis for your *actions*.

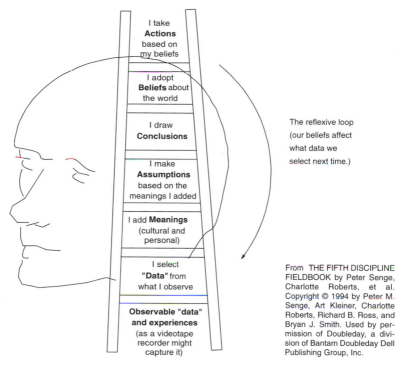

I take
Actions
based on
my beliefs

I adopt
Beliefs about
the world

I draw
Conclusions

I make
Assumptions
based on the
meanings I added

I add **Meanings**
(cultural and
personal)

I select
"Data" from
what I observe

Observable **"data"**
and experiences
(as a videotape
recorder might
capture it)

The reflexive loop
(our beliefs affect
what data we
select next time.)

From THE FIFTH DISCIPLINE
FIELDBOOK by Peter Senge,
Charlotte Roberts, et al.
Copyright © 1994 by Peter M.
Senge, Art Kleiner, Charlotte
Roberts, Richard B. Ross, and
Bryan J. Smith. Used by per-
mission of Doubleday, a divi-
sion of Bantam Doubleday Dell
Publishing Group, Inc.

Figure 6-3 The ladder of inference (from ref. 5, with permission)

Think back to the earlier design improvement done using a drawing tool and a technician. If a past noteworthy success using a fully automated tool heavily influenced the manager of this team or the key technical opinion leaders, such an experience might be internalized as a belief. It might work like this.

- You have discussed documenting designs with the manager. You have suggested various options all the way from hand drawings up to fully automated tools.
- The manager might think (select data): "I hear three solutions: (1) manual drawings, (2) a technician who enters manual drawings into a tool, and (3) engineers fully using a tool."
- The manager then might add meanings: "That last project was a great success largely because I was able to convince both management and the team to use a configuration management tool. They complained a lot at first, but we succeeded."
- Then, assumptions: "This design tool would produce a similar success."

- Then, conclusions/beliefs: "My project will fail if my engineers don't use this tool."

Thinking your way up to the top of the ladder happens quickly. In this example, the conclusions would make it hard to accept a semiautomated solution and virtually impossible to accept a manual approach.

Your probing questions and the use of a vision of a future desired state are ways to help people consider moving down the ladder of inference. You aren't necessarily adding "new" data. You may just be getting them to consider aspects of their own past experience that weren't integrated into a particular belief. You are essentially asking them to reconsider their conclusions, assumptions, or interpreted meanings.

Remember, you also are working from a ladder of inference. Consider, if your perception is that past success is attributed to teamwork and management expertise even though tools were used, you might see a tool as just a part of the environment or something that affects behavior. Your beliefs might assure you that their team has the flexibility for many possible approaches.

You need to remember the ladder of inference when you work with others to make process improvements. When you sense resistance, as in this example, consider where both of you are on your ladders of inference. What previous experience drives their conclusions and beliefs compared to yours? How should you integrate this new data into your conclusions? As long as you remain open to understanding their beliefs, you maintain a healthy balance between inquiry (asking for data and their meanings) versus advocacy (suggesting or trying to convince based on your own beliefs). [5] When others sense your openness, they will be more open to adjusting their beliefs, too.

This model suggests that there are no "right" or "wrong" reasons for people's reactions. Just as we saw represented in our earlier Figure 6-1 model, people interpret situations based on their frame of reference and understanding. To the extent that that frame can be opened to include other experiences and possibilities, they and you will have more options available and, possibly, greater chances for success.

CONCLUSION

Every time you hear a "reason" why an improvement won't or can't succeed, you are hearing important information. The people who give these reasons are not necessarily *negative* people. Their experiences are real. Probing their reasons helps you and them to better understand what to do to move forward more quickly and successfully. The many real examples in this chapter show how to do this. They hint at the experience maps behind common hangups, and they are designed to expand your map to enable you to try various approaches in similar situations.

Questions that probe the origins and boundaries of beliefs help clarify what's behind reasons for you and others. Information-oriented questions don't challenge the knowledge of belief-holders. They help to encourage people to discuss situations openly. These questions also help you to keep yourself open to learning. Ask them with curiosity, with interest, and without a personal agenda.

Sometimes probing questions don't work, because barriers seem too much to overcome. Helping someone mentally shift to a future desired state is a powerful way to get them open, creative, and more flexible. Both probing questions and thinking about a future desired state are ways to expand our own and others' experience maps to look at a current situation in a larger context.

Will asking questions this way help you to do software process improvements? Process improvement involves social change. The social aspects of change often are more challenging than technological ones. Most of all, these questions focus you on involving others and on moving forward. By doing so, you model leadership without being directive, and people adapt much more easily to changes when they feel they participate in the decisions. [8]

Even if solutions are clear to you, they may conflict with someone else's beliefs. Understanding the ladder of inference helps you to better balance advocacy with inquiry and to recognize when your questions have either shifted your beliefs or those of others. There are things to listen and watch for—words, facial expressions, body language.

- The most closed signs include negative words like "can't, won't, or don't"; facial signs like a negative head shake or a frown; or body postures like crossed arms or legs.
- Signs that a person is somewhat open to other possibilities are words like "might or could"; a thoughtful facial expression; or a neutral body posture.
- A person who is most open uses words like "can, might, should, or will." They nod their head positively, smile, and use animated gestures.

Will these techniques always work? If you view them as a way of learning, yes, most of the time. If you view them as a way of convincing someone else of something, they will work sometimes. Those times will especially be when the other person was already open to a change such as your proposed one.

Software process improvements are challenging. No two people are alike, and their beliefs can disable you at critical moments if you aren't resourceful. The examples in this chapter show you success in the face of serious process-improvement challenges. They show you behaviors that you can practice to improve *your* capabilities. With practice, you will be better prepared to work through the most challenging process-improvement"reasons not to succeed."

BIBLIOGRAPHY

1. Levitt, T., *The Marketing Mode: Pathways to Corporate Growth*, New York: McGraw-Hill, Inc., 1969, p. 180.
2. Grady, R., *Practical Software Metrics for Project Management and Process Improvement*, Englewood Cliffs, N. J.: Prentice-Hall, Inc., 1992, pp. 122-157.
3. Brooks, F., *The Mythical Man-Month*, Reading, Mass.: Addison-Wesley, 1975.
4. Finch, W., and R. Grady, "ATLAS: A Unit-Under-Test Oriented Language for Automatic Test Systems," *Hewlett-Packard Journal*, (Dec. 1975), pp. 2-13.
5. Senge, P., A. Kleiner, C. Roberts, R. Ross, and B. Smith, *The Fifth Discipline Fieldbook*, New York: Doubleday, 1994, pp. 243, 253-259.
6. Argyris, C., *Reasoning, Learning, and Action*, San Francisco: Jossey-Bass, 1982, pp. xvii-xviii, 176-178.
7. Argyris, C., R. Putnam, and D. Smith, *Action Science*, San Francisco: Jossey-Bass, 1985, pp. 56-58.
8. Lawrence, P. "How to Deal with Resistance to Change," *Harvard Business Review*, (Jan.-Feb. 1969), pp. 160-176.

7

Creating an Environment for Success

When I was young, my brother and I played Little League baseball. Somehow we got the idea that when we had a good game, it was bad luck to wash our uniforms. I'm sure we got this idea from watching athletes on TV. They often act like the most superstitious people in the world. What they are trying to do, though, is maintain or recreate past conditions under which they were successful.

Do we, as managers of software process improvements, act just as strangely when we imitate past success? Often we gained successes while managing development projects. While many things we did then also apply to process-improvement initiatives, others may be unnecessary superstitions or even counterproductive for process improvements. We should at least consciously explore our management methods to evaluate their usefulness to improvement projects.

As a development manager, I believed my most important job was to create and maintain a success-filled environment for my team. Looking back, I can see six facets to that environment: vision, people, suitability of product to customers, climate, infrastructure, and a good project plan. The following sections group these into the three categories on the left of Figure 7-1. Each facet is discussed from a product-development project view and then contrasted to the added risks you face to manage a process-improvement project. Ways to provide leadership to minimize those risks are then offered.

Figure 7-1 Aspects of a successful project environment

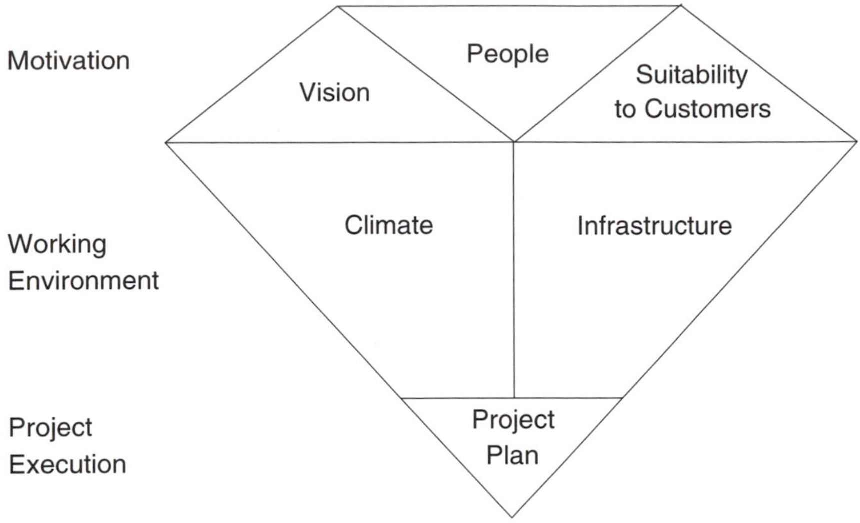

Motivation

People

Vision

Suitability
to Customers

Working
Environment

Climate

Infrastructure

Project
Execution

Project
Plan

MOTIVATE

There are several things you must do to create and sustain team motivation. First, you must show the team an exciting vision of the future. Second, people strongly influence the working environment. It is useful to assess key people's attitudes and work with those people to keep them supportive. Finally, you have to show the continuing suitability of your project, and do so often.

Create and Communicate an Exciting Vision

All projects should begin with a clear and exciting vision. The project manager is the project champion. You always must work to sustain team enthusiasm and other people's excitement for your project. You also must show how your project fits into the organization's larger picture.

Process-improvement projects also start best with a good vision. It must be a vision of people using a "product" to do things better. Such a vision must appeal to both the management team that reviews product projects *and* to the people who will use the improvement. Because you must try to satisfy both groups, extra effort is needed to create a vision that isn't fuzzy or that appeals only to one group or the other. Also, the management team isn't always clear how strongly they support process improvement versus product projects, and they sometimes appear to change their minds. It is very hard to compete with product projects whose visions show imminent sales and aggressive schedules. These challenges highlight the importance of a process-improvement vision statement. There are four things you need to capture in a process-improvement vision. Let's look at an example.

Clear benefits - Figure 7-2 is the way one group captured its vision. Their improvement will gradually pull together multiple, isolated information systems and databases into a single set of interfaces. It leaves a clear mental picture of how one internal customer will benefit from a series of process changes. The bubbles emphasize particular user needs while showing how a single system will provide a unified solution.

Long term - Their image is powerful in other ways, too. Because their system changes go beyond improvements for just marketing analysts, similar figures are equally effective in exciting other users and managers. A key success element is the figure's marketing analyst center of focus. This helps both internal customers and developers to internalize the customer-oriented approach. They also created a single architectural vision slide that unifies their technical approach. This architecture may take years to implement and evolve.

(Project goals) and intermediate results - A good vision statement is exciting, easy to visualize and remember, and can be articulated easily. It shows a desirable future state. It also is a vehicle to set goals and to discuss intermediate results. These are especially important when lengthy improvement projects compete for the same resources and sponsorship as more direct money-making projects. Clear goals with intermediate results can appeal even more than product projects, because you get them sooner. They also depend less on externally changeable markets. Chapters 3 and 4 offered some excellent examples of improvement goals and objectives, and Chapters 8 and 9 give additional guidance for how to develop them.

Alignment - A vision statement must be compelling for both upper management and engineers. Management must see a process improvement aligned to business needs such as new markets, cost constraints, or time-to-market pressures. Engineers must see such projects as well timed and aligned with what they believe their organization is ready to follow through with. Such projects should remove tedious, error-prone tasks and make their resulting jobs more fun and rewarding.

So, a good vision statement is just as important for an improvement project as it is for any other project. Just as there must be a compelling organizational vision, your process improvement will work best when you and your team create a compelling vision of how everyone will work after a series of improvements.

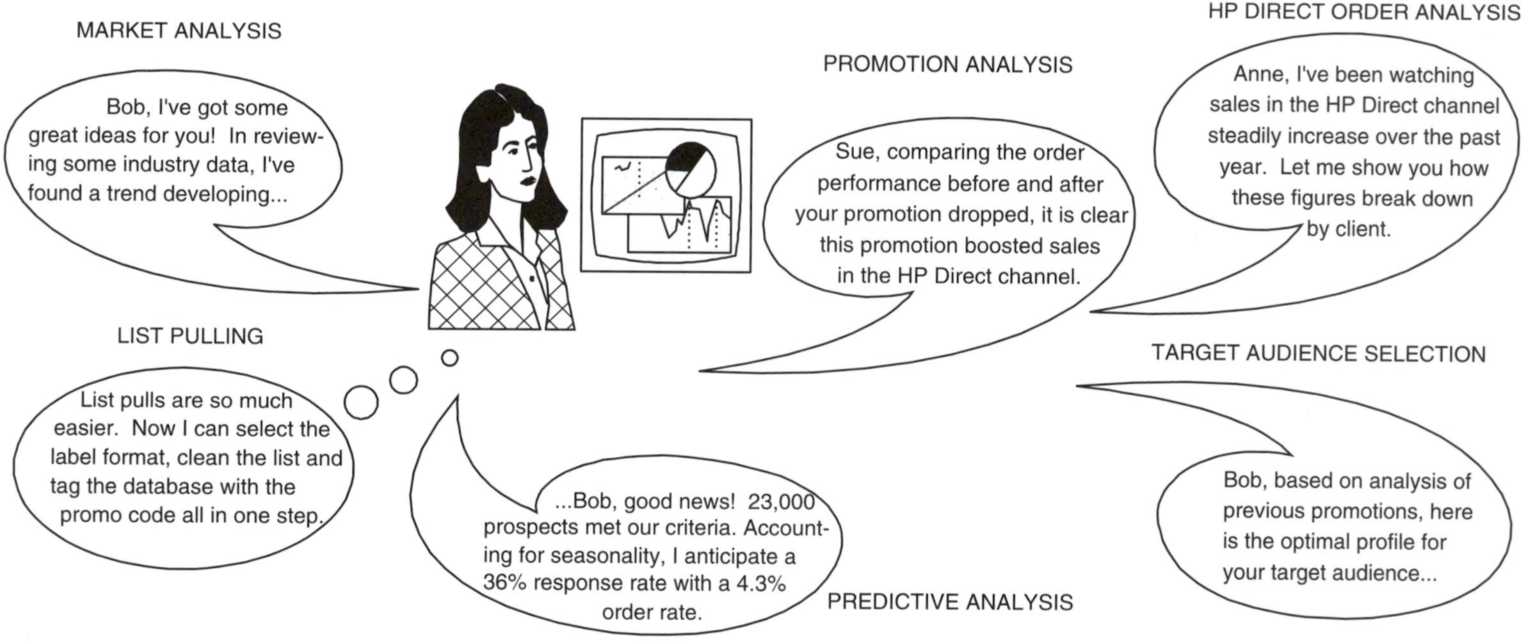

Figure 7-2 Marketing analyst vision

Identify and Sustain the Support of Key People

All projects can be made or broken by the people involved. The project manager plays a key role by ensuring that the people work together productively. This involves positive feedback, open listening, fairly resolving disagreements, sensing when people are stuck, and getting them unstuck.

A process-improvement project includes extra challenges. A manager has to be sensitive both to the improvement team's needs and to their customer's needs. This includes things that marketing, sales, and support usually handle for product projects. Improvement customers also are, in many ways, part of the project team, because both groups are often organizationally related. This can be an advantage if the improvement manager is seen as unbiased. It is a strong disadvantage if that manager is seen as pushing something onto the customers in an inflexible or insensitive way.

There are four key people and people-related aspects to assess and manage. An example of these is shown in Figure 7-3. Like the force-fields in Chapter 5, this is a way to simply visualize positive and negative influences. This figure's arrows were easy to draw after several meetings with management and improvement team people in one HP division. Having a sense for the commitment of these key people helps to focus efforts toward improving weak support. The champion, sponsor, and opinion leader roles were defined earlier in Chapter 1. These definitions are repeated here and expanded.

Figure 7-3 Force-field analysis of people effects on commitment

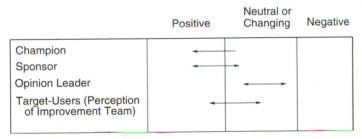

Champion - A project manager is generally also a project's champion. The champion role is key to success. A champion promotes an improvement throughout a project, removes obstacles, enthusiastically supports both people doing the improvement and future users, and leads through active involvement. Besides the project manager's actions as champion, it is often even more necessary for there to be a customer champion. When you get one, be sure to talk often with that person. Give lots of positive reinforcement for championing activities, both to the champion and to their management.

Sponsor - This is another key success role, so make certain that your project has an *active* sponsor. A sponsor is someone in a high organizational position who ensures funding and high-level public enthusiasm and encouragement. The sponsor is also a coach who keeps things progressing smoothly. Review progress with your sponsor often. End such meetings by asking "Is there anything else we should be doing to make sure our project contributes to our organization's success?"

Opinion Leader - Sometimes there are also less obvious technical leaders. Everett Rogers and other technological adoption researchers call them "opinion leaders." [1] They may not be as vocal as many technical leaders, but before other people will consider a change, they see if opinion leaders accept it. Be sure you know who the opinion leaders are in your improvement audience. Actively work to satisfy any concerns they might have. Remember that their vote of confidence is very influential.

Target User (Perception of Improvement Team) - This aspect is the reason to focus on your customer champions, sponsors, and opinion leaders. Target users will have a broad range of feelings about any improvement team. In HP, the words "we're from Corporate, and we're here to help" are sometimes treated humorously. Similar reactions can apply to other infrastructure groups. Organizational and technical leader allies will strongly help improve these feelings. You will also positively influence target users if you make it a point to *bring value to every meeting*. Your customer influence increases immediately when you help them solve problems.

Of all the responsibilities of managing a process-improvement project, the people area is often the most challenging. People aspects of process-improvement projects are more complex and less technically based than for most product projects, so consciously evaluate the four key aspects described here. Make sure that your plans include regular participation and reinforcement to hold the support you need. Remember that every member of your expanded project team is valuable. Draw on their individual and team expertise in making assignments, and follow their actions with support and positive reinforcement.

Flexibly Match Improvements to Suit Customer Needs

All projects are created for business reasons. A project's business purpose must be kept in front of a team so that they remain focused on high returns. Of equal importance, all projects compete for internal resources and management sponsorship. A good project manager must get and sustain strong sponsorship.

There are two big differences between product and process-improvement projects here. Improvement projects need stronger consensus to start and more frequent organizational reinforcement throughout their life. The consensus also must be sustained beyond the project team, and the reinforcement required may sometimes make you feel like you are always justifying your existence.

Just as you can assess your management's commitment to such projects, there are several aspects to evaluate for your project's suitability to the improvement customers' needs. Figure 7-4 summarizes these aspects. (It is taken from the same project as shown in Figure 7-3.)

Figure 7-4 Force-field analysis of suitability: aspects that influence process-improvement customers to support/not support a project

	Positive	Neutral or Changing	Negative
Perceived Connection to Their Project's Success			← →
Low Risk			← →
Local Success Story	←		
Timing		← →	
Measured Results	← →		
Personal Growth	← →		

Perceived connection to their project's successes - Do your process-improvement customers believe your project will improve their chances for success? Most product projects are tactically focused. Their teams will feel best if they see *detailed process-improvement plans* emphasizing immediate payback and little interference. Emphasize highly flexible solutions provided just when needed in their project's life cycle. Assume their starting attitude is the "if it ain't broke, don't fix it" philosophy. Show a strong enough connection between making an improvement and their success so that they're willing to change. Perceived connection is the weakest vector in the Figure 7-4 example.

Low risk - Risk is sometimes real, such as a potential mismatch of an improvement to an organization's current maturity. It can also be perceived risk, especially by adopting groups. Perceived risk may come from adopting teams overestimating the amount of training or adaptation time needed. It can also suggest they aren't yet convinced they will get much benefit from a change. In either case, you must visibly work to remove barriers and build their confidence.

Local success story - This aspect is one of the best ways of addressing the first two. When your customers know local people who have already adopted a process improvement, it is easier for them to accept. They have a day-to-day reminder that another group is reaping benefits. They can talk to the other group and ease their own concerns over how long the change will take and its potential risk. As a result, you don't have to spend as much time selling them on the benefits.

Timing - Timing when an improvement is first available can be a disaster or it can be an asset. One division asked a group I managed to create software design tools to help a large project improve tight schedules. Unfortunately, by the time we finished the tools, enough design work was done that the design team didn't have the time or motivation to learn how to use them. Faced with a similar situation later, we defined another tool well enough to do training when the lab was ready. We then created a manual equivalent of the tool that we staffed and ran until the automated one was ready. This time we were successful. Again, timing was a key aspect, and this time we used it as an asset.

Measured results - Even if you don't have a local success story, a measured success in another organization is still very convincing, especially for project managers. There are two things to remember. Present such results in ways that support local, compelling issues and your process-improvement customer's goals (quality, productivity, or others). Also emphasize how the results support shorter schedules, if possible, since almost all software project managers have schedule concerns.

Personal growth - Software is a young, evolving field. New processes, methods, and tools that engineers can see as improving their long-term skills will help gain their support. Improvements will be best applied when you match them well to your improvement customer's skills. This usually requires training and consulting until their abilities are optimized. Changing people's abilities takes time. You need to carefully plan this transition. You want your customers to be both excited about their progress and not satisfied until they are using their new skills well. You can only know this is happening when you spend some time talking with them individually about how they are using an improvement. Be sure to do this regularly.

In assessing your process improvement's suitability and in creating your plans, remember these projects are especially vulnerable if people see them as "overhead." It is crucial to maintain strong ties to product projects, to create local success stories, and to minimize risk by providing valuable intermediate results. Use Figure 7-4 to think about effective selling points when talking with your improvement customers, whether they are your own project team or a group in an entirely different organization.

OPTIMIZE THE WORKING ENVIRONMENT _____

A project's working environment includes all the physical, social, and cultural aspects that influence the team. For a process-improvement project, you must also include your customer's environment. Many times this will be essentially the same as yours. Other times, your customer may be organizationally different.

Major planning components can be grouped into project climate and infrastructure. The climate includes the physical and organizational interactions that influence your team's ability to be productive. The infrastructure includes existing processes, methods, and tools and their support framework. These are accepted parts of the management and engineering environment.

Create a Supportive and Enthusiastic Climate

Product projects last for many months, so project managers must create a positive climate that the team can count on. The team needs certain tools and training for the job, and they will be more motivated when they see strong management support in getting them. I like to draw an analogy to tanks and armor versus foot soldiers. My team would believe in our project's importance and urgency if I would help them get the "heavy guns." The best project managers minimize outside distractions and quickly remove barriers. This often means rolling up their sleeves and doing some "grunt work" to keep things moving.

Climate aspects may be much harder to control for a process-improvement project. Such projects are more likely to be strategic. This means high-level sponsorship is probably necessary, and usual project management approaches may not be enough. Sponsorship attention will wax and wane as other issues demand attention. Resources can be temporarily pulled to help with more tactical needs. Even tools and training for your team will often be a lower priority than for product teams.

Your "market acceptance" can also be very time dependent. Process changes will always be seen as time consuming, so you must tailor doing them to meet the target teams' desired timing and their ability to change. Adler and Shenbar's useful model of organizational learning is shown in Figure 7-5. [2] It graphically shows how you must think when matching a proposed change to your organization. It suggests that small changes involving only limited skills improvement and procedures take little time. Larger changes affecting structures or culture may take months or years. "Magnitude of improvement sought" in Figure 7-5 is probably best thought of as size and complexity.

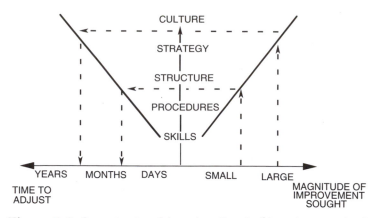

Figure 7-5 Organizational learning (level of learning required).

For example, changing design processes from traditional methods to object-oriented methods is far more complex than introducing inspections. In either case, the size of the change also heavily depends on the number of people you try to change at once. Size and complexity are two, more predictable change aspects.

Business and organizational aspects also strongly affect the change climate. Chapter 5 discussed ways to gain and strengthen commitment for 12 of these. As an improvement manager, you should especially organize your plans to blend with two of these: your organization's maturity and existing infrastructures. For example, suppose you plan a labwide process change, like configuration management. If existing processes are poorly defined and organized, you may need to first do manual procedures. On the other hand, if part of the lab already uses good configuration management, you can use their understanding and move faster. By intelligently planning your solution set to match your organization's maturity, you improve your chances for success.

You also help ensure a good climate by adding to the existing infrastructure. When people first work with a new process, ready access to someone to answer questions and remove roadblocks is critical. For example, a key part of speeding early HP inspections adoption was a local person who had specific process responsibilities, such as a "chief moderator." That person was a symbol of the organization's commitment to change and gave visible feedback for both management and the people doing inspections. This helped create an effective climate.

Mature usage of best practices like inspections and configuration management is similarly limited across an entire company if there is no group-level or company-level climate to encourage and sustain best-practice sharing. The limit here is on process optimization. Without a way to share improvements, individual labs can too easily stick with a far-from-optimum status quo. For example, HP's R&D labs widely adopted code inspections, but it wasn't until a companywide emphasis was shown and a support structure was created that inspections were widely expanded to include requirements and design inspections.

This discussion has focused on climate aspects that you can most directly control, both for your team and for your improvement audience. Just as certain crops can only grow in certain climates and soil conditions, process-improvement projects also depend on your organization's climate. Because most improvements are strategic, you need to plan for and often review your improvement's climate and your management's commitment to prevent loss of momentum.

Evolve Your Organization's Infrastructure to Speed the Adoption of Process Improvements

An organization's existing infrastructure is adapted and changed for every project. This happens because projects are created to do specific jobs effectively. So existing processes are adapted and complemented to achieve project goals. For example, I had to create a "defect-tracking binder" for some of my earlier software product projects. There was no automated system, so we needed a process to record and track defects. Most labs today have automated defect tracking, but teams still often complement such systems. Some systems don't provide for tracking defects found in inspections. Other systems don't provide for both prerelease and postrelease defects. It is usually easier for a fast-moving product team to complement its defect-tracking system than to try to adjust the existing infrastructure.

Product development teams *use* an infrastructure. Process-improvement teams *develop or change* one. You are swimming against a strong tide by trying to build a new infrastructure while not being a part of any affected product team. You must help some teams that are trying a new process for the first time to get started. You must also help other teams adapt earlier changes. For example, often when we work with an HP R&D lab on a new design method, some people are totally unfamiliar with the new method. They need basic training and skill building. Others in the same lab may already know the new method. They may need timely feedback and help in adapting the method to new situations.

An organization's infrastructure reinforces strongly held beliefs. In many ways, it sets the tone for learning. This affects both the speed and breadth of improvement adoptions. An infrastructure contributes to the standardization of a desired practice or process. Often it includes good information sharing. This can be as simple as regular meetings or more complicated, such as standard forms for data sheets or design documents. An infrastructure also reduces risk. For example, assigned personnel and standard procedures for software backups protect valuable work. An infrastructure increases efficiency. For example, creating optimal ways to debug or do builds saves many project hours.

An organization-level infrastructure spans many projects. Often it generalizes successful project practices, such as in the above examples. Sometimes it is created to support strategic needs, such as labwide software reuse.

The people who are part of an organization's infrastructure can be strong improvement allies. They won't have the same singular project focus as product teams. Labs with no one specifically responsible for quality or productivity will have a harder time changing. Their absence may suggest management sees infrastructure as "overhead." If so, you need to gradually change their thinking. One way is to draw an analogy to the role of transportation or communications in modern society. It's easy to see the weakness of such infrastructures in third-world countries. Such infrastructures are critical to rapid progress. Another way is to call the infrastructure something that doesn't trigger the "overhead" reaction. For example, we use "chief moderator" for the person who plays a key inspections infrastructure role, as opposed to "inspections support." The word "support" should particularly be avoided.

You will also need to convince project managers and engineers that infrastructure groups are valuable contributors. Here, emphasize the measurable results and personal growth parts of Figure 7-4. Speak in terms used by the organization, such as quality, productivity, time to market, or so forth. Talk about how engineers will spend more time doing better designs. This will reduce weekend test crunches and result in fewer rush fixes.

For any new improvement, start by creating a small infrastructure, and evolve it as the organization becomes ready. Both the size and function of an infrastructure will evolve. Make a strong case for staffing key infrastructure jobs with respected, enthusiastic people. Your goal is to get the maximum return from improvements that comes when an entire organization is optimally using new processes, methods, and tools. This occurs as a sequence of steps starting with individuals and teams. You will speed success and adoption by creating an infrastructure matched to an organization's maturity and ability to change. The people and processes in it will play key roles in encouraging usage and spreading best practices.

PLAN: What and Why?

Problem Being Solved or Opportunity (Assessment Decisions)
Business situation, challenges; issue statement; selection criteria (productivity, predictability, quality, and so forth)

Vision
Role of improvement in gaining vision; intermediate results

Process Model and Project Objectives
Before and after process views, features, objectives

Strategic Impact
Cost/benefit analysis, how effort supports core-competence strategy, examples of how improvement has led to success, key projects that depend on improvement, risk of not doing

DO: How, When, and How Much?

Development/Purchase/Evolution Plan
Approach, way of pacing user training/knowledge/readiness, form of reporting status, reviews, metrics, quality objectives and verification including FURPS+, support life

Implementation Tactics
Major deliverables, organizational maturity considerations, key role of infrastructure, coordination with other groups, timing to match user projects, hand-off criteria

People and Resources
Sponsor and champion roles, user partners, people and expertise needed, hardware, software, space

Schedule, Risks, Contingency Plans
PERT chart, Gantt chart, risks, contingency plans

CHECK: How Will You Know It Worked?

Measuring and Validating
Baseline measurements, prechange environment characteristics, expected measurable changes

Postproject Review, Degree of Adoption
Postproject review, percentage of engineers using improvement, range of uses, maturity of usage

ACT: How Do You Plan to Fully Adopt?

Standardizing the Changes
Renewed sponsorship, matching organizational readiness, expanding user base, items in various deliverables/releases, points for acknowledged stages of completion and celebration

Support Strategy
Infrastructure changes, documentation, training, consulting, packaging, maintenance, feedback

Issues
Technical, organizational, priority conflicts, timing

Figure 7-6 Process-improvement plan outline

PLAN AND EFFECTIVELY EXECUTE IMPROVEMENTS AS PROJECTS _____

A project plan generally answers what, why, when, how, and how much about your project. The size and content of a good project plan varies. A plan can be as short as a set of slides or as long as a 20-page document. A project plan is the design of how you will run a project. Its primary purpose is to record and communicate key project assumptions, strategies, and tactics so that your team knows where they are going and how. Besides other key topics, it should include all the aspects discussed so far: vision, people, suitability to customers, climate, and infrastructure.

Since earlier sections showed how process-improvement projects include significant sociological issues beyond those seen in product projects, be sure to think them through and emphasize them in a process-improvement plan. Figure 7-6 shows an outline that will help you to do that.

The outline in Figure 7-6 is stated in the plan/do/check/act form, since process improvements are closer to iterative quality improvements than they are to product projects. In preparing your plan, think about your process improvement in iterative stages and your current changes as one of those iterations. You are describing your tactics, risks, and anticipated results for each of the four parts. As with all project plans, match the length and detail of yours to risks associated with your improvement. Because you will probably face more complex sociological challenges than any of your product projects will have prepared you for, it is even more important to create and manage from a good project plan than it was for those product projects.

Use the Spiral Model of Process
Improvement to Strengthen Your Planning Process

Chapter 1 introduced a spiral model of process improvement. It and part of its discussion are repeated here, since it represents the key mental model you need when you plan a process-improvement project (Figure 7-7).

The figure shows a progression from first-time practice usage (in the center, "project plans new practice") to widespread organizational adoption. Normal *product (development) projects* aren't organized to go through this entire spiral. At best, there may be a product-line architecture that could ideally do so if all the planned products were done. The figure gives some useful insights for *process-improvement projects* that can help us assess to what extent an improvement has been adopted.

The model includes several patterns across the plan/do/check/act quadrants. These reflect

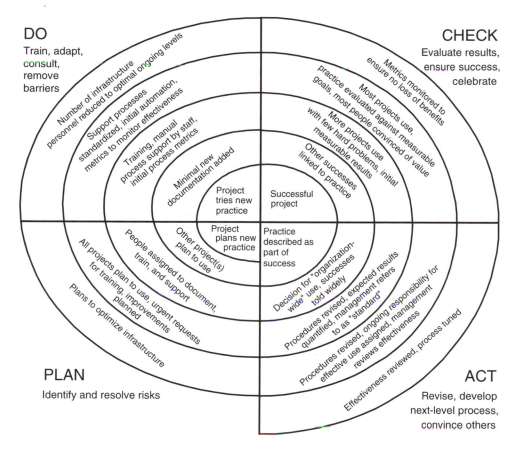

Figure 7-7 Spiral model for process-improvement adoption

- increasing people and resource investments,
- greater management understanding, attention, and commitment, and
- better control with process metrics.

Let's briefly revisit the meaning of outward movement within each separate quadrant. This time, we will specifically look at the differences between product projects and process-improvement projects.

Plan - The plan quadrant suggests a major change from single product projects: Product project teams seldom do the activities in the outer rings, unless they become involved in a long-term, custom solution contract. Marketing departments usually provide training. Support groups help resolve questions asked when products start being used in unanticipated ways. And customer groups ultimately optimize usage for themselves. Process-improvement teams must plan for and accelerate all of these things.

Do - Only projects for mature hardware product lines approximate all the Do segments. Successful process-improvement adoptions continue to improve infrastructure and support beyond the minimal documentation of the second segment. Many product projects stop there, and people move to other projects.

Check - For product projects, "Check" is normally discussed in detail in a quality plan and in less detail in a project plan. Setting the stage for moving outward in this quadrant is a major, improvement-project challenge with today's software developers. Few have taken the time to even loosely apply the experimental methods taught in chemistry, physics, and engineering labs they may have attended. While applying these methods in industrial settings will lack the precision of academic, controlled experiments, they are still a key to understanding and convincing others of improvement results.

Act - Gaining ever-increasing management commitment as you move outward on these segments suggests the critical elements of follow-through and "sales" that are necessary for process improvements. You can think of this sequence as pursuing "market share" for adopting a practice.

The emphasis for the process-improvement spiral model is on new practice adoption. This changes the primary focus from technological for product projects, to sociological for process improvements. [3] It reinforces the need for a good project plan, like one derived from Figure 7-6, where you have recorded your ideas for dealing with these new challenges.

Change Your Project Management Frame of Reference

At the start of this chapter we raised the question, Are any of our development product management techniques counter productive for process improvements? While none seemed to be, there were some subtle differences in many of the contrasts between product projects and process-improvement projects.

First, there was the difference in a process-improvement project manager's perception of the team. A view that includes people other than developers suggests that a project manager's "protective" view of a project team may get you in trouble if you accidentally fall back into thinking of only the project team as the people directly working on an improvement.

Second, if you are used to strong help from other functional groups like marketing and customer support, you need to adjust your thinking to much more proactively fill these roles for your internal customers.

Third, the evolutionary nature of a process-improvement project also suggests that an intense product-development focus on completion may have to change. Using a spiral model calls for thinking in terms of a series of results. Otherwise, you will set expectations that an improvement will be soon "done," resources will be free for other purposes, and sponsors can shift their enthusiasm to something else.

Fourth, the long-term nature of a fully adopted process improvement dramatically impacts how you have to sell your project. You must approach this selling differently than you have for product projects, or everyone will view your project in these familiar terms. You need to sell to different audiences. You need to sell more often. You need to do many of the things that product projects depend on marketing, sales, and support to normally do.

When you think of these key differences, you begin to change your project-management approach in subtle, but important ways. You will have a new frame of reference.

CONCLUSION

Although all our successful project-management methods seem to still apply to process improvements, it seems clear that we need to complement them with others and assume a new frame of reference. Better initial planning is a key step. While this planning may seem like a new "project management superstition" to colleagues, it is the best way to improve your team's chances for success. There are also many ways to extend your leadership on process-improvement projects. This chapter has emphasized different aspects and suggested ways to assess and act. These acts include:

Motivate

- Include clear goals and intermediate results in your improvement vision to make it even more exciting. Also spend more effort aligning customer needs.
- Make sure that there are both a committed sponsor and an enthusiastic champion in the customer organization. (One or both of these can be you when you are making improvements for just your product project.)
- Understand who the customer's opinion leaders are and cultivate their support.
- Coach and encourage your process-improvement customers. "Your team" is part of "their team."
- Flexibly match improvements to your customer's needs, regularly present the improvements from each new practice, and ensure that everyone stays committed until the practice is effectively adopted organizationwide.

Optimize the working environment

- Create a supportive and enthusiastic climate by matching each new practice to your customer organization's maturity and infrastructure.
- Create an appropriate infrastructure in the customer organization. Protect it like an endangered species.

Plan and effectively execute

- Plan your improvement more carefully and on a broader time scale than you would plan a product project.
- Use the spiral model to define deliverable intermediate results. Structure these as points of celebration and project-team recognition.

Managing a process-improvement project will challenge you and stretch your skills as no product-development project has. By using the tools here and developing your ability to meet those challenges, you will make the difference in your project's success. You will also get a stronger sense of accomplishment and confidence than you've ever felt before.

Postscript

One of this chapter's reviewers wouldn't let me stop here without completing the Little League story. How did our mother put up with our dirty uniforms? Well, despite a lack of management experience, she handled this "change management" issue pretty well. She knew that the trend of good play was important to us, so she simply waited for a downturn to wash our uniforms. Then she emphasized how a clean uniform caused us to do well in the next game (if we did), or suggested that we hadn't done any worse than with the dirty ones. Eventually, we accepted the evidence that clean uniforms didn't hurt how we did, so her major challenge after that was repairing pants legs that always seemed to be torn after sliding.

BIBLIOGRAPHY

1. Rogers, E., *Diffusion of Innovations*, 3rd Edition, New York: Macmillan Publishing, 1983.
2. Adler, P., and A. Shenbar, "Adapting Your Technological Base: The Organizational Challenge," *Sloan Management Review*, Vol. 32, No. 1, (Fall 1990), pp. 25-37.
3. Griss, M., "Software Reuse: From Library to Factory," *IBM Systems Journal*, Vol. 32, No. 4, (1993), pp. 547-566.

8

Telling the Story of Software Process _Improvements_

One of the first steps I take when I plan a trip is to find some books with pictures and maps of the places where I plan to go. These help to build excitement for some aspects of the trip and give some sense of priorities and timing. They are a preview of the coming experience. If they represent the coming trip reasonably well, then the trip is more likely to be a success.

We can do the same thing for process improvements. We can put together a set of pictures and maps of where we plan to go. A particularly successful format for presenting HP after-the-fact results has been the "TQC Storyboard" format. [1,2] Why not plan our "process-improvement trips" by creating a storyboard in advance and then track our progress against it?

This chapter walks through an example of such a storyboard. The slides follow the typical TQC Plan/Do/Check/Act sequence. They are adapted from the preimplementation planning of a real HP division that we will call "DIV." Figure 8-1 shows an introductory summary slide for the project dubbed "Rosetta Stone." It outlines the total storyboard and ties subsequent discussion to Plan/Do/Check/Act. Next to this slide and the others in the chapter are suggestions for both what you might include and how you might present it.

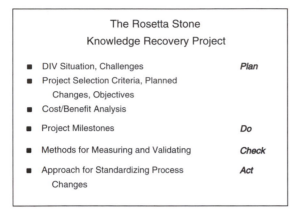

The Rosetta Stone
Knowledge Recovery Project

- DIV Situation, Challenges   *Plan*
- Project Selection Criteria, Planned
  Changes, Objectives
- Cost/Benefit Analysis

- Project Milestones   *Do*

- Methods for Measuring and Validating   *Check*

- Approach for Standardizing Process   *Act*
  Changes

Figure 8-1 Overview slide

Purpose of slide: Give the audience a preview of the entire talk. Set expectations that the material is pertinent and well organized. This slide can be reused as a reminder to summarize the major talk sections and to reinforce the overall message and flow.

Points to emphasize: At the start, emphasize the overall talk structure. After completing individual sections, use to summarize what was just covered in each section.

After stepping through the example storyboard, this chapter briefly discusses how much effort is needed to create a storyboard. This will help you to know what steps to take and about how long they might take. You can use this outline to create an advance picture of *your* process improvement. For those sections that ask questions in the "points to emphasize" sections next to the slides, you may or may not include answers on the slides. If you don't, then at least be sure that you have thought through the answers. The questions may be asked when you present the slides. There are no rigid rules about the number of slides. Sometimes you will need more than one slide where this outline has only one. Because these slides are prepared early in a project, I encourage you to keep your script notes so that you remember all of the thinking that went into their preparation.

The captions in these slides are specifically targeted for an R&D or IT (Information Technology) management audience. You need to think about what additional comments and possible other slides you would add when engineers are also in the audience.

PLAN

DIV 1993 Software Situation

- DIV was created to maintain mature software.
- The software is old, developed by different people in several divisions, poorly documented, and because of its previous modifications, very poorly structured.
- Expectations are that, with time, DIV will maintain more products and do it with fewer engineers/product.

Figure 8-2 Situation

Purpose of slide: Define the current situation as a framework to the improvement that you are trying to make.

Points to emphasize: Often it is useful to give a one-sentence summary of background history followed by the more precise improvement statement described in the next slide.

This slide states the situation nicely. It establishes a clear frame of reference that is understandable by people who are either familiar or unfamiliar with this business. This is particularly useful when you present such a slide set to other groups who want to benefit from your experience.

DIV Software Challenges

In order to be successful, DIV must

- Find better ways to understand and evaluate the effects of changes.
- Help customers to get timely, cost-effective responses to change requests.
- Be seen as providing the same or better productivity as the original software-supplying divisions.

Figure 8-3 Issue statement

Purpose of slide: Define the improvement that you plan to make.

Points to emphasize: Make sure that your issue statement is aligned with your organization's primary business goal. It is a good idea to either include the business goal or to paraphrase it as part of your issue statement. Also make sure that you are describing the root issue—ask "why" (better yet, "in order to . . . ?") until you get to the right level (refer to discussion below).

In an ideal TQC project, the issue is driven by an analysis of process data. The issue statement is then just a summary of your findings. Process data is not always available, though. In such cases, projects are driven by assessment data of some sort. Such data is subjective and indirectly approximates what you might learn from process data. Assessments can range from short, informal assessments to longer, formal ones. The following discussion is relevant to projects driven from both types of data, but it is particularly important that you follow these recommended steps when you start with assessment data.

A business goal is the highest-level statement of what you want to do. This goal is a key point, and the issue statement in Figure 8-3 must be closely related to this goal. It must be a high-level organizational business goal. My experience is that organizations *primarily* focus on one of three areas: customer satisfaction, engineering effort and schedule, or sustaining product integrity and market. [3] The primary focus often also helps improve the other two, though perhaps not as quickly as some managers would like.

DIV's business goal is a subset of one of these focuses, namely, to minimize engineering effort and schedule. In particular, it addresses just maintenance effort. Their goal is

> Goal: Optimize engineering effort to do defect repairs and minor enhancements.

It is confusing to have separate slides for both a business goal and an issue statement, so this slide set doesn't. Just remember that business goals drive issue statements. Both can be tricky to state. While the next discussion focuses on issue statements, the comments apply to both. If your organization doesn't have a clearly articulated business goal, you should try to state one first.

Sometimes an issue is stated too broadly. One possible version might be, "DIV will exceed expectations of all the customers of inherited mature software products while substantially reducing defect backlogs and experiencing high-profit margins." While no one can argue that such effects are desirable, this statement is so broad that it provides little useful context in which to plan and design an improvement project.

Issue statements can also be too narrow. For example, "DIV will take no longer than one engineering day to do any software change." Again, this is a statement that might sound reasonable. Here it is too restrictive. It could lead to poor management and engineering practices. For example, fixes requiring more than a day might be avoided, or they might be divided into multiple smaller fixes that would take much longer than if they were managed as one.

Issue statements are sometimes stated with too much of a solution-specific bias. For example, "DIV will substantially reduce its time to fix defects by using the XYZ tool." This might actually happen, but seldom are changes so restricted. Such a tool would probably be accompanied by other changed methods and processes. Along with an "XYZ" tool, added or improved inspections might play a crucial improvement role. By stating the issue statement as above, you might mislead people into focusing only on the "XYZ" tool. This can lead to disappointment or failure.

Test for these types of potential problems by asking "why" until you are confident that your statement describes your issue in a clear and compelling way. Let's test the Figure 8-3 issue statement. First, it has elements of both customer satisfaction and productivity, but its bias is toward "timely, cost effective . . . same or better productivity." It even answers a broad "why" by saying "In order to be successful . . ."

Is it stated too narrowly? An area of focus is given: ". . . must find more effective ways to understand products and evaluate the effects of changes." This focus is open to a combination of processes, methods, or tools. Similarly, the statement doesn't assume any specific solution. Other organizations can evaluate what was done and decide whether new techniques might work even better for future projects.

Purpose of slide: Explain why this improvement was selected rather than others.

Points to emphasize: What business issues were affected? What would the change allow you to do? What cost savings would accrue? What was the motivation level of different people? How easy would it be to make changes? What changes would your customers see and how would these improve their opinions of your products? How did all these add up to addressing this issue?

Reasons for Doing Initial Process Improvements

- Understanding unfamiliar code is a very immediate and obvious problem.

- Engineers have expressed the need for tools to help.

- Risk is minimum, since good tools are available and they complement existing processes.

Figure 8-4 Selection criteria/rationale

Often, the people who decide on an improvement are so close to the decision that it seems very obvious. There are always other choices, and often other people might feel more enthusiastic about those choices. By including a why-selected slide, you acknowledge the importance of other choices while stating some of the more important criteria that influenced this decision. This is particularly important for lengthy process changes. *Conditions change and people may need to be reminded why they are doing the changes.*

Note that the example in Figure 8-4 gives good reasons that would appeal to engineers, but it could be strengthened by directly addressing more of the questions in the "points to emphasize" comments.

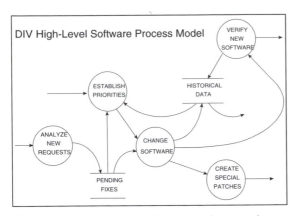

Figure 8-5a Process model with changes shown

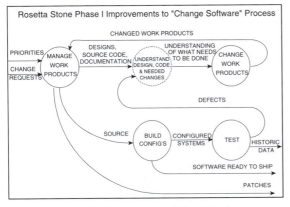

Figure 8-5b Process model with changes
shown (expansion of change software bubble)

Purpose of slides 8-5a and 8-5b: Describe the process before the proposed improvements were made. Show the planned process changes superimposed onto a model of your current process. (Note: you may need two slides here, as this example does: one that shows a high-level process model and a second that expands the affected parts of the process.)

Points to emphasize: Were there any constraints on the approaches taken or the extent of changes allowed? What frustrated managers and engineers?

The dotted circle shows where the process improvements are.

Like the why-selected slide, your process may seem very obvious. It won't necessarily be obvious to others, though. It turns out that these slides have been the most difficult to get from divisions who are making changes, yet they are key slides. First, they visually show the change. Simple verbal explanations of the same thing can be misleading, because people may hear different things depending on their perspectives. Pictures pinpoint your changes.

Second, visual images make additions, deletions, and changes very obvious. This starts people thinking about what trade-offs are being made. In the example shown, the step of "understand design, code, and needed changes" has changed. This pinpoints what new things engineers must do. It also paves the way for later benefit-calculation slides.

Rosetta Stone Project Objectives

- Successfully deploy program-understanding technology to optimize engineering effort to do defect repairs and minor enhancements.

- Measure the deployment effort and benefits and use the results to help future process changes.

- Use the savings gained from program understanding to fund subsequent changes.

Figure 8-6 Project objectives*

Purpose of slide: Describe the primary thrust of the project.

Points to emphasize: Be more specific here about the bounds of your project than you have been so far. Use this slide to set clearer expectations. Some people prefer to present this slide before the process model(s). I prefer it after, because I feel it clarifies the ideas in

Figures 8-5a and 8-5b. Notice that these objectives incorporate the business goal into the first bullet. Such a strong link helps ensure ongoing management commitment.

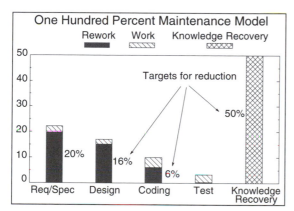

Figure 8-7 Software business cost model*

Purpose of slide: Frame the expected process-improvement benefits by using a summary cost model.

Points to emphasize: This is a variant of the Chapter 4 cost model (which was based on 55 percent maintenance, whereas this organization only does maintenance). Note that it attributes

rework costs to the activities where defects were *caused*, even though those costs are experienced in later phases, such as test. You might want to adjust the model to your environment or replace it with a different high-level model. Highlight the part of your model that is targeted for improvement.

Now that you have a clear goal and understand how and why you plan to change the process, you usually have to justify the changes or at least set some expectations for the payback. The clearest way of stating payback, particularly when addressing high-level managers, is return on investment (ROI). Sometimes people resist measuring ROI when the primary improve-

---

*Slides flagged by an asterisk are not typically part of a TQC after-the-fact storyboard. They've been added for preproject planning purposes.

ment goals are not directly stated in money terms. For example, decreased time to market is difficult to state in terms of money savings. Another example is measuring increased customer satisfaction. Not only is this difficult to state in money terms, but it also can be very subjective and the results will depend on many uncontrollable market factors.

You can't avoid trying to define ways of measuring improved time to market and customer satisfaction benefits. But be aware that there is often an implied assumption accompanying such benefits. It is that engineering efficiency will not decrease because of other improvements. My recommendation is to always measure changes in engineering effort, as well. Efficiency may temporarily decrease, but you must be prepared to confidently talk about why and to explain what to expect in the future.

Because the example goal is to reduce engineering effort, the primary measure of success must show how to do that. The Figure 8-7 model is useful, because it gives a visual framework for the current relative costs. It also shows which of these you expect to reduce. This sets the stage for the next slide.

```
Projected Savings from Rosetta Stone

                                        Percent of
                                        Total Costs

■ Reduce program understanding time   =>    12%
■ Reduce effort to do rework          =>    11%

  Total potential engineering              23%
     cost reduction

■ Improved engineering morale
■ Improved customer satisfaction due to fewer new
  problems introduced with successive software releases.
```

Figure 8-8 Expected benefits*

Purpose of slide: Analysis of expected costs and benefits.

Points to emphasize: On this slide, you should combine estimated savings and costs. Typical net savings are in the 5 to 10 percent range (Table 4-1 is a good source of ideas here). Point out that future costs will be less, since they will not include startup costs beyond a certain point. What other less quantifiable benefits were expected (e.g., customer satisfaction, time to market, flexibility)? How do you plan to measure these, if at all?

Figure 8-7 is based only on nonoverhead engineering effort. Some studies suggest this is about two-thirds of total effort. Nevertheless, when benefits are derived from the model, we can directly use its percentages. This is so because when we save an amount reflected by the model, that percentage directly translates to the amount of extra engineering resource available in the future, irrespective of the overhead percentage. If we can save 10 percent on a 10-person project, we need one less engineer for the same work.

With this in mind, this project team feels that knowledge recovery time can be cut by one-fourth (of 50 percent), and that design and coding rework can be cut by almost half (of 22 percent). Figure 8-8 shows how this would result in their ability to do 23 percent more work with the same number of people in the future. In addition, they expect this project will improve engineering morale and customer satisfaction.

Increased costs are not explicitly shown, since this team used net reductions to calculate improvements. On the other hand, they didn't include one-time charges associated with tools and training. Be sure to be able to back up simplified slides like this one with how these costs affect total project ROI. Chapter 14 of *Practical Software Metrics for Project Management and Process Improvement* has a good discussion of justifications, [3] and Chapter 12 expands on it to discuss how to tailor your slides to different audiences.

DO

Rosetta Stone Milestones	Target Completion
1. Decision on which tool and methods to use	7/15
2. XYZ acquisition complete	8/19
3. Tool installed	8/21
4. Project-team training complete	9/28
5. Baseline data analysis complete	12/15
6. Start necessary new data collection	12/15
7. Begin pilot system/integration test	2/1
8. Preliminary XYZ evaluation report	3/15
9. Plan for process standardization	4/15

Figure 8-9 Action plan

Purpose of slide: Describe the key actions to be taken.

Points to emphasize: The key project steps and deliverables. This is a high-level summary of your project plan with rough dates. Including dates at this early point starts setting expectations and gauging level of commitment.

CHECK

The difference between success and failure often depends on whether you have a way of measuring progress and final success. The goal/question/metric paradigm is a useful way to define measures of both progress and results. It was created by Vic Basili and his associates at the University of Maryland while working with the NASA/Goddard Software Engineering Lab. [4] Here, the paradigm starts with the business goal defined earlier. You then brainstorm questions that will help you to measure whether you are being successful in reaching the goal. In particular, the focus is on questions that are potentially measurable. These will be used to derive the metrics and graphs that will help you to establish baselines and to track and validate your results. Chapter 3 of

Practical Software Metrics for Project Management and Process Improvement has a valuable list against which to compare questions and metrics. [3]

Once you pass the hurdle of a good goal statement, brainstorming related questions is the next step. Take some care to focus on measurable questions while not constraining the creative suggestions of the group generating the questions. The following questions (Q's) and metrics (M's) were developed to go with the earlier goal. They were split into two groups after brainstorming. The questions and metrics directly relate to understanding both whether you're achieving the goal while you are making the changes and the degree of success after the changes are made. The methods of displaying results follow. The slides have "Q" references to these questions.

Goal: Reduce engineering effort to do defect repairs and minor enhancements.

Q1: Is the average amount of time to do a fix or enhancement decreasing with time?

   M: Average engineering time to do defect fixes, enhancements
   M: Estimate the amount of time it took to do each fix/enhancement. Classify them by <1 day, 1-2 days, 2-4 days, 4-7 days, >7 days. Do a histogram of how many fit into each category and look for a shift to the left with time.

Q2: How much time and effort is spent on each subprocess step?

   M: As a minimum, a breakout of program-understanding time for different time-to-fix categories. Ideally, engineering time by product/component/activity by time-to-fix categories

Q3: How variable are the times spent on making changes?

   M: Engineering time by time-to-fix categories

Q4: How much rework occurs as a result of changes we make?

   M: Percent new defects introduced when fixing old or existing defects (including only those found in system test or later)

Q5: Do the engineers perceive that their working environment has improved?

   M: Ask the engineers to rate the efficacy of the tool(s)
   M: Ask the engineers to estimate their usage of the tool(s)
   M: Ask the engineers what other changes have improved their effectiveness and how much compared to the change of interest

The next questions are significant to the goal, but it seems unlikely that answers will be available for them in the pilot project timeframe. Note that the metrics represent alternative ways of answering a question and that they are not necessarily all required.

Q6: Is the maintainability of the components degrading over time?

> M: Incoming problem rate
> M: Code stability
> M: Average complexity by product
> M: Number of modules changed per release cycle

Q7: Is the quality of the components degrading over time?

> M: Incoming problem rate
> M: Average complexity by product

Measuring and Validating—Figures 8-10a through 8-10e

Purpose of the following slides: Describe the measurements taken to validate success. Note that it is also desirable to select a subset of them to post in your area during the project. They will help remind your team of the project goals and provide positive feedback as you make progress.

Points to emphasize: What baseline measurements existed before changes were made? What change-unique measurements were taken to measure benefits, and what results were expected? How did you expect to get these results? What measurable results did you get? How much better can you expect results to be the next time? Also show what slide(s) you will use to track progress during the project.

I like to make sure that there are defined graphs that address all the brainstormed questions. From these you can then pick the two or three that best help you to know whether you are accomplishing your goal. Use these to present continuing and final project results. The other graphs are backup material that is often needed.

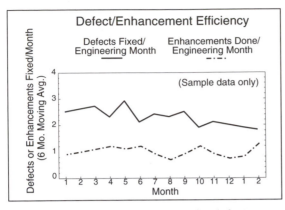

Figure 8-10a Measuring and validating

Q1: Is the average amount of time to do a fix or enhancement decreasing with time?

This is a bottom-line question that directly addresses your goal. As a minimum, this data must be tracked.

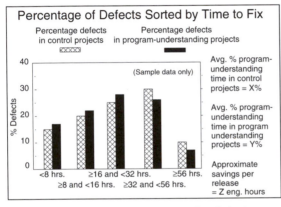

Figure 8-10b Measuring and validating

Q1: Is the average amount of time to do a fix or enhancement decreasing with time?

Q3: How variable are the times spent on making changes?

This bar chart adds additional information to Figure 8-10a. If the bars in the program-understanding projects have greater percentages of defects in the left bars, not only is the average efficiency better, but also you will understand what a typical mix of times is. The chart might also show that the improvements are more effective for easy or difficult fixes.

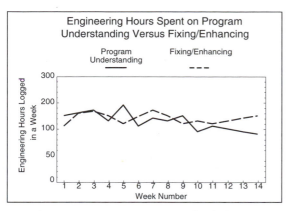

Figure 8-10c Measuring and validating

Q2: How much time and effort is spent on each subprocess step?

This graph helps you to confirm the part of the original justification related to reduced program understanding time.

For this project, this graph also serves as an ongoing check that data is being collected. You particularly need such a graph when you ask people to collect data that they haven't reported in the past.

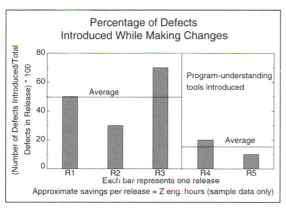

Figure 8-10d Measuring and validating

Q4: How much rework occurs as a result of changes we make?

This chart helps ensure that you aren't improving fix time at the expense of bad fixes. Remember also that part of the justification in Figure 8-8 specifically related to reduced rework.

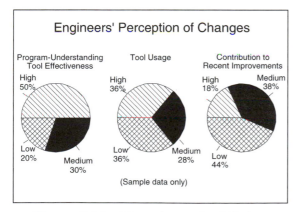

Figure 8-10e Measuring and validating

Q5: Do the engineers perceive that their working environment has improved?

This slide helps you to understand engineer's acceptance of the changes. This allows you to interpret other possible differences between results and expectations that you might see in Figures 8-10a through 8-10d. It also confirms or denies one of the other key benefits listed in Figure 8-8.

After defining these graphs, it is useful to summarize what data you need to collect and what historical data you need for comparison. You should do this because the graphs sometimes appear overwhelming to some people. Summarizing the necessary data helps to put the data-collection task into perspective. Chapter 9 goes into a more detailed discussion of other aspects of data collection. For these Figure 8-10 graphs, the data needed is

- engineering time by week spent on defect fixing, enhancing, and time spent on program understanding,
- total number of defects by release,
- number of defects introduced while making fixes/enhancements, and
- data from a simple survey of engineers.

In most HP cases, many of the necessary metrics are already collected in some form. Added metrics can be approached as a one-time activity for the duration of a pilot or as a desirable long-term business measure. Assess your organization's business needs and willingness to change when you decide what metrics to use.

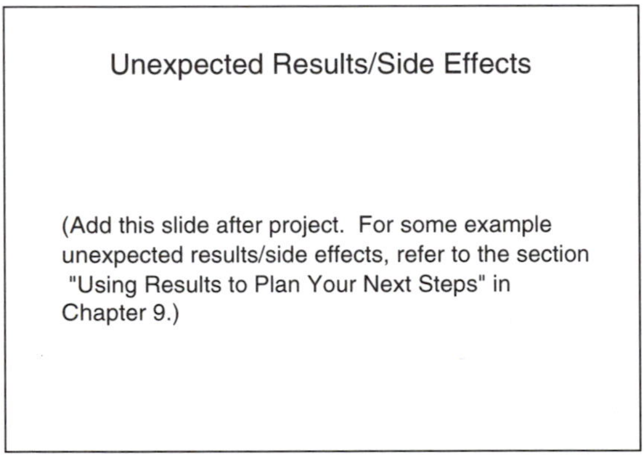

Unexpected Results/Side Effects

(Add this slide after project. For some example unexpected results/side effects, refer to the section "Using Results to Plan Your Next Steps" in Chapter 9.)

Figure 8-11 Unexpected results/side effects

Purpose of slide: Describe any observed side effects. (You cannot do this slide before the project is done. It is included here so that you don't forget it when presenting your results at the end of your project.)

Points to emphasize: What limiting or enhancing effects did these have on your results? What made some results hard to anticipate?

ACT

Standardizing the Changes

1. Spread usage of initial methods/tools within local DIV lab.
   - Update/optimize training
   - Improve method and tool access
   - Consult and monitor to ensure adoption and optimum usage.
2. Spread usage outside local DIV lab.
3. Spread usage to products written in different languages.

Figure 8-12 Standardizing the changes

Purpose of slide: Show how improvements can be standardized.

Points to emphasize: What temporary processes were used to help with change adoption? How much longer will they be needed? What feedback mechanism will you use to tell you when temporary processes are no longer needed? What needs to change in the improvement process itself? Emphasize that the total benefits won't be achieved until the improvements are standardized.

Remaining Issues

(Add this slide after project. Possible topics to consider include:

- People availability
- Potential schedule conflicts/dependencies
- Needed resources
- Third-party support
- Conflicting organizational practices)

Figure 8-13 Remaining issues

Purpose of slide: Describes remaining issues. (You cannot do this slide before the project is done. It is included here so that you don't forget it when presenting your results at the end of your project.)

Points to emphasize: Were these issues already present, but possibly hidden? Are they temporary? Would other organizations expect to experience similar issues?

PLAN

Future Plans

(Add this slide after project. For example:

	Target Completion
• Increase XYZ usage in	
Erin's team	9/30
Sean's team	11/15
Jan's team	1/15
• Identify the top 10 error-prone modules	2/25
and start replacing them	
• Reevaluate engineer's perceptions of	4/30
change and net savings)	

Figure 8-14   Future plans

Purpose of slide: Describes future plans for the next adoption stage around the spiral model. (You cannot do this slide before the project is done, although you should include your current thoughts about this in your process-improvement project plan. It is included here so that you don't forget it when presenting your results at the end of your project.)

Points to emphasize: Do these plans focus on refining the initial solution, replacing the solution, resolving related issues, addressing new issues, or some combination of these?

PREPARING A STORYBOARD

From the example, you should be convinced of the usefulness of using a storyboard approach early in a project, as opposed to afterward. You should also have a general idea of how to do one. Let's complete the picture by reviewing some helpful hints on storyboard preparation and how long it should take.

The first thing for you to decide is, who are you doing it for? Your effort will be dictated by its intended use. I recommend that you initially approach a storyboard as a document only for use of the team responsible for process change. This minimizes your initial effort to create a useful document. Expect it to evolve to a document or presentation that you share, but don't worry about the final presentation initially.

The next question then is, who does one? Ideally the project manager prepares a storyboard along with a project plan. A first pass can be done by someone who isn't on the project team, using information already created by the team, for example, a consultant or a quality or productivity manager. One advantage of this approach is that a person not too close to the project helps to force early clarification. Before long, the ownership of a storyboard must change to the project manager.

How long will it take? We have learned from experience with many storyboards that the following sequence works best, and that the timing of the steps will be close to the times shown.

1. Start by pinning down the primary business goal. Then use the goal/question/metric paradigm to brainstorm questions and metrics. This normally takes about 1 1/2 hours.
2. Sanity-check your prior answers with an appropriate version of the Chapter 4 cost model. Then create first-pass sample graphs (like Figures 8-10a through 8-10e) that answer your questions from step 1. This step should only take about 1 hour, especially if you can look at past storyboards that had similar goals and questions.
3. Fill in the other slides generally in sequence. If a rough project plan already exists, this should only take about 2 hours to adapt information from it to create all the other first-pass diagrams besides the process (8-5a and 8-5b) and schedule (8-9) diagrams. Our experience is that these last two items are often not yet available at this point.
4. A process diagram has typically been difficult to get. It is not unusual for this to take 2 to 4 weeks, although this is calendar time, not engineering effort. This might be faster if the project manager is the person creating the storyboard. Fortunately, not having this at first doesn't seriously affect project progress.
5. The project schedule is ready when a completed project plan is ready. Accurate schedules depend on completion of the high-level design of process changes, so wait for a good schedule.

How do you know that you are done? If you are not the project manager for the change, you are done when you have a reasonable storyboard and the project manager has assumed ownership of it. If you are the project manager, you are done when you are confident that your vision of results is clear and that you have a way of measuring your progress.

This level of confidence usually takes three passes: The first pass is a prototype to organize your thoughts and to review with a limited audience. The second pass is generally a management pass, and if the project manager wasn't the originator, this is the pass where that manager buys in. The third pass includes modifications resulting when you start to share this project vision with others in the organization, including doers. The whole process will take from 1 to 8 weeks.

Whether you are the project manager or a consulting agent, you should keep a scripted version of the storyboard handy. Your GQM brainstorming results, the assumptions regarding your software development costs, your thoughts about how data will appear and be interpreted, and so forth, are all important information that must not be lost.

What happens if you wait until project end to create a storyboard? In the best case, your project may be successful and you may have a hard time proving it. Worst case, you may fail because you focused on the wrong things. Then your project may be cancelled, redirected, or starved. The difference between the two is like the difference between conscious and unconscious control of your project.

CONCLUSION

The example in this chapter came from our work with one HP division. It presents a clear vision for a journey. Like many vacation journeys, there are unknowns, but our goal is clear and we have ways of measuring our progress toward our destination. This storyboard format is a valuable tool for planning for success.

- It creates a presentation-formatted summary of a project plan and describes a vision of the future.
- It focuses the project on measurable results.
- It defines the metrics that will be used to validate project success and the graphs that will be monitored during the project.

These three key features draw upon the strength of our experiences with postproject storyboards. They also are explicitly guided by three techniques added by this preimplementation approach.

- This new approach starts with a clear statement of an organization's key business goal.
- It includes a consistent approach for calculating engineering cost savings based on an economic model of software costs.
- It incorporates the goal/question/metric paradigm to derive meaningful measures for both monitoring and measuring final success.

Remember that a storyboard is a tool for focusing a project on measurable results. More than anything else, when you create a storyboard, you are clearly stating a vision.

BIBLIOGRAPHY

1. "TQC Storyboard Format," Corporate Quality Training and Development, (Oct. 1991). (Not available outside HP.)
2. Scholtes, P., *The Team Handbook*, Madison, Wis. Joiner Associates, Inc., 1988, Appendix 2.
3. Grady, R., *Practical Software Metrics for Project Management and Process Improvement*, Englewood Cliffs, N. J.: Prentice-Hall, Inc., 1992, p. 24.
4. Basili, V., and H. D. Rombach, "Tailoring the Software Process to Project Goals and Environments," *IEEE Proceedings of the Ninth International Conference on Software Engineering*, Monterey, Calif., (Apr. 1987), pp. 345-357.

Part Three

CHECK

Evaluate Results, Ensure Success, Celebrate

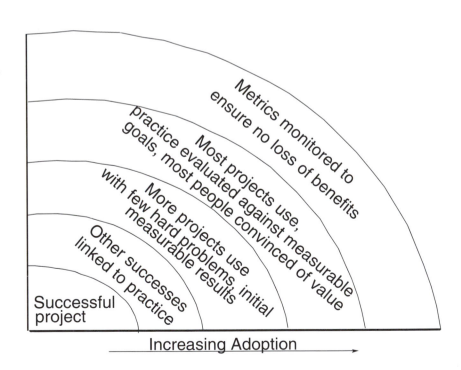

Metrics monitored to ensure no loss of benefits

Most projects use, practice evaluated against measurable goals, most people convinced of value

More projects use with few hard problems, initial measurable results

Other successes linked to practice

Successful project

Increasing Adoption

The DO section has given additional valuable tools that will help you to effectively implement process improvements. CHECK is all about measuring success. While individual improvements can succeed with few measurements being taken, the CHECK quadrant at left suggests that you are unlikely to achieve widespread usage without them. This is why the storyboard chapter so naturally separates DO and CHECK. In DO you use a storyboard to keep your story fresh and in front of everyone involved throughout implementation. In CHECK, you evaluate your project's final results in the original storyboard context and present them to motivate further adoption of improvements.

"Validation of Process Improvements" shows how to drive process improvement from key business goals and gives practical advice and a model for how to validate improvements.

"Tracking and Reporting Process-Improvement Results—Mission Possible!" then uses a wide range of examples from real projects to show how the model works and what you need to do to measure your project's progress and results.

9

Validation of Process Improvements

For hundreds of years, until the 1600s, Aristotelian methods dominated scientific thinking. These methods were based on deductive reasoning. If you knew certain things were true, you could safely conclude that other things were, also. Unfortunately, many scientific "truths" had become accepted without experimental validation, and subsequent conclusions were wrong. Galileo changed these methods. His way of combining experimental results with theory became the basis of modern scientific method.

What methods have we used to help us evolve software development and maintenance? We certainly continue to use Aristotle's deductive reasoning. There is nothing wrong with that, as long as we don't derive conclusions from assertions instead of facts. Unfortunately, many assertions have not been adequately validated. It is time to change that. Not only will experimental validation provide a better basis for subsequent conclusions, but it will also give us more persuasive arguments to convince others of the value of changes.

This chapter describes a minimal way to validate process improvements. Even a minimal approach is idealistic in most high-pressure software development environments. However, it will give your process-improvement project an advantage when you move to propagate its results. It is organized to include:

- How to define clear goals for making improvements
- How to capture baseline data required for validating most improvements
- How to define change-unique metrics that will help you to better understand results
- How to use measured results to help guide your next steps

GOALS FOR SOFTWARE PROCESS CHANGES

What are typical goals for process change? In their simplest form, they are "improve results X of entity Y by doing Z." X typically takes the form of productivity, time to market, quality, predictability, and so forth. For example, "double the number of products per year that our division can produce by increasing the amount of software we reuse."

The goal/question/metric (GQM) paradigm introduced in the last chapter is a valuable method for clarifying such goals. [1] This paradigm suggests that for each goal there is a set of questions that you might ask to help you understand whether you are achieving your goal. Many of these questions have answers that can be measured. To the extent that the questions are a complete set, and to the extent the metric data satisfactorily answers the questions, you can measure whether you are meeting your goals.

Let's look at an example from a real, process-improvement, brainstorming session.

Goal: Improve software project productivity.

Q1: What is the current productivity?
M: Delivered output/input (e.g., NCSS/eng. mo., methods/eng. mo., function points/eng. mo.)

Q2: How much can you expect to improve productivity?
M: Percent change

Q3: What is included in productivity?
(No metric here, rather definitions of subprocesses)

Q4: What is the productivity of subprocess components?
M: Some measure pertinent to a specific work product/eng. mo.

Often a manager or group will start with a goal to improve productivity. However, almost all improvements should improve productivity, so such a statement isn't as good as one that ties more specifically to business needs.

If you find yourself with such a start, try clarifying the goal by "Improve software productivity *in order to . . .*" You can add the phrase "in order to . . ." as many times as needed to seek clarity. (The previous chapter discusses forming good goal statements in more detail.)

Once you achieve this clarity, the resulting GQM-derived metrics will be a more powerful tool in tracking and validating progress toward your goals. For example, a statement more specifically tied to business needs is "Maximize the innovative product functionality done in a fixed product-development time period."

The example above poses four questions that explore the typical issues of baseline, expectations, scope, and detail. It's unusual when any of these issues are missing. In fact, initial questions such as these often lead to new goal statements that have a narrower scope. For example, the group stated the following subgoal as their brainstorming proceeded from the initial goal stated above.

Goal: Characterize a particular process activity.

Q1: What is the calendar length of the activity?
M: Weeks/activity

Q2: What is the quality of the activity?
M: Defects (that should have been eliminated by activity)/total defects found at system test

Q3: What kinds of defects are found or prevented by the activity?
M: Defects by type found or prevented by the activity

Note that while this second goal is a valuable goal to pursue, it is much weaker than the first. It only represents a means to an end. Characterizing a process may be a necessary step to improvement, but *make sure that you tie your primary goals to measurable results that solve key business needs.*

The measures that you want from the GQM process help you to focus your activities and to validate your results. They must answer three general questions:

Q1: *Did the process really improve? By how much?*
Q2: *Were there any unexpected side effects?*
Q3: *Were there any confounding factors?*

A combination of metrics provides the answers to these questions. Some are metrics that are basic for understanding virtually all changes, and others are unique to some particular changes being made.

BASELINE MEASUREMENTS FOR ALL
SOFTWARE PROCESS-IMPROVEMENT PROGRAMS _____

We have initiated changes as a result of past HP failure analysis activities in various divisions. One of the lessons that these analyses have taught us is that we seldom recorded adequate data to understand what progress we made. As a result, the following recommendations were developed. Each recommendation includes reasons why you need the data and an example of how it might look. An abbreviated version of a similar example first appeared in Appendix B of *Practical Software Metrics for Project Management and Process Improvement*. [2]

Recommendation: Capture Process and Product Descriptions

The primary reason that you need process and product descriptions is that you must have this information to understand *environmental aspects that have an effect on process changes.* For this reason, you should capture this high-level information both at the start of a process change and upon completion. The artificial example below shows postproject data.

Also, no two organizations develop software in the same way. In order for people to apply your results to their own processes, they need to have some understanding of what processes you used.

Describing processes, products, and level of training doesn't call for sophisticated surveys and analyses. All you need is a summary that is complete enough to identify conflicting changes and aspects that might affect your results. This data should take no longer than an hour or two to collect.

Example: Process and Product Descriptions

> *Development type (underline one): Applications, Systems, Firmware,*
> *Other (specify) _____.*
> *Language(s): C++*
> *Types of products (include any particularly unusual requirements):*
> *Measurement system software.*

Table 9-1 Example development method characterizations

Method/Tool	Percentage of Team Trained	How Extensively Applied	Applied by This Team Before	Team Opinion Of Value
Requirements				
Prototypes	0	4 iterations with customers	Limited	High
Design				
Structure charts & data dictionary	100	100% high-level design	Yes	Necessary
Design inspections	75	50% high-level 25% low-level	No	High
Code				
Complexity tool	25	50% code	No	High
Code inspections	75	20% high-risk modules	Yes	Mixed
Test				
Branch coverage	100	All modules, 85% goal	Yes	High
Goel-Okumoto reliability model	15	Throughout test	No	Mixed

Recommendation:
Collect and Summarize High-Level Process Measurements

The goal of all process-improvement programs is to improve total results. While high-level results alone generally won't be conclusive, it is important to look at them to make sure that they haven't changed in some unexpected way. For example, you might have improved productivity at the expense of product quality.

Often a process change is just one of a series of changes. Recording these data against time is a significant way to measure success for the complete series and to show progress along the way. One of your greatest challenges when doing so will be to normalize your data so that comparisons are meaningful. High-level process measures like these can be much more sophisticated than this simple example. Of course, more complete information with trends over time would help make improvement results even more useful.

Example: High-Level Process Measurements

Product size: 50,000 NCSS (non-comment source statements)
Effort: 125 eng. mo.

Productivity before changes: 350 NCSS/eng. mo. (20 % avg. reuse)
Productivity after changes: 400 NCSS/eng. mo. (25 % avg. reuse)

Activity breakdown before changes: specif./requirements = 14%, design = 19%, coding = 30%, test = 37%
Activity breakdown after changes: specif./requirements = 18%, design = 25%, coding = 29%, test = 28%

Defects before changes: 250; defect density:
    5 defects (system test)/KNCSS
Defects after changes: 200; defect density:
    4 defects (system test)/KNCSS

Project calendar time before changes: 19 months
Project calendar time after changes: 18 months

Recommendation: Determine Your Defect Failure-Analysis Baseline

Possibly the most useful technique today for measuring the effects of process change is a detailed failure analysis. You use processes, methods, and tools to eliminate particular classes of defects. By characterizing your defect patterns, you can determine whether your changes helped.

We have been using a failure-analysis model for many years in HP that will be described in Chapter 11. It was originally described in [3], and *Practical Software Metrics for Project Management and Process Improvement* describes the most current definitions and examples of its application. [2] Also, HP's Software Metrics Class includes a section that trains project managers and engineers to classify defects and do root-cause analysis.

Example: Defect Failure Analysis Before and After Process Changes

Figure 9-1 shows the top eight defect types from the HP failure analysis model that were found in test before and after the process changes in our artificial example. Since each set of eight bars shows only the top eight

Figure 9-1 Percentages of the eight most frequent defect source types

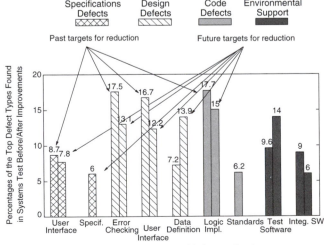

Left bars are for before changes; right bars are for after

categories, each total is less than 100 percent, although each set represents about 90 percent of the division's total. Also, there are nine categories shown, since "specif." replaced "standards" in the second set as one of the top eight.

CHANGE-UNIQUE MEASUREMENTS TO VALIDATE RESULTS _____

The metrics defined in the previous section will measure your process-improvement success in many cases. In other cases, additional change-unique metrics that give more detail are desirable. For example, to validate changes to the design process, it would be useful to know the percentage of design defects in test before and after the changes to complement the other metrics described in the previous section. This might help you to decide whether your design process changes merely shifted previous problems instead of eliminating them.

Other times, you need process-specific data. For example, the number of builds or the ratio of planned to unplanned builds are almost certainly needed to validate configuration management changes. These are cases where the goal/question/metric paradigm is a very useful tool to keep your measurements focused on desired results. Let's use this last example to explore how to apply GQM to define change-unique metrics.

One HP improvement program derived the following GQM.

Goal: Reduce the engineering time it takes to correctly create a target software environment.

Q1: How many builds are necessary?
  M: Number of builds

Q2: How long does an average build take?
  M: Calendar time, engineering effort

Q3: How many unplanned builds are there?
  M: Number of planned builds versus unplanned builds

Q4: How many failed builds occur?
  M: Number of failed builds versus successful builds

Q5: What are the steps in each build?
  (No metric here; rather, definitions of subprocesses)

Let's go back to the three key questions asked in the first section. You can test whether these metrics, along with the baseline metrics, provide you with a strong, results-based focus.

Will you know whether the process really improved? By how much? You can look at the high-level process measures for some sign of improvement, particularly if you plot them for multiple products/releases. More specifically though, a reduced number of builds, a reduced average build time, and a reduced percentage of unplanned builds will be more convincing results.

Will you be able to recognize any unexpected side effects? The high-level measurements are probably the best indicator of this. For example, the percent time spent in the various phases may change in some unexpected way. The product defect density might go way up or down. The next section gives some additional guidance about how to make sure that here you take into account training and startup time.

Will you be able to recognize any confounding factors? The process and product descriptions help you to understand the sources of potential confounding factors. For example, in the earlier example, our imaginary organization introduced design inspections, a complexity analysis tool, and a reliability model. All three of these can help reduce some unplanned builds or the software integration time.

Alternatively, both complexity analysis and a reliability model could also *increase* the number of builds if you use them to significantly increase quality over past projects. It is useful to anticipate such potential side effects so you will be better prepared to explain your results.

These examples provide you with a concrete starting point for measuring process improvement. Use them to help you write the validation part of your process-improvement plan.

USING RESULTS TO PLAN YOUR NEXT STEPS

Now you have a set of baseline metrics and you have seen several examples of how change-unique measures supplement the others. What do you do once you have your data? A key first step is the analysis of your results. In previous sections, you saw three key questions that asked about improvements, side effects, and confounding factors. Your analysis must answer those questions.

Did the Process Improve? By How Much?*

		Design Insp.	*Complexity*	*Reliability*	*Total*
Costs:	Training	36 eng. hrs. $1240	4 eng. hrs. $400	20 eng. hrs.	60 eng. hrs. $1640
	Startup	96 eng. hrs.	8 eng. hrs. $3600	20 eng. hrs.	124 eng. hrs. $3600
	Purchased SW				

---

* The calculations here are similar to those in Chapter 14 of *Practical Software Metrics for Project Management and Process Improvement*. [2] For those of you familiar with those examples, you will see two primary differences here. The starting defect density is lower than in those examples, and the average times to find and fix defects are longer. These new assumptions fit more aggressive defect-removal processes both before and during test than used in the referenced book.

Savings for reducing user interface, error checking, and logic code defects:

> *(22 prev. proj. UI rqmts. def. - 16 UI rqmts. def.) × 40 find & fix hours/def.*
>   *= 240 eng. hours*
> *(42 prev. proj. UI design def. - 24 UI design def.) × 25 find & fix hours/def.*
>   *= 450 eng. hours*
> *(44 prev. proj. error chk. def. - 26 error chk. def.) × 25 find & fix hours/def.*
>   *= 450 eng. hours*
> *(44 prev. proj. logic code def. - 30 logic code def.) × 10 find & fix hours/def.*
>   *= 140 eng. hours*
> *4 serious defects normally found postrelease × 150 find & fix hours/def.*
>   *= 600 eng. hours*

Were There Any Unexpected Side Effects? Any Confounding Factors?

- *Overall project metrics improved (350 -> 400 NCSS/eng. mo.). Increased reused code (20 -> 25%) undoubtedly improved these metrics, although we can't say whether the planned improvements directly caused the increased reuse.*

- *Earlier project activity percentages increased (rqmts. 14 -> 18%; design 19 -> 25%) as expected, while test decreased (37 -> 28%). The percentage change was higher than expected, though, so there may have been some other changes that we don't understand.*

- *The new appearance of specifications defects (6%) in the top eight category wasn't expected. With design inspections, we expected to (and did) find some specifications defects earlier, not later. Also, the four prototype iterations should have helped to uncover most specifications problems early.*

- *The reliability model use encouraged us to test longer. This probably led to finding some of all the targeted defect types that we would normally find postrelease, so our percent improvement is probably better than the data shows.*

State Your Recommendations

Draw from all your data, and make sure that you feel that you can justify your conclusions both to your managers and to your team. This part is shown in Figures 9-2 to 9-5 as part of a slide set that might be presented to your management. The slides shown here would normally be preceded by project background slides (see Chapter 8). Note how the process/product descriptions, high-level process measures, and the failure-analysis baseline are combined with the cost and savings analysis plus next-project expectations to create recommendations.

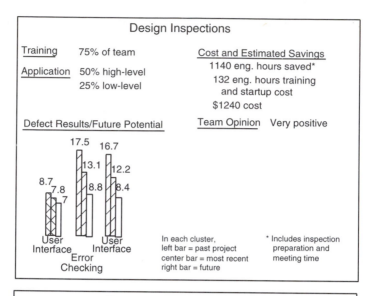

Design Inspections

Training   75% of team

Application   50% high-level
            25% low-level

Cost and Estimated Savings
  1140 eng. hours saved*
  132 eng. hours training
    and startup cost
  $1240 cost

Defect Results/Future Potential

Team Opinion   Very positive

In each cluster,
left bar = past project
center bar = most recent
right bar = future

* Includes inspection
  preparation and
  meeting time

Design Inspections (cont.)

Next Project Expectations
We should get even fewer defects on
the next project, as the team's
experience with design inspections will
both improve our efficiency and
increase the number of inspected
artifacts.

Potential Next Project Savings
  1595 eng. hours saved
  24 eng. hours cost

Recommendations
- Increase design inspection usage.
- Have a meeting to figure out how to
  detect more data definition defects
  during next project inspections.
- Start requirements/specifications
  inspections.

Figure 9-2 Design inspections

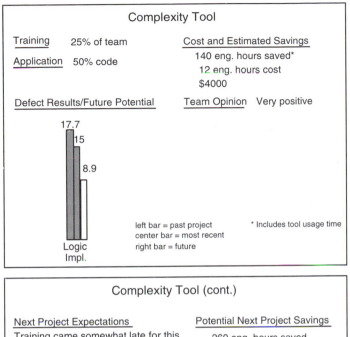

Complexity Tool

Training   25% of team

Application 50% code

Cost and Estimated Savings
140 eng. hours saved*
12 eng. hours cost
$4000

Defect Results/Future Potential

Team Opinion   Very positive

17.7
15
8.9

left bar = past project
center bar = most recent
right bar = future

* Includes tool usage time

Logic
Impl.

Complexity Tool (cont.)

Next Project Expectations
Training came somewhat late for this
project, so we believe that the tool's
earlier use in the next project will
encourage better coding practices
and further reduce logic defects.

Potential Next Project Savings
260 eng. hours saved
24 eng. hours cost
$1200

Recommendations
■ Continue tool usage.

Figure 9-3 Complexity tool

Reliability Model

Training   15% of team

Application   Throughout test

Cost and Estimated Savings
    600 eng. hours saved*
    40 eng. hours cost

Defect Results/Future Potential

We won't know how effective
the model was in decreasing
postrelease defects until the
first 12 months postrelease.
The team strongly believes that
they found 4 major defects
they normally wouldn't have.

Team Opinion   Mixed

    * Includes analysis time

Reliability Model (cont.)

Next Project Expectations
Some team members were unhappy
about the mixed messages they felt
they were getting about releasing
sooner than the model suggested.
Model use will work if our goals are
more clearly set.

Potential Next Project Savings
    900 eng. hours saved
    20 eng. hours cost

Recommendations
  ■ Have a discussion by the division
     staff to explore ways to give better
     reinforcing messages to the project
     teams.

Figure 9-4 Reliability model

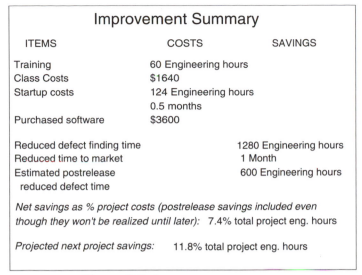

Figure 9-5 Improvement summary

This analysis and these recommendations are the essence of change. The better your results, the stronger your recommendations should be and the wider the scope of change. Technology transfer is aided in many ways. Your goal should be to sufficiently document the new process and train people so that your improvements are quickly and effectively adopted.

Consider all these ways:

- Written results in the form of management summaries and technical papers
- Verbal presentations; be sure to consider several potential target audiences (for example, engineers, project managers, functional managers)
- Integrate changes into project management training
- Integrate changes into lifecycle documentation
- Include tools in standard lab system configurations

If you developed a storyboard framework for your project during its early stages, then you already have a powerful way to present and sell your results. Remember, your actions immediately after completion will strongly determine whether a particular process change will last and propagate.

CONLUSION

Just because we use a new method and successfully finish a project doesn't mean that the new method caused the success. Without reasonable supporting measurements and analysis, this is just jumping to conclusions.

The goals for various process changes are *based on key business challenges*. Most successful long-term change efforts demonstrate a clear understanding of these goals and are focused on measurable results closely tied to the goals. The GQM method is a valuable way to arrive at this clarity.

There are *baseline measures and descriptions* that apply to most software improvement efforts. They include

- process and product descriptions,
- high-level process metrics of productivity, time, and defect density, and
- a defect-source profile.

They are the minimum set you need to clearly see if you are meeting your goals, and they can probably be considered the basis for a software engineering "scientific method."

Also, *change-unique metrics*, like the ones shown earlier for a build-process improvement, are useful for measuring progress and for making sure that change programs are correctly tuned to business goals.

Even after you've validated your improvement with metrics that support your business goal, you must continue to *present and sell your results*. The transition to widespread use of proven practices isn't easy. Capturing data, as in these examples, will at least help you to base your conclusions on solid facts instead of claims. As our industry more widely embraces such measures and demands this type of proof, it will signal the exciting start of a software engineering renaissance similar to the one Galileo triggered. While many changes will still be hard, history has proven that repeated measurable proofs help to speed adoption of significant practices.

BIBLIOGRAPHY

1. Basili, V., and H. D. Rombach, "Tailoring the Software Process to Project Goals and Environments," *IEEE Proceedings of the Ninth International Conference on Software Engineering*, Monterey, Calif., (Apr. 1987), pp. 345-357.
2. Grady, R., *Practical Software Metrics for Project Management and Process Improvement*, Englewood Cliffs, N. J.: Prentice-Hall, Inc., 1992, pp. 228-230.
3. Grady, R., "Dissecting Software Failures," *Hewlett-Packard Journal*, (April 1989), pp. 57-63.

10
Tracking and Reporting Process-Improvement Results—Mission Possible!

My wife and I used to be great fans of TV's "Mission Impossible." At the start of each program, the mission leader, Mr. Phelps, listens to a self-destructing tape that describes the mission. You then see him sorting through files with agent's pictures to select a team. That's what I imagined when I was sorting through process-improvement articles for this chapter. Each one has one or two key pictures of success. As a whole, they show a wide range of effective ways to approach improvements and describe results, and a subset will probably work for any specific improvement "mission."

This chapter shows you a wide variety of reported process-improvement successes. Its goals are to:

- greatly shorten the original reports;
- capture the essence of their results; and
- model background data and issues so you can effectively track and present your project results.

All the stories are from published articles from Hewlett-Packard and other companies. Remember that the major thrust of these brief descriptions is to give you minimal information while still enabling you to understand the key original results. In doing so, you will end up with a much better understanding of how to track and report your process-improvement projects.

CASE 1: STRUCTURED METHODS FOR REAL-TIME PERIPHERAL FIRMWARE

A project team was faced with doing the firmware and being on the critical path for a project with a short schedule. They were also keenly aware that the firmware had to be highly reliable to avoid costly field upgrades. Their goal was to improve their planning, analysis, design, testing, and metrics tracking. [1, 2] The key pictures of their results are Table 10-1 and Figure 10-1.

Table 10-1 Project estimation quality factors (EQFs)

Activity	EQF	Estimated Elapsed Months	Actual Elapsed Months	Estimated Engineer Months	Actual Engineer Months
Analysis	9.0	4.5	5.0	20.0	22.5
Design	7.5	1.7	2.0	6.5	7.5
Coding	9.3	1.1	1.25	6.25	7.0
Functional Testing	11.5	4.2	4.6	21.0	23.0
System Integration	5.0	4.0	5.0	12.0	15.0
Total Project	8.1	15.5	17.85	65.75	75.0

Figure 10-1 Cumulative defect and code coverage

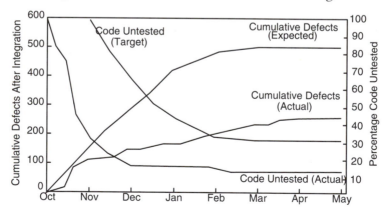

The original article summarized baseline practices very well. The team included four firmware engineers. Two had used structured analysis (SA) before, and they all had used structured design (SD). Classes in SA/SD, real-time extensions to SA/SD, and structured testing were all taken by the team. Finally, they applied configuration management (CM) to both documentation and code during the project.

While they didn't report previously measured high-level process metrics, they did show project phase estimates, defect estimates, and expected code coverage. Since the article says they finished on time, we can infer their prior productivity rate (since the firmware size was 24,000 Non-Comment Source Statements, they averaged 320 NCSS/engineering month). Their defect density in systems test was 11 defects/KNCSS, which is close to HP firmware project averages for that time period. [3]

EQF in Table 10-1 is a metric created by Tom DeMarco. He defines EQF as the reciprocal of the average estimating discrepancy. [4] For example, the first EQF in Table 10-1 is 22.5/abs (22.5 - 20) = 9.0. DeMarco defines a "good" EQF as ten or more. Their results are respectable, since the first-time use of new methods complicates estimation. They were able to test more thoroughly than they had expected (85 percent coverage versus their target of 70 percent), and the number of defects at a stable release point was half what they had expected.

Most articles will leave a reader with some unanswered questions. For example, how did this project compare to previous projects—size, effort, productivity, percent time spent in phases, defect density? We were only able to infer some of these. Also, what types of defects were found in test and how did they compare to previous defect patterns? It would have been particularly rewarding to see that their use of SA/SD reduced the number of specifications and design defects found late in their project. Since we are focused here on the essence of each article's results, the brief summaries here will leave these questions and others unanswered. This is ok. By noting questions, you will know what else *you* have to do when you choose to track your project in a similar way.

This project had aggressive objectives to improve their analysis, design, and testing practices. They characterized their practices and the changes to them well. They also summarized their results well, using a table that gave the accuracy of their estimates and a graph that showed better testing and fewer defects than in the past. One is left with a sense of their accomplishment, particularly since first-time experiences with new methods can be costly and disruptive.

CASE 2: IMPROVING EARLY LIFE CYCLE PRACTICES

This next article came from a very progressive HP division that did PC application products. They were a leader in early adoption of best practices. This article's project faced an inflexible introduction date, yet they still wanted to continue to adopt new practices and improve their old ones. A key shift of previous code and test emphases to analysis and design for their project (code name Renoir) is shown in Figure 10-2. However, Figure 10-3 shows that productivity declined. [5]

Figure 10-2 Engineering months for Renoir versus other PSD applications

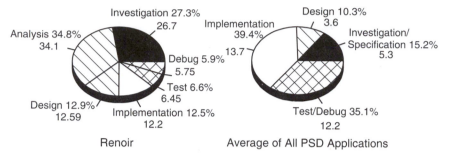

Renoir

Average of All PSD Applications

Figure 10-3 Productivity versus release date for PSD new projects

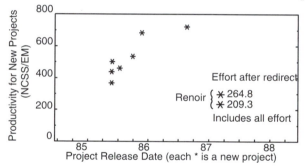

Again, this article summarized baseline practices well. They used incremental development with throw-away prototypes. They were the first in the division to use SA/SD, so they arranged for classes for the team. They also had workshops with two consultants to ensure they were using the methods well. They trained the team in inspections. They inspected their data-flow diagrams, and all modules with structure charts were formally inspected. Modules designed using other methods were seldom inspected. For code, they did 100 percent desk checks. Finally, they did special usability testing with customers. Their results were complicated by interfaces to an unstable software environment, two major project redirections, and a "brick wall" release date.

The report did show several high-level baseline metrics. Their defect density in system test (about 8 defects/KNCSS) compared well with the division average. Productivity was 264.8 NCSS/EM if you didn't include time spent before the first project redirection. Only one previous project beat their EQF of 10, although the author attributes this at least partially to the "brick wall" release. Figure 10-2 shows a dramatic shift of effort to analysis and design compared to previous projects. The two project redirections account for some increased front-end work, but probably not all. One very revealing data point was their defects in test showed only 18 defects for the design-inspected modules and 113 for those not inspected.

There were some unanswered questions. The article left a strong impression that many designs were inspected, but the data for defects found in test would be more meaningful if we knew the percentage of designs inspected. Finally, while the article did show a stable prerelease defect discovery graph (not shown here), was the postrelease defect density also low?

Like the first success story, this one also had aggressive objectives to improve analysis, design, and testing. Unlike the first, they had two major project redirections. Fortunately, they also characterized their practices and the changes to them well. Their descriptions show us that you can still make process improvements in the face of such change, although the benefits may suffer. Their results showed the shifting project emphasis from testing back to the early development phases, although other complicating project aspects and their lower productivity leave their "success" in question. Despite their project's setbacks, the article strongly concluded that the team felt the methods had been worthwhile and planned to continue using them.

CASE 3: AN EVOLVED PEER-REVIEW PROCESS

This project team had three challenges: an aggressive schedule; a new firmware architecture for a multifunction, printer product family; and providing more adequate and complete documents than previously. They read about the Cleanroom process and felt it might solve many of their problems. When they took Cleanroom training, their reactions were quite different, despite past promising reports. [6, 7] They felt "overwhelmed by the scope of this approach in its academic purity." [8]

Instead, they attacked their challenges by organizing into well-segmented responsibilities and by using a well-defined peer-review process. Their goal was to enable them "to deliver a high-quality implementation with the lowest overall schedule and cost." They set a process objective to peer review all work products. Figure 10-4 shows their peer-review matrix, and Figure 10-5 shows their results emphasis. [8] Each Figure 10-5 bar was calculated by multiplying the number of major defects times 9.8 hours and then subtracting the time spent for one inspection.

Figure 10-4 Peer-review matrix

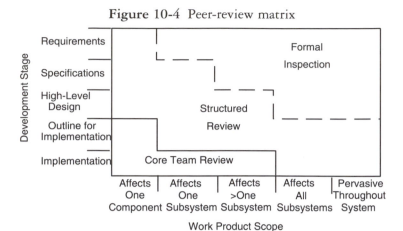

Figure 10-5 Return on investment (major defects)
(assumes 9.8 hours for late life cycle rework)

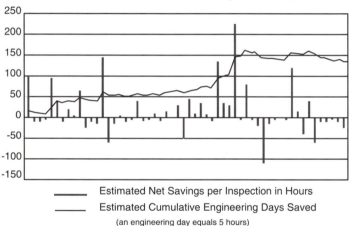

The article focused on their inspection process. It gave no other development practice descriptions. It did describe help they got from their division's software quality group—inspection and moderator training, process support, and facilitation. The team size was about 15 engineers. It is safe to assume from their process metrics descriptions that they used the inspection process widely used in HP. (see Chapter 13)

The article was written before project completion, so no defect density, productivity, or time reduction data were given. The savings shown in their key graph, Figure 10-5, is based on an estimated cost of 9.8 hours for late rework. Other HP divisions have measured similar values ranging from 4 up to 22. This division selected 9.8 hours, based on the number measured by a HP division in a very similar business. Another successful aspect was the positive perceptions of the team for the peer-review process.

There were several unanswered questions. What form of specifications and design work products did they use? How large did they expect the product to be? What defect types appeared in test? What qualifies as "late-to-fix defects," and what were the actual times that they measured for similar defects that they found? Finally, did they meet their high-quality, on-time objectives?

This HP division's story is an excellent example of a second- or third-generation adaptation and improvement of a particular method. The team was driven to make significant improvements by very aggressive project goals. Its success leveraged

- team confidence in inspections,
- timely training tuned to HP's most successful practices,
- a valuable, proven way to focus their inspections on their most risky items,
- the timely support of a local quality team, and
- process metrics that gave them immediate feedback that the process was working.

Their process performance chart not only reinforces their effective inspections use for themselves, it also excites others to make similar improvements.

CASE 4: LESSONS FROM THREE YEARS OF INSPECTION DATA

This article, from Bull HN Information Systems, takes a much broader view of improvements than the first three articles. It doesn't discuss the organization's motivation for the improvements or give any goals. At the article's end, it does talk about using improvements as a valuable tool for software developers and managers to predict product quality and reliability. We can infer that they were looking strategically at improved quality and reliability. Figure 10-6 shows one important result from inspecting defect fixes before testing them. [9]

There were no organizationwide defect density, productivity, or time-related baseline data. Neither did the article describe other practices. This is understandable, since the article summarized results from over 6,000 inspections. Some companies (including HP) use many different practices in different groups. There is some hint of this here. For example, they discuss 16 types of analysis and design documents inspected. There are also some inspection process hints: team sizes of three or four, and the effectiveness of code inspections after unit test (I know of no HP cases where we inspect after

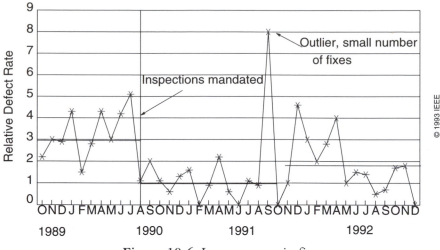

Figure 10-6 Improvement in fixes

unit test). Finally, one included case study described how inspections found 70 percent of all defects detected after code complete.

A key strength of the article was its inspection process metrics. Figure 10-6 convincingly shows what other groups have also found: Fixing defects is a defect-prone activity that inspections can help. [3] There are also results for defects per thousand lines of code at various process points, by team size, and numbers of defects versus inspection rate. There were two unanswered questions: What was the effect of inspections on key business aspects, and what were the benefits (some are shown in [10])?

Inspections were among the earliest documented process improvements. Later reports both confirmed earlier results and extended them to improve our understanding of how inspections can be adapted. For example, this report showed variations of defects found for a variety of different work products (also see [11]). It showed that they got better results with four inspectors than three (also see [12]). Figure 10-6 dramatically confirms results that we had also seen in HP. [3] However, there is nothing quite as convincing, and probably necessary, as reporting these kinds of results for your own environment.

INTERLUDE _____

Despite the brevity of their descriptions, these first four cases captured a wide range of tracking and reporting process improvements: better estimates, reduced defects, higher productivity, better designs, and ROI. Some appear more successful than others. For example, Case 2 may not appear as successful as Case 1, because its productivity compared poorly with past projects. However, it isn't necessarily fair to conclude that it wasn't a success. The graph doesn't tell us anything about the relative complexity of Renoir versus the other projects. We would get a better sense of this if we had data for multiple projects that used the new methods, as Case 4 did.

All the remaining cases show results for multiple projects and longer efforts. As you read them, think about what you need to do to include or exclude data points. Case 4 showed one approach. It included one outlying point with an explanation. Remember, the emphasis here is on pictures that effectively track and report improvements. The brief descriptions here can't possibly capture everything from the original articles.

CASE 5: IMPACTS OF OBJECT-ORIENTED TECHNOLOGIES

The NASA/Goddard Software Engineering Lab (SEL) was created in 1976 to investigate the effectiveness of software engineering technologies. They have done pioneering research work in a production environment. The goal of a series of projects was to evaluate whether object-oriented (OO) technology would lead to high reuse and reduced cost of developing new code. Figure 10-7 shows the way they presented key results for three projects (UARSTELS, EUVETELS, AND SAMPEXTS). [13]

Previous articles and this one give excellent descriptions of SEL practices. They develop flight dynamics ground-support systems, mostly in FORTRAN, with Ada use starting in the 1980s. The article talks about ten experiences from 2- to 4-year projects, each of which had 100K to 300K lines of code. Their initial application of OO principles was done in FORTRAN during coding, rather than being consciously planned during design. While it was limited to grouping data and operations on data, its success led to training in a variety of design methods, including Booch's object-oriented design. They gradually evolved these methods and started using Ada. Their next major step was to look across separate systems, using domain analysis. This helped them to plan for variations and exploit commonality across projects.

Although this article didn't give baseline data, other SEL articles do give historical error rates, costs to develop, productivity, and percent effort spent by activity. [6, 7] They considered their initial projects' OO usage "modest." Even so, their results were impressive. "This basic grouping of data and operations on the data . . . alone enabled an increase in code reuse from the baseline 20-30 percent to 75 or 80 percent." [13] Their continuing results, as shown in Figure 10-7, are also impressive, despite their limited data. Another figure in the Basili et al. article shows their percent reuse has

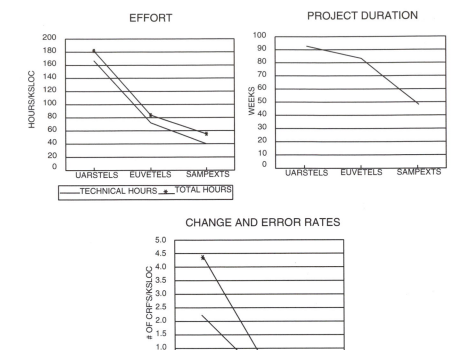

Figure 10-7   Key results for three projects

increased to 96 percent. [6] A final note says that, subjectively, OO methods were not as intuitive as expected. [13]

There are two unanswered questions. Did the improvement trend continue? Have they seen any OO-related reduced costs for developing *new* code?

This story centered on the changes resulting from a single technology. Many people have praised the benefits of OO, so it is good to see well-documented results from one environment. Their story is very persuasive with its views of effort, time, and quality improvements. Still, as the following two examples show, the results reflect the benefits of increased reuse, and OO is just one strategy to improve your reuse.

CASE 6: A SUCCESSFUL FIRMWARE REUSE PROGRAM

A HP division ran a successful reuse pilot program over several years by creating common components on a project-by-project basis. From this, they achieved 30 percent reuse along with reduced schedule and budget risks.

Their management decided that consolidating resources to work across all projects would increase those benefits. Figures 10-8 and 10-9 show how increasing reuse enabled them to greatly reduce their time to market for new products. Each bar is a separate product release. [14]

Figure 10-8 Proportion of code new, leveraged, and reused

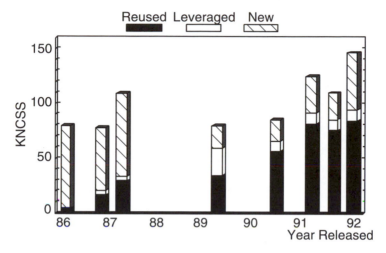

Figure 10-9 Time to market (TTM)

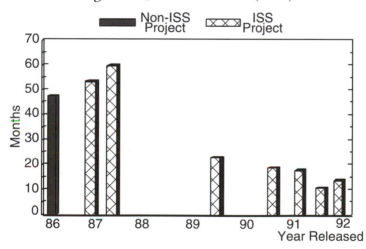

This article gave a very good description of their baseline practices. They make telecommunications instruments that include about 150 KNCSS of firmware. They have standardized on a common programming language, a common design approach, common file and function names, and they carefully track defects. Their reuse pilot gave them common code for instrument displays, state management, remote control, printout, and operating system interface. It also gave them what they called "spin-off benefits"—rapid prototyping, a known development environment, and a constant software architecture.

They developed a questionnaire that helped them focus on what users and managers wanted most from a reuse group. Besides providing the components needed, they developed one tool that has particularly helped. It takes a high-level definition of an instrument in a text file and compiles it into tables and code that configure a runtime system. This gave them the ability to simulate an instrument on a workstation. Thus, they could do fast iterations of evolving designs.

Productivity was the only baseline metric the article gave. It has increased from 540 to 1,830 NCSS/engineering month. The reuse team was three engineers for the period described. They spent one-half or more of their time doing reuse support. Their proportions of new, leveraged, and reused bar chart and their TTM bar chart give the most valuable information. They estimate that they have saved $1,430,000 in development costs.

The main unanswered questions are: Did defect levels change and what kinds of defects do they see now? They did say that they have lower defect rates in their reused components, but without knowing how much the rates went down, we couldn't even approximate what we might expect in another environment.

The basis of improvement from reuse makes it a long-term effort. Sustaining long-term support is a major challenge. This story's bar charts show a way of tracking results that has also proven helpful in other organizations. Since a reuse program affects so many people and products, economic calculations, as given here, are generally also needed.

CASE 7: EFFECTS OF REUSE ON QUALITY, PRODUCTIVITY, AND ECONOMICS

This article compares the reuse results of HP's Manufacturing Productivity Division and the San Diego Technical Graphics division. MPD started reuse to increase engineering productivity to meet critical milestones. STG wanted lower development costs and consistent functionality across products. Figures 10-10 and 10-11 show how both divisions have sustained significant results with their multiyear reuse programs. [15]

The article doesn't discuss either division's baseline practices beyond simple division and reuse program profiles. MPD created large software applications for manufacturing resource planning. They created 685 reusable work products of 55 KNCSS in size. STG created firmware for plotters and printers. Their reusable work products were 20 KNCSS.

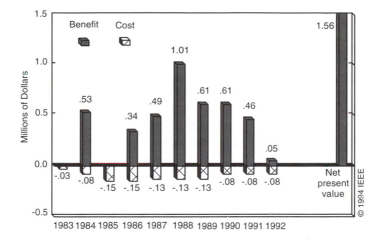

Figure 10-10 Cost/benefit of MPD reuse program

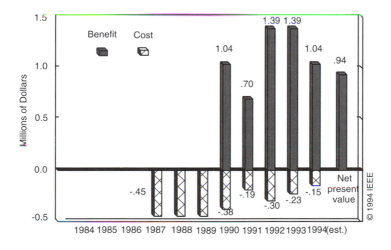

Figure 10-11 Cost/benefit of STG reuse program

The article shows good comparisons of baseline metrics to results. There was a bar chart for defect density in system test. (For MPD, 4.1 defects/KNCSS new code versus 0.9 defects/KNCSS reused code. For STG, 1.7 defects/KNCSS new code versus 0.4 defects/KNCSS reused code.) There was also a productivity bar chart for new code only versus product code, including both new and reused code. (For MPD, .7 KNCSS/EM new code versus 1.1 KNCSS/EM product code. For STG, .5 KNCSS/EM new code versus .7 KNCSS/EM product code.) It also described how STG reduced their time to market from 36 to 21 calendar months.

The reuse program results are best shown in the multiyear cost/benefit charts in Figures 10-10 and 10-11. These show (and the article describes) that the two divisions followed different strategies with different, but positive, results: STG followed a "pay up front" strategy, whereas MPD followed a "pay as you go" strategy. The productivity, quality, and TTM data add to the convincing cost/benefit charts. The main unanswered question is, What things should you consider when trying to decide which of the two strategies to follow? A second unanswered question is, What happened in 1992 at MPD to cause the reuse savings to drop so much?

By showing the results of more than one organization, this story both strengthens the argument that reuse is generally useful and suggests that the ways of showing reuse results are generalizable. While the bar charts here only reflect costs versus benefits for two HP divisions, the original article also has charts that show the same effort, duration, and defect improvements that we saw earlier in the OO/reuse example.

INTERLUDE

Cases 5, 6, and 7 added reduced effort, project duration, and time to market to our growing set of successful results. These three stories all involved longer change periods than the first four. Which of them would appeal most to your manager? What unique challenges did tracking their progress present?

As process-improvement efforts grow, the effort required to track and report their progress also grows. Imagine that each project must track data that is like data in one or more of the first four cases. Then, you also need to collect the data similarly enough across projects so you can aggregate it as Cases 5, 6, and 7 did. The next four cases have done exactly that. Each also captures an organizational vision for what is important.

CASE 8: A DOLLARS AND CENTS VIEW OF RESULTS

This article is unusual since its results are entirely oriented to high-level managers. Raytheon felt their processes weren't adequate to deal with the diverse needs of customers across seven business areas. They did a self-assessment (based on the SEI CMM) that led to an initiative whose goal was to continuously improve their development and management processes through process stabilization, control, and change. The persuasive graph of their results in Figure 10-12 has been cited as a good example many times. [16]

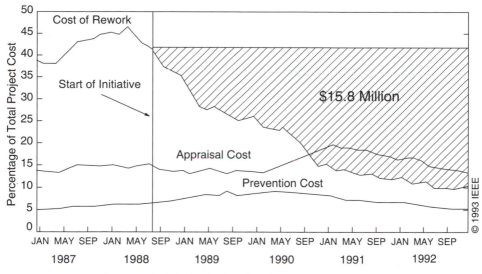

Figure 10-12 Analysis of savings over 15 projects

The article gave a good description of practices, considering its focus on process improvement's financial aspects. The organization described has 400 software engineers. They build electronic systems, and there is one reference to large, real-time, embedded software systems. We learn the most about their practices from their training program details. They teach SA, formal inspections, Ada, SCM, unit testing, and project management. Courses under development are in design techniques, OO, measurement and root-cause analysis, and software integration.

They had baselines for several high-level metrics, since they reported relative progress. The rework savings shown in Figure 10-12 are their most impressive results. They reduced rework from 41 percent to 11 percent. Much of this came from cutting integration rework by 80 percent. There is a productivity graph showing 204 percent relative improvement, and there was a $9.6M schedule-incentive bonus (which wasn't included in Figure 10-12) for just one large project. Finally, they have progressed to CMM level 3, and they calculated a 7-to-1 return on their process-improvement invest-ment. A key unanswered question that practitioners always want to know is: What are the correlations between the use of specific practices and the result-ing savings?

The broader the scope of your process-improvement effort, the larger the expected return will be. This story shows a very effective way to show value to high-level managers who manage large businesses and think in terms of millions of dollars. It is particularly effective, because the author supports this well-constructed graph with backup data for ROI, productivity, and rework. While most readers won't have to make such a strong case, it's valuable to understand how your improvements may ultimately be rolled up into a larger picture.

CASE 9: A QUALITY VIEW OF RESULTS

This interesting article presents a variety of ways that Hitachi tracks and evaluates software quality. It doesn't give any specific business challenges, but it does imply that a high-level goal is to minimize system failures at customer sites. Figure 10-13 shows how they have tracked this since 1981. [17] The field-failure ratio is the number of system failures per month per 1000 systems.

Figure 10-13 System failures at customer sites

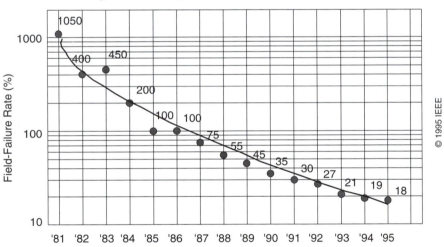

They don't describe their development or testing methods. Rather, the article focuses on quality planning and tracking methods. The only baseline high-level metric is on Figure 10-13, which also shows dramatic progress. The article also gives a bar chart of the percent defects detected at each life-cycle stage. A surprising part of it is three bars that are tied to inspections—"cramming" before inspection, inspection, and "cramming" after inspection—that add up to only 4.8 percent (they don't explain what "cramming" is). This inspection percentage is much less than in other industry reports. [6, 8, 9, 11, 12]

There are many unanswered questions. What message do they give to their Hitachi developer customers about what practices need to improve? To what do they attribute the low percent defects found by inspections? Finally, what are the correlations between the use of specific practices and the resulting improvements?

This story features a simpler graph than the Raytheon graph. Yet, it is still persuasive for many high-level managers. Other businesses besides software have proven that other benefits usually accompany quality improvements, so goals and long-term tracking of quality improvements are very effective.

CASE 10: HP'S 10X IMPROVEMENT PROGRAM

HP was traditionally an electronic instrumentation company until the 1980s. Then, our product software content rapidly increased. We had made excellent progress toward meeting a factor of 10 (10X) hardware improvement goal triggered by foreign manufacturing competition, so our company president set a 10X software challenge. There were two goals to meet in five years. The first was to reduce product postrelease defect density (for the first 12 months after release) by 10X. The second was to reduce the number of open serious and critical defects by 10X. [3, 12] Each division tracked their improvements against their own starting points. Figure 10-14 shows our impressive results during the five years of the challenge.

Figure 10-14 HP 10X postrelease discovered defect density

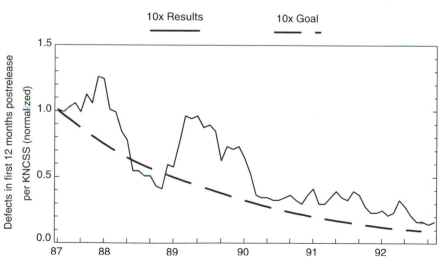

We did a survey that summarizes the state of HP practices at the start of the 10X challenge. [18] The most astonishing thing we learned was that 69 percent of HP's engineers felt their primary job was to develop software. The 69 percent was divided roughly equally among engineers who developed firmware, systems software, and applications software, and the amount of software was growing rapidly. Inspections were the most widespread common practice, but they were still largely focused on code. There were no consistent specification or design practices, though there were SA/SD experiments with reports of success. There was a strong move toward developing in the UNIX® environment (in 1983 about 10 percent of developers used UNIX; by 1985 the percentage was up to 35). We had a metrics database that already showed the advantages of reuse. It also contained good baseline metrics for productivity, prerelease defect density, and percent engineering time per phase. [3]

Figure 10-14 shows that we achieved a 6X companywide defect density improvement. There are strong indications from recent group-reported data that at least three of five HP groups had beaten 10X by 1995. The absolute number of open serious and critical defects remained level. In retrospect, it is clear that this metric should have been normalized, as was the postrelease defect density metric. HP averages 20 percent revenue growth per year. Assuming shipped software grows at the same rate, this alone would lead to a 2.5X increase in open serious and critical defects if nothing were done differently. When you add the clearly identified, increased software content in virtually every product (for example, firmware in our printers increased over 10X in five years), I believe that keeping the number of open serious and critical defects level was a huge, well-disguised improvement. The combination of these goals fostered the sustained adoption of key practices, and this has led to strongly increased HP competitiveness.

We have the same key unanswered question as for several of the organizationwide results given earlier. What are the correlations between the use of specific practices and the resulting improvements? We can see from the HP practice-specific results in this chapter that

- inspections yield the fastest, good results;
- better analysis and design practices yield some results the first time you try them, and they promise even more for later projects;
- reuse and OO require the largest investment, and they offer the largest return.

When HP's 10X improvement program started, it was hard to believe that such improvements were possible in such a short time. Its success shows the importance of a clear improvement vision and a visible way of tracking progress toward it. The HP and Hitachi stories, and the next story about the Space Shuttle Onboard Software project, strongly argue that a high-level quality graph may be the best way to focus efforts and to track progress.

CASE 11: A REPORT FROM ONE OF THE BEST

This article shows how the Space Shuttle Onboard Software project has successfully approached two decades of improvements. Their organization is driven to improve their processes and quality continuously, since they support a highly visible, increasingly complex, life-critical application. Figure 10-15 shows how they summarize their progress. [19]

Figure 10-15 Onboard flight software releases

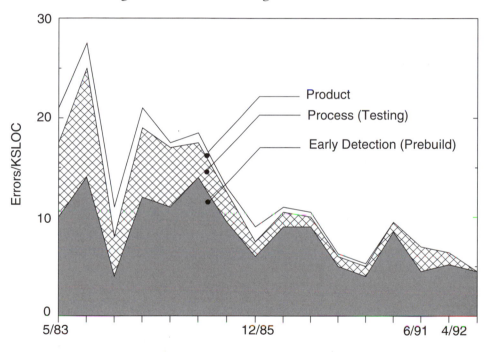

They give an excellent description of the evolution of their practices since the 1970s. In the 70s, a big challenge was to establish a system architecture. Reviews were the quality method of choice, though they were informal without specific documents, checklists, or follow-up. Their requirements process was out of control. In the 80s, they sought a balance of control versus responsiveness. They controlled requirements. They improved their inspections, started an incremental release process, independent verification, and causal analysis and defect prevention. They applied various process assessments—NASA Excellence, Baldrige, and an early version of the CMM. In the 90s, they have created process-ownership teams. One major switch has been from unit and functional testing to scenario testing.

The only baseline metric data the article gives is their product errors in 1976. Figure 10-15 shows their impressive record of reduced defects in their key areas of early detection, process, and product. The product error rate was around 8 defects per KSLOC (thousands of source line of code) in 1977. This rate dropped to 0.72 in 1986 and to 0.3 in 1993. Finally, the article says they have been evaluated as a level 5 on the SEI Capability Maturity Model.

There are two key unanswered questions. How well do their rigorous practices apply to commercial product organizations? With no productivity data, it's hard to know whether continued quality improvement to their level doesn't hit a point of diminishing returns. Finally, what do their current defect patterns suggest are their best current opportunities for improvements?

The Space Shuttle Onboard Software project has one of the strongest published software process-improvement records available. That makes its view of results important. Again, it's a quality-oriented view, although it is significant that it also includes *process* elements.

CONCLUSION

Now that you've sorted through this "mission" portfolio, which tracking and reporting methods appealed the most to you? Remember, the figures here aren't models. They are all from real projects. They may all be incomplete in different ways, yet they are exciting, particularly when viewed as a whole.

Imagine that you had been responsible for one of these projects or programs and had presented its results to managers from another company. Some of the questions they would surely want answered are:

"What kinds of savings did you get?"
"What did it cost you?"
"How does your project compare with others?"
"What did you learn that should be passed on to other projects?"

Most of these articles answered these questions reasonably well, even if the brief summaries here didn't. There were some unanswered questions, and you probably had others. The examples did show that when you tell your story, you need a similar key graphic message.

These cases reinforce the model introduced in Chapter 9. It will help you to select the information you need to track for your process-improvement project. It was created after many questions about HP improvements and after hearing others give their results. Let's examine its four parts for the cases summarized here.

Process and Product Descriptions - These are probably the hardest to understand well enough to translate to your own environment, especially with the abbreviated descriptions in the cases. It is particularly easy to make incorrect assumptions when you read a paper. The most complete descriptions for these cases were for the single-project ones. They took a variety of forms. If we look across them all, we see requirements, design, code, test, configuration management, prototyping, desk checks, inspections, languages, defect management, project size, amount of code reused, team size, experience levels, and training. Even within specific practices like design or inspections, there can be wide variety. One way to think about what you need here is to imagine you are at a conference. What things would you ask a speaker after a talk that would help you to understand their practices?

High-Level Process Measures - These included product size, effort, productivity, activity breakdowns, defect density, and calendar time. All the articles here were picked for their original completeness and persuasiveness. Most of them gave excellent baseline metrics. Despite this, several left unanswered questions in this key area. Cases 1, 3, 5, 6, and 11 all failed to include important metrics, and some of the others didn't give some baseline metrics that would have just answered points of curiosity.

Defect Failure-Analysis Baseline - Possibly the most useful technique today for measuring effects of process change is a detailed failure analysis. While we saw better high-level process metrics for almost all the cases, many would have been much more persuasive if they had had data that showed reduced targeted defects. Cases 1, 3, 8, 9, and 11 would especially have been better. Chapter 11 and *Practical Software Metrics for Project Management and Process Improvement* show other project results that particularly emphasize such measures. [12]

Change-Unique Measurements - Defect failure-analysis data are a special case of measures that help you to understand the results of particular improvements. These articles showed a wide range of others: EQF, percent code untested, time in inspections, number of major defects found, number of fixes and defects in fixes, new/leveraged/reused code, rework/appraisal/prevention effort, field-failure rate, and product/process/early detected errors. All these played a key role in showing the success of their associated process improvements.

Process and product descriptions, high-level process measures, a defect failure-analysis baseline, and change-unique measures form the basis for effective tracking and reporting process-improvement results. All the stories here showed a variety of exciting results, and these will help you to better plan and present your own. They also showed a process-improvement range of single projects through multiyear, business-level efforts. I freely admit that these cases were chosen on the basis of their success. Still, you want such a bias when setting a vision for your own improvements and deciding how you will check your progress and results. So, when you plan your improvement, imagine the "Mission Possible" theme song in the background, and set your vision for what the cover of your process-improvement folder will look like when you're done.

BIBLIOGRAPHY

1. Robinson, P., and P. Bartlett, "CPB's Use of Structured Methods for Real-Time Peripheral Firmware," *HP Software Productivity Conference Proceedings*, (August 1988), pp. 285-295. (Not available outside HP.)
2. Bartlett, P., P. Robinson, T. Hains, and M. Simms, "Use of Structured Methods for Real-Time Peripheral Firmware," *Hewlett-Packard Journal*, (Aug. 1989), pp. 79-86.
3. Grady, R., and D. Caswell, *Software Metrics: Establishing a Company-Wide Program*, Englewood Cliffs, N.J.: Prentice Hall, 1987, pp. 112, 127.
4. DeMarco, T., *Controlling Software Projects*, New York: Yourdon Press, 1982.
5. Witkin, L., "The Renoir Project at PSD: Reflections on Our Experiences," *HP Software Engineering Productivity Conference Proceedings*, (May 1987), pp. 1-87 thru 1-104. (Not available outside HP.)
6. Basili, V., G. Caldiera, F. McGarry, R. Pajerski, G. Page, and S. Waligora, "The Software Engineering Laboratory—An Operational Software Experience Factory," *ACM Proc. Intnl. Conference on Software Engineering*, (May 1992), 370-381.
7. Basili, V., M. Zelkowitz, F. McGarry, J. Page, S. Waligora, and R. Pajerski, "SEL's Software Process-Improvement Program," *IEEE Software*, (Nov. 1995), pp. 83-87.
8. Hollis, J., "Establishing A Peer-Review Process for Work Products," *HP Project Management Conference Proceedings*, (April 1996). (Not available outside HP.)
9. Weller, E., "Lessons from Three Years of Inspection Data," *IEEE Software*, (Sept. 1993), pp. 38-45.
10. Herbsleb, J., A. Carleton, J. Rozum, J. Siegel, and D. Zubrow, "Benefits of CMM-Based Software Process Improvement: Initial Results," *Technical Report, CMU/SEI-94-TR-13*, (Aug. 1994).

11. Kelly, J., J. Sherif, and J. Hops, "An Analysis of Defect Densities Found During Software Inspections," *Journal of Systems Software* 17, (1992), pp. 110-117.
12. Grady, R., *Practical Software Metrics for Project Management and Process Improvement*, Englewood Cliffs, N. J.: Prentice-Hall, Inc., 1992, pp. 122-157.
13. Figure 10-7 is reprinted by permission of the publisher from Stark, M., "Impacts of Object-Oriented Technologies: Seven Years of Software Engineering," *Journal of Systems and Software*, No. 23, (1993), pp. 163-169, Copyright 1993 by Elsevier Science Inc.
14. Rix, M., "Case Study of a Successful Firmware Reuse Program," *HP Software Engineering Productivity Conference Proceedings*, (Aug. 1992), pp. 125-137. (Not available outside HP.)
15. Lim, W., "Effects of Reuse on Quality, Productivity, and Economics," *IEEE Software*, (Sept. 1994), pp. 23-30.
16. Dion, R., "Process Improvement and the Corporate Balance Sheet," *IEEE Software*, (July 1993), pp. 28-35.
17. Onoma, A. K., and T. Yamaura, "Practical Steps Toward Quality Development," *IEEE Software*, (Sept. 1995), pp. 68-76.
18. Grady, R., and E. Brigham, "A Survey of HP Software Development," *HP Software Productivity Conference Proceedings*, (April 1986), pp. 1-126 thru 1-141. (Not available outside HP.)
19. Billings, C., J. Clifton, B. Kolkhorst, E. Lee, and W. Wingert, "Journey to a Mature Software Process," *IBM Systems Journal*, Vol. 33, No. 1, (1994), pp. 46-61. Reprinted with permission.

Part Four

ACT
Revise, Develop Next-Level Process, Convince Others

Increasing Adoption

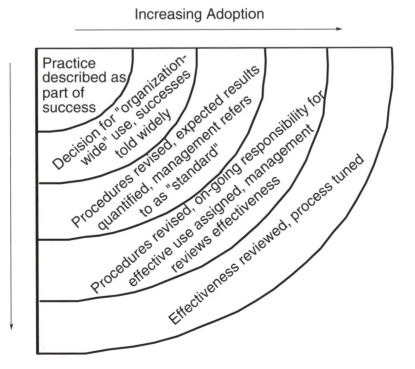

ACT is a key part of TQC continuous process improvement. It represents the feedback part of the improvement process. More importantly, it also represents increased organizational commitment, so the ACT quadrant at left emphasizes management involvement, reviews, and decisions.

"Software Failure Analysis for High-Return Process-Improvement Decisions" could have been put in PLAN, since root-cause defect data can help you to quantify the potential return of various improvement areas. We also saw how these methods played a key role in the CHECK quadrant. So, this chapter provides a natural bridge to ACT. No process is as likely to continue to play as key a role in motivating change once you start doing root-cause defect analysis.

"Placing a Value on Software Process Improvements" then describes a powerful model of process-improvement value, of how different people look at value, and of how you can adjust your presentation of value to anticipate the needs of different audiences. It builds on the idea of the experience map introduced in Chapter 6, the cost/benefit analyses done in Chapters 1, 8, and 9, and the core-competence discussion in Chapter 3.

"Key Lessons from Adoption of a Software Engineering Best Practice" gives an in-depth study of how software inspections adoption has evolved over many years. This shows an exciting, successful journey around the complete spiral model through all of its stages. From this experience, we draw key lessons that you can benefit from when following through with any improvement.

The book ends with "Your Mileage May Vary," a recap of many of the key models used in the book.

11
Software Failure Analysis for High-Return Process-Improvement Decisions

When I was growing up, my father was fond of using sayings to encourage me to remember important lessons. One of his favorites was "Do you know the difference between a wise man and a fool?" He would then go on to say that a wise man only makes a mistake once. A fool makes the same mistake over and over again.

Applying my father's saying to software defects, it sometimes seems as if there are many "fools" among software developers. However, there aren't. Individually, we learn from our mistakes. What's missing is *organizational learning* about our software mistakes. I guess that many organizations have earned my dad's "fool" label.

One of the most powerful, convincing arguments for changing a particular process is that the process results in costly defects and rework. By evaluating your software defects and acting on your results, you have a way to transfer process learning from individuals to organizations. It includes analyzing software defects, brainstorming the root causes of those defects, and incorporating what you learn into training and process changes so that the same defects won't occur again. There are five steps:

1. Extend defect data collection to include root-cause information. Start shifting from reactive responses to defects toward proactive actions.
2. Do failure analysis on representative organizationwide defect data. *Failure analysis is the evaluation of defect patterns to learn process or product weaknesses.*
3. Do root-cause analysis to help you decide what changes you must make. *Root-cause analysis is a group-reasoning process applied to defect information to determine organizational understanding of the causes of a particular class of defects.*
4. Apply what you've learned to do training and to change development and maintenance processes.
5. Evolve failure analysis/root-cause analysis to an effective continuous process-improvement process.

How do these steps differ from other popular methods for analyzing processes? One popular method is process assessments, like those described in Chapter 2. Most assessments document people's answers to subjective questions that are designed around somebody's model of ideal software development practices. If such models are accurate and if people's answers reflect reality, the models provide a good picture of an organization's status. Thus, the results may or may not be timely, representative, or motivational.

The combination of failure analysis and root-cause analysis are potentially more valuable than subjective assessments, because they quantify defect costs for your specific organization. The key point to remember is that software defect data is one of your most important, available, management information sources for software process-improvement decisions. Furthermore, subsequent data will give you a measurable way of seeing results and evaluating how methods can be further adapted when you are done with a specific set of changes.

THE REACTIVE USE OF DEFECT DATA (A COMMON STARTING POINT) _____

After initial analysis, everyone reacts to defects by either fixing them or ignoring them. Customer dissatisfaction is minimized when you react quickly to fix problems that affect your customer's business. This is often done with fast response to issues and by following up with patches or workarounds, when appropriate. Some Hewlett-Packard divisions track the resolution of "hotsites." Figure 11-1 shows an example. [1] Such a chart is a valuable way to track responsiveness, but it does little to prevent future defects. Furthermore, hotsites and patch management are very expensive.

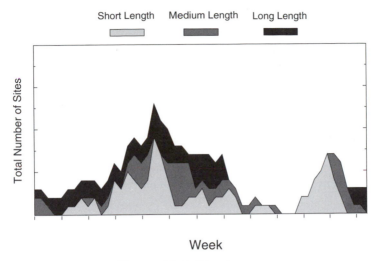

Week

Figure 11-1 Hotsite status

Cumulative defects for long-lived software products are also tracked. For example, Figure 11-2 shows the incoming SRs (service requests) or DRs (discrepancy reports), the closed SRs or DRs, and the net progress for one NASA software project. [2] Some HP divisions also track progress like this, [1] although HP's progress measure subtracts incoming defects from closed defects so that positive progress represents a net reduction of defects. NASA appears to do the reverse.

Figure 11-2 Software maintenance request closure analysis

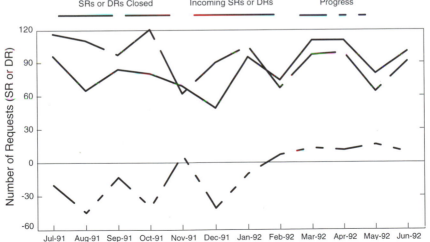

Both the hotsite graph and the defect closure progress graph show reactive uses of defect data. In the examples, the respective organizations were using the data to try to improve their immediate customer situations. The alternative is to ignore the data or to react much more slowly.

Ignoring defect data can lead to serious consequences for your business. For example, the division producing one HP software system decided to release their product despite a continuing incoming defect trend during system test. The result was a multimillion-dollar update shortly after release, a continued steady need for defect repairs, and a product with a bad quality reputation. This is the kind of mistake that can cause an entire product line's downfall. A recent article describes how one company learned this lesson the hard way. [3]

You also cannot limit your responses only to reaction. Besides endangering customer satisfaction and increasing your costs, here are some other dangers if you don't complement your reactive processes with proactive steps to eliminate defect sources.

1. Your people can get in the habit of reactive thinking. They can come to believe that management finds shipping defective products acceptable.
2. Your managers get in the habit of primarily rewarding reactive behavior. This further reinforces fixing defects late in development or after release. Late fixes are both costly and disruptive.
3. People place blame too easily in highly reactive environments because of accompanying pressure or stress. This is demoralizing, since the root causes of most defects are poor training, documentation, or processes, not individual incompetence.

Remember that effectively reacting to defects is an important part of successfully producing software products. However, because business conditions change rapidly, many organizations can't seem to find the time to break old habits of using defect data reactively without considering ways of eliminating similar future problems. You must also include the elimination of the causes of potential future defects in any successful long-term business strategy.

FAILURE ANALYSIS (CHANGING YOUR MENTAL FRAME OF REFERENCE)

The proactive use of defect data to eliminate the root causes of software defects starts with a change in mental frame of reference. The reactive frame generally focuses on single defects and asks "How much do they hurt?" It also considers how important it is to fix particular defects compared to others and asks "When must they be fixed?" The proactive frame asks "What caused your defects in the first place? Which ones cause the greatest resource drain? How can you avoid them next time?"

Various reports have described successful efforts to analyze defects, their causes, and proposed solutions. But, the terminology among them has differed, and the definitions could mean different things to different people. In the fall of 1986, the HP Software Metrics Council addressed the definition of standard categories of defect causes. Our goal was to provide standard defect terminology that different HP projects and labs could use to report, analyze, and focus efforts to eliminate defects and their root causes. [4] Figure 11-3 is the model that has evolved from our original definitions. [1]

The model is used by selecting one descriptor each from origins, types, and modes for each defect report as it is resolved. For example, a defect might be a *design defect* where part of the *user interface* described in the internal specification was *missing*. Another defect might be a *coding defect* where some *logic* was *wrong*.

Figure 11-3 Categorization of sources of software defects

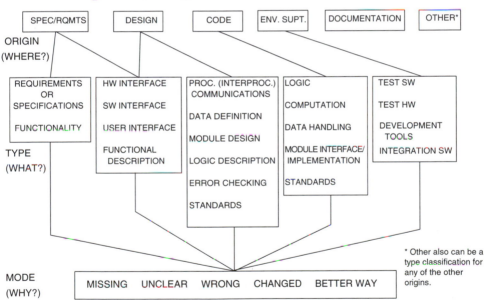

Figure 11-4 gives you some idea of how defects vary from one entity to another. [5] The different shadings reflect the origin part of Figure 11-3. The pie wedges come from the middle layer of Figure 11-3, the defect types. The eight largest sources of defects for different HP divisions are shown in each pie. All four results profile defects found only during system and integration test.

We can immediately see from just looking at the shadings that the sources of defects vary greatly across the organizations. No two pie charts are alike. These differences are not surprising. If everyone developed the same way and experienced the same problems, then we would have fixed those problems by now. Instead, there are many different environments. While many proposed solutions to our problems apply to different situations, they don't necessarily apply equally well to all problems or all environments.

Figure 11-4 Sources of defects for four HP divisions (defects found in test)

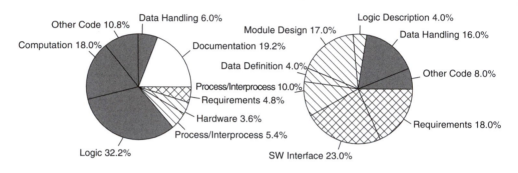

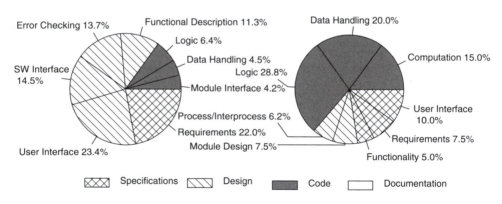

Some of the differences are due to inconsistencies in people's use of the origin and type definitions. Because the definitions are just a means to focus process-improvement efforts on the costliest rework areas, groups resolve inconsistencies when they define root causes to problems and brainstorm potential fixes. It is the triggering of these discussions that makes the data in Figure 11-4 so important. Discussing root causes is a way for you to instill a process-improvement attitude in your organization. Your data will provide a measurable basis for decisions that you must make. By continuing to track your defect data, you can also measure how successful your solutions are.

Acting on Causal Data

Collecting defect source data is only the first step. Persuasive as the data might be, improvements won't happen automatically. Both managers and engineers must agree on what the data means and the importance of acting on it. One of the best ways to help ensure this is to tie proposed improvements to stated business goals. This also keeps improvement priorities high enough to help ensure sustained management support.

Besides management support, some first-line managers and engineers affected by a proposed change must be motivated to do something and be assigned responsibility to plan and do the necessary changes. Finally, as for any effective project, there must be a way of monitoring progress and gauging success.

As a group, software developers now have several decades of software development experience. It is time to break out of our pressure-driven reactive habits to use our accumulated knowledge to drive lasting improvements. Failure analysis changes the way managers and developers look at software defects. This finally opens the way to a proactive frame of reference.

ROOT-CAUSE ANALYSIS PROCESSES

There are many possible ways to analyze root-cause data. Any successful way must be sensitive to project pressures and personnel motivation. HP has used several approaches in different organizations. For this discussion, I will label three that seem to evolve naturally from each other as "one-shot root-cause analysis," "postproject root-cause analysis," and "continuous process-improvement cycle." The three include many common steps. Since the first is an introductory process, the most detailed explanation is saved for the postproject root-cause analysis.

One-Shot Root-Cause Analysis

A good starting approach for divisions that have not previously categorized their defect data by root causes is a one-shot root-cause analysis. This approach minimizes the amount of divisional invested effort by using someone from outside the division to facilitate the process. Fortunately, the information already recorded in most HP divisional defect-tracking systems has been complete enough to extract such data. HP Software Initiative consultants have facilitated these with many HP divisions. (SWI is a corporate program whose people work with divisions to accelerate companywide adoption of software best practices.)

The one-shot process has six steps.

1. Introduce a group of engineers and managers to the failure-analysis model (Figure 11-3) and the root-cause analysis process. (About 1 hour) Make it clear that the goals of the one-shot process are to:

   • Create a rough divisional picture of their defect patterns

   • Identify some potential improvement opportunities

2. Select 50 to 75 defects from the defect tracking system using a random process. Make sure the defects have enough information so the team thinks that they will be able to extract the necessary causal information. (About 2 hours, some time before the meeting)

3. Have the people in the group classify one defect per person and discuss the findings as a group. Then have them classify enough defects so that you have about 50 total. Draw a pie chart of the top eight defect types. (About 2 hours)

4. Pick two defect types to focus on. Create fishbone diagrams from the combined root causes and additional comments (like Figures 11-7 and 11-8). A fishbone diagram is a brainstorming tool used to combine and organize group thoughts. [1, 6] (About 1/2 hour)

5. Develop some recommendations for improvements. (About 1/2 hour)

6. Present the results and recommendations to management. Make assignments to do initial changes. (About 1 hour)

Participants in this process have been generally surprised and excited that they could learn so much in a very short time. They have also been uniformly interested in adopting the analysis process permanently. How quickly they have followed through has varied, depending on many business variables (for example, immediate product commitments, other in-progress process changes, or tight economic climate tend to delay immediate adoption).

Postproject Root-Cause Analysis

The major difference between this process and the one-shot process is that divisions that start with the one-shot process have not previously collected causal data. Divisions that already collect failure-analysis data and have an understanding of their past defect patterns analyze their data and act on their results more efficiently. The steps in this explanation follow the meeting outline shown in Figure 11-5. Note that the timings below are intended to force the meeting to keep moving. It is best to schedule a full two hours, since that time will be needed. The example used here to illustrate the various steps came from a root-cause analysis meeting done at an HP division shortly after a team released a new product.

Premeeting

Identify the division's primary business goal. This goal is an important input when prioritizing which high-level defect causes should be addressed first. It also will help you to frame management presentations to ensure sustained management support. A typical business goal might be framed around maximizing a particular customer group's satisfaction, or evolving a product line to some future state, or in controlling costs or schedule in order to attract new customers.

Division champion and root-cause facilitator analyze data. The champion is a person who promotes a process or improvement, removes obstacles, enthusiastically supports implementers and users, and leads through active involvement. The facilitator is a person who will run the root-cause analysis meeting. They are skilled in meeting processes and dynamics and also should be familiar with software development and its common defect types.

Figure 11-5 Root-cause analysis meeting outline

PREMEETING
    Identify the division's primary business goal
    Division champion and root-cause facilitator analyze data
    Champion sends meeting announcement and instructions to engineers
            - Pick two defects from their code from chosen categories
            - Think of ways to prevent or find defects sooner
MEETING
    State goal: *Use insights gained from failure analysis data to*
                   improve our development and support practices

    Select issues (10 minutes)

    Review defects brought (15 minutes)

    Analyze defects (15 minutes)

    Break (10 minutes)

    Brainstorm solutions (10 minutes)

    Test for commitment (10 minutes)

    Plan for change (10 minutes)

POSTMEETING
    Division champion and root-cause facilitator review meeting process
    Division champion captures software development process baseline data

One simple data-analysis approach is to enter the data into an electronic spreadsheet. Draw pie charts of the top eight defect types by quantity and by find-and-fix effort (either actual or estimated). Figure 11-6 shows the system-test data we first saw in Figure 1-5 for four projects. The shading represents defect origin information, and the pie wedges are defect types. The left pie chart shows the eight most frequently recorded causes of defects. The right pie chart shows the data adjusted to reflect that design and specifications defects found in system test cost increasingly more to fix than coding defects do. The weighting factors are based on the relative costs to fix defects in Figure 4-3, since the HP division for this case had not collected their own defect-fix times. The right pie chart was prepared by multiplying the left pie chart wedge percentages (or counts) by the appropriate weighting factor and then converting back to 100 percent.

Figure 11-6 Top eight causes of defects for one division

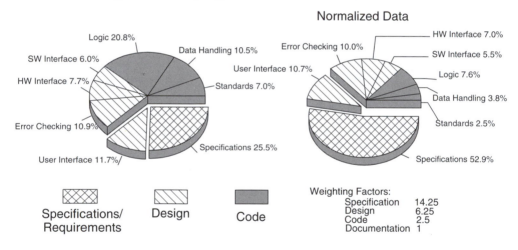

Select two defect types to brainstorm, based on your best estimate of division concern or readiness to implement solutions. The two defect types selected for this meeting were user-interface defects and specifications defects. The specifications defect type was picked because it was the largest *division* category (there were 64 in this project team's 476 defects). User-interface defects were picked because they were the largest *team* category (110 defects) that the particular brainstorming team had experienced. Both categories represented significant divisional improvement opportunities.

Send out instructions to engineers. Meeting attendees typically are 10 to 15 engineers and project managers from one or more teams. The division champion should have each engineer bring hardcopy information for two defects from their code from the chosen categories. Tell invitees to think back to the most likely root cause for each defect and propose at least one way to prevent or find each defect sooner.

Meeting

State the meeting goal: Use insights gained from failure analysis data to improve our development and maintenance practices. Present the defect categorization model; show typical patterns for other divisions; and show your division's pattern. Set a positive tone for the meeting. Remind attendees that they will be looking at *process* flaws, and that they *must* avoid even joking comments that might belittle the data or solutions discussed.

Select issues. Reiterate the reasons for selecting this meeting's particular defect types. Let people make initial comments. Address concerns about potential data inaccuracies (if they come up at this point) by emphasizing the solution-oriented nature of the brainstorming process. Suggest that inaccuracies matter less when combining pie wedges to consider solutions. For example, for this division's meeting, some engineers had a hard time calling some defects "user interface" as opposed to "specifications." We simply used both labels for such defects during the meeting instead of getting sidetracked on resolving the differences. You want to get people ready to share their defects by discussing a future time (like their next major product release) when they have eliminated the reasons for the defects occurring at all.

Review defects brought. Have engineers read off their defects/causes/solutions. The major reason to do this is to get attendees involved in the meeting in a nonthreatening way. Thus, don't criticize those who did not prepare, rather encourage them to contribute real time. Unlike inspections, root-cause analysis meetings require very little preparation time for attendees. After their first meeting, attendees will realize this, and it will be easier to get them to quickly review their defects before the next meeting.

Foster a creative brainstorming mood by showing everyone that all their inputs are "right," and begin to form a shared understanding of terminology, definitions, and an acceptable level of ambiguity. This section also gives you some idea whether there is some energy around any particular defect types. You can use such energy later to motivate action.

Here are examples of two defects out of the ten that this division's engineers selected. About 12 engineers and managers attended the meeting.

1. User interface/specifications defect: There was a way to select (data) peaks by hand for another part of product, but not for the part (being analyzed).

Cause: late-added features; unanticipated use.

Proposed way to avoid or detect sooner: walkthrough/review by people other than own team.

2. Specifications defect: Clip doesn't copy sets of objects.

Cause: inherited code, neither code nor error message existed. Highly useful feature, added, liked, but never found way back into specifications or designs.

Proposal to avoid or detect sooner: do written specifications, control creeping features.

Analyze defects. Create fishbone diagrams [1,6] from combined root causes and additional comments. Use this discussion to bring the group from their individual premeeting biases regarding defects to a group consensus state. A useful technique for grouping the defects is to write the suggested causes on sticky pieces of paper. Then have the group silently move the papers into groupings of related areas. If some papers move back and forth between two groups, duplicate them. The resulting groupings are called an "affinity diagram." [7] These groupings are major bones of the fish that the group must name. Don't expect the fishbone to be perfect here or even complete. The next section will potentially contribute more. Also, don't get concerned about form. Let the group know that a fishbone is just a means to an end, that you will clean it up after the meeting, and that it is likely to change even after that point.

This particular root-cause analysis meeting was the third that was done in roughly a two-month period at this division. They brainstormed the Figure 11-7 fishbone diagram. [8] They also refined the Figure 11-8 fishbone diagram that had been created in the other two meetings.

Break. This type of meeting takes a lot of energy and focus. It's hard to sustain that for two full hours. You will need a break.

Brainstorm solutions. Use this time as an orthogonal approach to analyzing the issues at hand. This is also the transition from analysis to action planning for change. Notice which topics the group is enthusiastic about and help them to choose to target those improvements.

A lot of group energy was present for both defect types. Because a task force already was working on specification defects as a result of the previous root-cause analysis meetings, planning focused on user-interface defects. Here is the solution list they created. Note that some of these seem vague. Remember that the brainstorm list is only an intermediate step toward defining action steps. Just be sure that the group understands

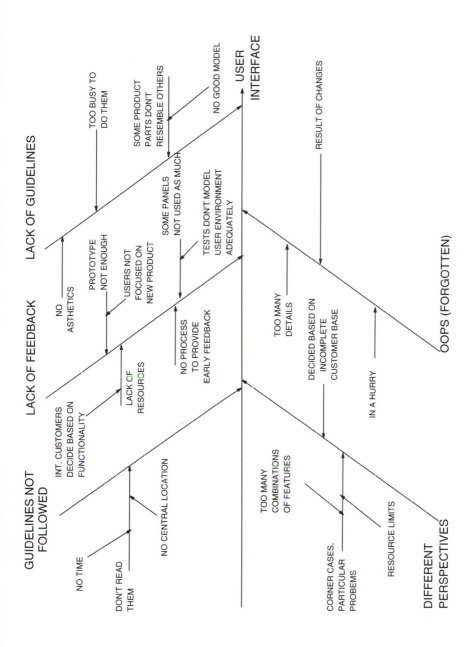

Figure 11-7 Fishbone diagram for the causes of user-interface defects

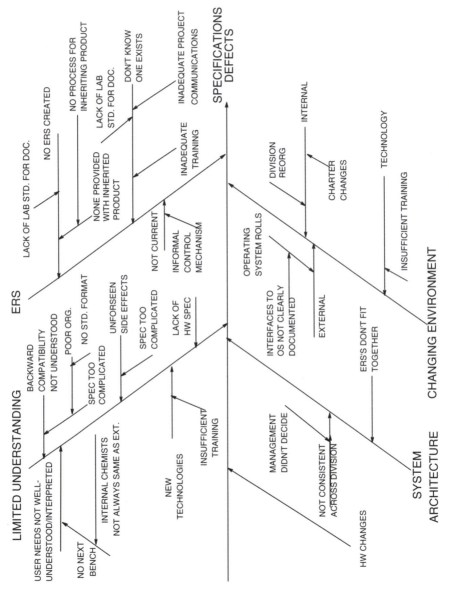

Figure 11-8 Fishbone diagram for the causes of specifications defects

what they mean by the solutions. If they seem to, you don't need to slow down the brainstorming process for more precise definitions. These can be added later.

1. Learn from past experience. Track user-interfaces, particularly when changes occur.
2. When new functionality is thought of or added, ALWAYS also design and specify user-interface implications.
3. Evaluate other applications.
4. Checklist for when designing panels.
5. Use Caseware tool.
6. Complete entire feature when you do it.
7. Give it to someone else to use right away.
8. Solicit thoughtful feedback. Create guidelines for feedback use. Watch users use interfaces.
9. Usability walkthroughs/training.
10. Use standard modules—common dialog boxes.

Test for commitment. Normally you won't need this section, but some organizations that are more tightly controlled than others may not feel empowered to implement solutions. Don't let them get away with this! Find out what they feel they are empowered to do and direct the solutions to that end. When those solutions are successful, they can be more broadly or completely applied. You may need to test for what the roadblocks to change are.

Our example division seemed very committed. This was reinforced in the next step when several people volunteered to initiate specific changes.

Plan for change. Discuss which defects can be eliminated with the proposed solution. Create an action plan with responsibilities and dates. A model action plan looks like this:

1. Establish working group.   10/8
2. Meet and define outputs.   10/15
3. Present objectives and gather inputs.   11/1
4. Create change process and artifacts.   12/1
5. Inspect and fix process and artifacts.   12/15
6. Celebrate.
7. Use and measure results.   2/1

This team decided to create guidelines for user-interface designs that addressed many of their fishbone-diagram branches. This was their action plan.

1. Patty will create a checklist for designing panels. (First pass by 12/17)
2. The project manager will set expectations that all new functionality will be accompanied by design and specification implications. (Consider using new specification formats.)
3. Artie will give the project team a presentation on Caseworks.
4. Follow up the project presentation with a discussion on the use of prototyping.

Remember to end the meeting with a clear understanding of ownership and responsibility. Use standard project-management techniques to plan and schedule follow-up, including ways to monitor success.

Postmeeting

Division champion and root-cause facilitator review meeting process. Review the process and brainstorm changes to meeting format, data collection, analysis, and responsibilities. Redo the fishbone diagram, but be careful not to change it so much that attendees no longer feel that it is theirs. Promptly send out meeting notes that include it, the responsibilities and action items, and the schedule dates.

Division champion captures process baseline data. Part of structuring a process-improvement project for success is to record minimal before and after information. It is particularly important to summarize what your basic divisional processes are so that when your improvement is done, you can better understand other influences besides the particular changes you made. In this example, the team didn't do this step.

Results from Eliminating Major Defect Root Causes

The team from the example above created their checklist and used it during their next project. It had 30 items to watch out for, based on their previous experience and their defects. Figure 11-9 shows an excerpt.

Over 20 percent of the defects on their previous project had been user-interface defects (though the divisionwide average was lower). The results of their changes were impressive.

- They reduced the percentage of user-interface defects in test for their new, year-long project to roughly 5 percent of their total system test defects.

> ∙
> ∙
> ∙
>
> 7. Are fields case sensitive or not? What implications are there?
> 8. Are abbreviations kept to a minimum?
> 9. Are there any spelling mistakes on the panel?
> 10. Does the panel have a title which matches the action of the panel?
> 11. Is the screen too crowded? For data entry, less than 50 percent of the panel should be writing. Controls should "fill" the panel without cluttering it.
> 12. Is "Help" available to the user? Is there a help line to aid the user in understanding the field?
> 13. Has the Help writer been updated with information on the new panel?
> 14. Are the units for edit fields given when appropriate?
>
> ∙
> ∙
> ∙

Figure 11-9 Excerpt of review checklist for dialog boxes

- Even though the project produced 34 percent *more* code, they spent 27 percent *less* time in test.

Of course other improvement efforts also contributed to their success. But the clear user-interface defect reduction showed them that their new guidelines and the attention they paid to their interfaces were major contributors. [8] (See [9] for a similar success story involving JPL safety checklists.) Finally, the best news is that customers were very pleased with the user interface, and product sales were very good.

Two other project teams finished their projects subsequently, and their results were equally impressive. Both projects used new, standard, divisional specification templates created to eliminate many of the root causes shown in Figure 11-8. A cross-project team task force had created two 2-page specifications templates (one for user-interface-oriented routines, one for software-interface-oriented ones) that they felt would help. Both teams substantially reduced specification defects compared to their previous project levels. While one reduction could possibly be due to the project being second generation, the other project's reduction couldn't have been, since it wasn't second generation.

Although the action steps discussed here follow those of successful improvement projects at one HP division, they can also be applied in organizations with different defect patterns and business needs. One of the division people who worked with all three project teams summarized their results: " . . . we must conclude that the root-cause approach is an effective mechanism to identify and introduce change into our software development process." [10]

Continuous Process-Improvement Cycle

Some organizations have shown root-cause analysis to be so beneficial that they now use it to pursue continuous process improvement. It appears to be a natural evolution from postprocess, root-cause analysis successes. This approach extends the supporting infrastructure and requires ongoing management commitment.

The first step that a division generally takes is to widely adopt root-cause information logging by engineers. Causal information is then included as a normal part of the defect-handling process. Analysis is triggered in a variety of ways. It is often triggered by a product or system release. Sometimes it is triggered by the end of a development phase or a series of inspections. It can also be triggered by an arbitrary time period. Figure 11-10 shows how one HP division runs its process. [11] Root-cause solution teams are empowered by lab management to initiate smaller process improvements. More far-reaching improvements still require lab management approval.

Figure 11-10 Root-cause analysis process

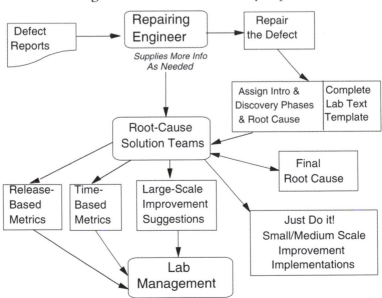

Knowing which defects occur most often in test or later helps us to focus improvement efforts. We saw two examples of this in the postproject, root-cause analysis discussion. The continuous process-improvement cycle encourages you to examine similar data throughout your development process. Take the HP division whose test data was shown as the lower right pie chart of Figure 11-4. They also captured data for specifications, design, and code inspections. All these data are shown in Figure 11-11. [5] Some caution should be used in interpreting this specific data, since it was not uniformly collected. In other words, there may be more or less data shown for any one of the inspection types than for any other or for test. Nevertheless, this figure suggests some interesting questions and reveals possible insights.

Figure 11-11 Defect profile

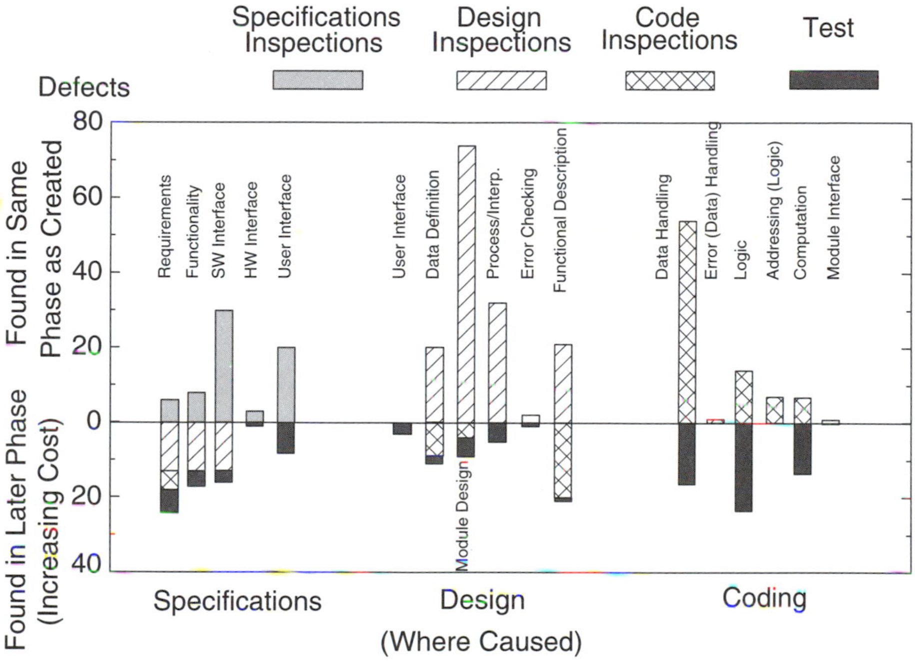

The bars above the center line show counts for different defects that were found in the same phase in which they were created. Tall bars represent good opportunities to reduce these defect sources significantly. For example, the large number of module design defects suggests that a different design technique might be needed to replace or complement existing methods.

The bars below the line show counts for defects found in phases after the ones in which they were created. The later you find them, the more expensive they are to fix. Therefore, the tall bars here are sources of both better prevention and earlier detection opportunities. For example, the requirements, functionality, and functional description defects combine to suggest that designs may be changing due to inadequate early product definition. It might be useful to use prototypes to reduce such changes.

It is clear that this type of data can contribute to more informed management decisions. It also gives you a way of evaluating the results of changes with better precision than in the past. The amount of effort required to sustain a continuous process-improvement cycle will vary, depending largely on the cost of implementing the changes suggested by your analyses. Which changes you choose to do will depend on other business aspects besides the projected costs and benefits. Just remember that the cost to sustain failure analysis practice and modest improvements is small, and the returns have proven to far outweigh those costs. [1, 5, 8]

CONCLUSION

Process-improvement projects are started in many ways, for many reasons. In the software field especially, processes are changing and adapting daily, and software products and businesses are also rapidly evolving. One of the most effective ways to both motivate and evaluate the success of your net improvements is to look at your defect trends and patterns. This chapter has shown how software defect data is a powerful management information source. Using it effectively will help you to achieve an optimal balance between reacting to defect information and proactively taking steps toward preventing future defects. HP divisions have used several successful approaches with defect causal data. The three root-cause analysis processes described here are positioned against a suggested five-level maturity model in Figure 11-12.

Like many other best practices, failure analysis can be applied with increasing levels of maturity that lead to different possible paybacks. HP's experience says that the biggest benefits of driving to higher maturity levels are

- increased likelihood of success when implementing process changes, particularly major ones,
- accelerated spread of already-proven best practices, and
- increased potential returns because necessary infrastructure components are in place.

Our successful results from three failure-analysis approaches are very encouraging. While the time it takes to progress to higher maturity levels will vary among groups, our experience suggests that failure analysis starts providing returns almost immediately, particularly in visualizing progress.

Level 5: Optimizing - Divisional goals to achieve competitive advantage via specific software capabilities. People with primary responsibilities that include process improvement through root-cause analysis.

Level 4: Managed - Root-cause analysis meetings are a regular part of development process. May be people responsible for improvements. Not all root-cause analysis meetings result in action items, but management reviews data.

Level 3: Defined - Defect source information uniformly collected, root-cause analysis meetings held, but not as a standard part of process. Data validating subsequent improvements is mostly anecdotal.

Level 2: Emerging - Defect source information collected, not necessarily uniformly, not necessarily validated. General agreement on what requirements, design, and coding are.

Level 1: Initial/Ad hoc - Defect source information not regularly collected. No recognized divisional defect source patterns. Incomplete R&D process descriptions.

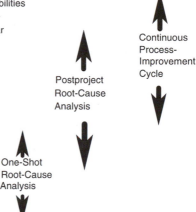

Figure 11-12 Software failure analysis maturity model

Ironically, the main limiter to failure-analysis success is that many managers still believe that they can quickly reduce *total* effort or schedules by 50 percent or more. As a result, they won't invest in more modest process improvements. This prevents them from gaining 50 percent improvements through a series of smaller gains. Because it takes time to adopt any improvement *organization-wide*, these managers will continue to be disappointed.

It has not been difficult to initiate use of the Figure 11-3 defect model and the root-cause analysis process. The resulting data has led to effective, sometimes rapid, improvements. There are few other available sources of information that are as useful in identifying key process weaknesses that are specific to an organization. This information will help you to successfully drive process-improvement decisions and commitment in your organization, too. Perhaps this will help us to reverse the "fool" perception many have of software developers.

BIBLIOGRAPHY

1. Grady, R., *Practical Software Metrics for Project Management and Process Improvement*, Englewood Cliffs, N. J.: Prentice-Hall, Inc., 1992, pp. 37, 79, 129, 130, 137-157.
2. Figure 11-2 is reprinted by permission of the publisher from Stark, G., L. Kern and C. Vowell, "A Software Metric Set for Program Maintenance Management," *Journal of Systems and Software 24*, (1994), pp. 239-249, Copyright 1994 by Elsevier Science Inc.

3. Clark, D., "Change of Heart at Oracle Corp.," *San Francisco Chronicle*, (July 2, 1992), pp. B1, B4.

4. Grady, R., "Dissecting Software Failures," *Hewlett-Packard Journal*, (April 1989), pp. 57-63.

5. Grady, R., "Practical Results from Measuring Software Quality", *Proceedings of the ACM*, Vol. 36, No. 11, (Nov. 1993), pp. 62-68.

6. Ishikawa, K., *Guide to Quality Control*, Tokyo: Asian Productivity Organization, 1976.

7. Brassard, M., *The Memory Jogger Plus+(TM)*, Methuen, Mass.: GOAL/QPC, 1989.

8. Grady, R., "Successfully Applying Software Metrics," *IEEE Computer*, (Sept. 1994), pp. 18-25.

9. Lutz, R. "Targeting Safety-Related Errors During Software Requirements Analysis," *SIGSOFT '93 ACM 0-89791-625-5/93/0012*, (Dec. 1993), pp. 99-106.

10. Tischler, M., e-mail message, Aug. 10, 1994.

11. Blanchard, D., "Rework Awareness Seminar: Root-Cause Analysis," March 12, 1992. (Not available outside HP.)

12

Placing a Value on Software Process — Improvement —

The value of many process improvements seems so obvious that we're amazed by how long they take to propagate. Frederick Mosteller told an incredible story in "Innovation and Evaluation" about the adoption of fresh fruit by the British Navy to combat scurvy. The first ship test was done in 1601, but it was called off when too many sailors who were in the control group died. Despite the evidence of the first test, a second one wasn't done until 1747. Even after its clear success, it took another 48 years to wipe out scurvy in the British Navy. Even more remarkably, it took another 70 years to adopt a similar policy for the merchant marine. [1]*

One can just imagine their ship specifications: "An extra 100 percent crew-quarter space for the sick and dying." If that sounds ridiculous, how about a software process specification: "An extra 100 percent testing time to fix some of the problems that we didn't take the time to prevent earlier." In both cases, daily decisions were made to do certain things instead of others. As Rogers says in retelling the Mosteller story, "Other innovations like new ships and new guns were accepted more readily." [2]

---

* Abstracted with permission from Mosteller, F., "Innovation and Evaluation," *Science 211*, (1981), pp. 881-886. Copyright 1981 American Association for the Advancement of Science.

Adoption of any practice requires widespread convincing. In HP's most successfully adopted software practice, inspections, almost every key adoption aspect included convincing a key individual or setting up an infrastructure that supported convincing many people. (This is described in detail in Chapter 13.) The heart of convincing anyone to change is their perceived value of the change. How do we express the value of changes better so that we can leverage proven successes more quickly?

A DEFINITION OF VALUE

In simple terms, the value of anything is its benefit minus its cost. Figure 12-1 shows a value model that is especially biased toward software development, although the model won't change much for other businesses. It suggests three major software costs: development, rework, and knowledge recovery. A detailed rationale for their selection was discussed in Chapter 4.

Figure 12-1 Model for the value of a software development process improvement (development organization's perspective)

The figure also offers four benefits as answers to common questions. Will an improvement

- get you more/better products? *(Product Capability)*
- get you products sooner? *(Time to Market)*
- get you products to meet commitments? *(Timeliness)*
- help make your products long-lasting and easy to evolve? *(Product Evolution)*

A basic premise of all the examples in this chapter is that improvements start when you change the "cost" part of the model. For example, you can cut the percentage of rework or knowledge recovery that your process requires. With the same resources as before, the organization can then use such a savings to gain one or more of the benefits shown.

Another key premise of this chapter is that these benefits represent more exciting and persuasive aspects of value than cost savings, so present-ing proposed improvements in benefit terms backed by cost savings can help ensure better project focus and stronger organizational commitment. Let's look at an example.

Different Perspectives of Value

Both benefits and costs are always filtered and interpreted from various peo-ple's viewpoints. These include individual and organizational contexts, as well as timing contexts. For example, have you ever noticed how colleagues' opinions seem to change depending on whether you are talking to them alone or with your boss present? This probably doesn't mean that they are dishonest with you. It may just be that they don't think of a larger organi-zational context without the boss there. Figure 12-2 shows how these differ-ences might look. Each box represents value as seen by a group. Overlaps suggest shared values.

Figure 12-2 Different perspectives for the value of a software development process improvement

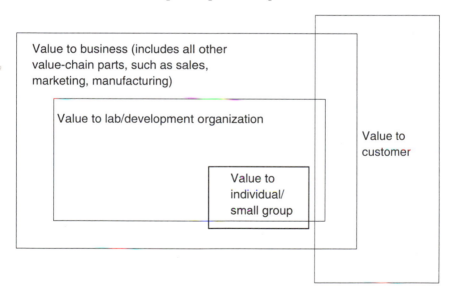

Suppose the figure shows people's views of a process improvement that will increase the number of reusable software assets in your organization. Such a project might have a large value to the business, so the *value to lab/development organization* (think of this value in the benefit terms of Figure 12-1) is large and entirely contained within the *value to business* perspective.

The *value to individual/small group* would depend on whether the initial reuse asset work would benefit their project. In Figure 12-2 it is assumed to largely overlap the lab's values.

The *value to customer* here is entirely different from the *value to individual/small group*, but overlaps both the *value to lab/development organization* and the *value to business*. An example of this might be that the small group has been producing products that customers already value, but the group has had to make great personal sacrifices to do so. Thus, customers will only see increased value from other products or services than those provided by the particular small group shown.

Of course, depending on *what* is being valued, the perspectives of the various boxes will shift. It is these different viewpoints that challenge quick adoption of improvements like reuse. Far-reaching process changes aren't created all at once. They start small. As people see their advantages and implications, the extent of wider change is assessed, proposed, and sold.

This chapter builds on a small, real improvement introduced in the next section to show how potential change benefits can far exceed your initial, modest calculations. In doing so, it shows you how to restate the value of an improvement so that other management and organizational viewpoints are better understood and, ultimately, aligned. With this knowledge, you will then be better prepared to present necessary strategic changes. As the introductory scurvy story dramatically shows, full benefits will not be realized until a large number of people believe in an improvement enough to act on their beliefs.

COST SAVINGS: COMMUNICATING WITHIN R&D

Every day we see better ways to do things. For example, whenever I turn on my sprinkler system it reminds me that some sprinklers no longer cover their areas. Until I replace them, I need to manually water spots. Is it worth my time to change them? My rationale says that the couple of hours it will take will be repaid easily, but usually there is something else I want to or need to do with my weekend time.

We face similar decisions at work every day. They involve both strategic and tactical aspects with influences from many parts of an organization. Therefore, the reasons to make a change finally derive from much more than just a desire to reduce costs. These were reflected as the resulting benefits in Figure 12-1. However, thinking still commonly starts with a cost savings. Let's look at another example that finally gets translated to a time-to-market benefit.

An HP division that developed electronic instruments needed to improve its specifications process. They found that specifications problems caused one-fourth of the software defects found in system test (Figure 11-6). This helped motivate them to create standard specifications templates to reduce the defects.

Usually, the first step in setting a proposed improvement's value is to calculate the cost savings. Always state your assumptions. Then, if anything changes, it is much easier to reevaluate the value. For example, here are assumptions for making the specifications changes for just a one-year project.

- Time to create templates, discuss them, and gain agreement—say, 6 people will take 12 hours each plus 1 hour of training for a project team of 6 people.
- Increased desk checks and inspections—about 80 engineering hours.
- Next project without changes: 6 people will produce about 25,000 NCSS (non-comment source statements); specifications/design/code/test at a rate of 350 NCSS/engineering month. [3]

  -> Total project effort = 71 engineering months.

- Rework without changes—about 33 percent of total development time before the changes (and we will see savings there). (Chapter 4)

  -> Rework = 71/3 = 24 engineering months.

- The number of specification defects will go down, say from 25 percent to 15 percent. However, specification defects fixed in test are more *costly* than defects introduced in later phases [3]—10 percent savings in number of defects is more likely to yield a 20 percent or more time savings.

  -> Savings = 24 × .2 = 4.8 eng. months ×
  160 eng. hours/eng. month = 768 eng. hours

  ->768 eng. hours/(6 eng. × 160 hours/month) = .8 months

Figure 12-3 shows the estimated cost savings* (for similar cost/benefit analyses, see *Practical Software Metrics for Project Management and Process Improvement* [3]).

These are impressive, but if we think back to Figure 12-1, they are only a way to get to even stronger returns shown on the benefit side of Figure 12-1. Such benefits can be more motivating than just cost savings, and they are more likely to represent the value to the entire organization (as suggested in Figure 12-2). For example, one way that we have emphasized the time-to-market savings of various front-end process changes is to include a diagram

---

*The HP division on which this example is based went ahead to cut their specifications defects from 25 percent of their total to 15 percent in two years (the calculations above were scaled down to one year).

ITEMS	COSTS	SAVINGS
Create specifications templates	72 eng. hours	} One-time costs
Training	6 eng. hours	
Increased desk checks & inspections	80 eng. hours	
Reduced defect find/fix time		768 eng. hours
Reduced time to market		.8 Month

Assuming at least 2 projects use the new guidelines,

ROI > 9:1 in first year and doubles in subsequent years.

Figure 12-3 Cost/benefit analysis of specifications changes

like Figure 12-4. Of course, the example becomes much more dramatic for larger projects than a one-year, six-person effort.

Figure 12-4 Time-to-market savings for specifications improvements

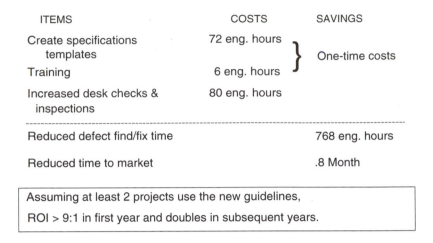

Specifications   Design   Code   Test

Current

Proposed

Time savings in test = .8 months with more

confidence that customer needs are met.

You can emphasize the other Figure 12-1 benefit components similarly. For product capability, the extra time can be used to provide an additional feature, to test longer, or to tune performance. For timeliness, the reduced defects, particularly in test, will lead to fewer last-minute fire drills and better on-time deliveries. Also, customer acceptance of a product that has fewer postrelease defects will be quicker and longer lasting. For product evolution, key designs and documentation can be reinspected and improved to better ensure future growth and adaptation. For each of these approaches, you have translated initial cost savings into benefits that are more persuasive to both yourself and others.

We can only speculate how the person responsible for the successful 1601 scurvy test using lemon juice presented the results. Perhaps they said that lives would be saved. Perhaps they said that the results were promising, but the test was inconclusive since healthy sailors moved from the main ship to operate the other ships. Neither of those statements would have been as persuasive as *"If all the sailors had been as healthy as the ones on the ship that used lemon juice, we would have completed our mission one month sooner. That would have increased crown revenues from that East India Company venture by 25 percent."*

Cost justification of process improvements is a natural first step toward determining value. Often, translating cost savings into strategic business needs will be all you need to get management support for your process improvement. Keeping the expected benefits visible and celebrating successes toward getting them will also help ensure sustained momentum for your improvement's complete adoption.

INCREASED PRODUCT VALUE: EXTENDING COMMUNICATIONS TO THE BUSINESS TEAM

The translation from cost savings to other benefits shown in the previous section is only a first step in an expanded understanding of value. It focused on reduced time to market. We often hear about the advantage of reducing time to market. What does that really get you? There are several concrete examples that are familiar. They include a chance to

- win a big contract.
- beat the competition to announce a new, better product.
- free up resources to work on another key project (which will probably result in one of the first two).

Each of these is a means to desired *customer* ends, also. The next step in understanding value is to figure out how your improvement makes this link. Figure 12-5 expands on Figure 12-1 to do this. It shows an example that could easily be based on the specifications improvements in the previous section. The arrow from *value to you/rework* to *time to market* (1) shows the first translation from cost savings to benefits. The arrow from *value to you/time to market* to *value to your customer/rework* (2) shows that your benefits might be directly useful as a cost savings for your customers. For example, using your new electronic instrument might combine and simplify previous, error-prone measurements for them. Reducing these, in turn, could translate to any of

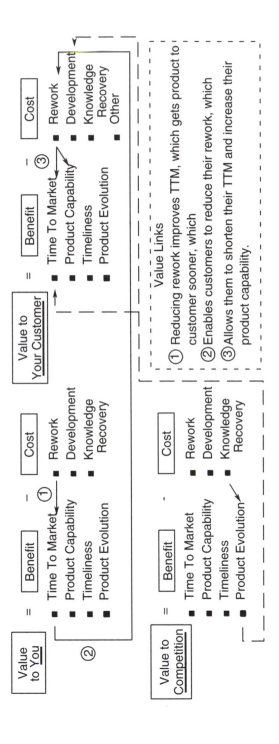

Figure 12-5 Linking your values to your customer's values

their four benefits. The ones picked for this example that *they* feel are important are both *time to market* and *product capability* (3).

Note also that the cost part of the customer side of the model has been expanded to include "other." The Figure 12-1 model was designed around a development organization's terminology. A more general model also includes other costs for manufacturing, marketing, and so forth.

The example also shows some paths from your competitors. Never forget that they are also making improvements. If they understand your mutual customer's needs better than you, they can use this knowledge to gain a competitive edge. Of course, you can do the same thing. Figure 12-5 underlines the importance of extending your analysis to better understand customer needs. Not only do you further leverage your improvement's benefits, but you also better focus your products to your market's needs. This eventually helps virtually every part of your business' value chain.

Can you quantify these other benefits? Certainly. Just as with the example in the prior section, you need to start with a set of assumptions. The following assumptions lead to the analysis in Figure 12-6.

- Your rework improvement is leveraged across many project teams in a 150-engineer lab. Since their efforts interrelate in all phases, your net time to market savings for a key product will be 2 to 3 months. This will increase revenue once by $10M from one key customer (including hardware).
- Similarly, other product development cycles will be reduced by an average of 5 to 10 percent. This will accelerate revenue for new products by 5 percent.
- Current business revenue is $100M -> accelerated revenue = $5M
- Scale up savings from 6 to 150 eng. (ignore specif. template creation in Fig. 12-3; assume savings yield proportionately more revenue) -> increased product revenue = $100M × ((150 eng./6 eng.) × (768 eng. hrs. - 86 eng. hrs.) × (1 eng. mo./160 eng. hrs.)/(150 eng. × 12 mo.)) = $5.9M.

The idea of accelerated revenue is described in detail by Smith and Reinertsen in *Developing Products in Half the Time*. [4] They suggest that, for certain products, earlier introduction leads to a steeper sales growth. This can be especially good for new products, because early market-share capture can lead to a long-term sustained hold on a market. A cautionary contrast is in Von Braun's articles about "The Acceleration Trap." They suggest there are limits to how short you can make your development cycle before the risk of just one product failure outweighs the potential benefits of your short cycle times. [5, 6]

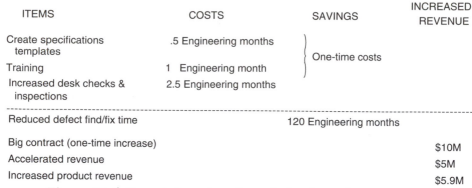

ITEMS	COSTS	SAVINGS	INCREASED REVENUE
Create specifications templates	.5 Engineering months	}	
Training	1 Engineering month	} One-time costs	
Increased desk checks & inspections	2.5 Engineering months	}	
Reduced defect find/fix time		120 Engineering months	
Big contract (one-time increase)			$10M
Accelerated revenue			$5M
Increased product revenue			$5.9M

Figure 12-6 Extended cost/benefit analysis of specifications changes (per year for a lab of 150 developers)

Increased product revenue is more straightforward. Because this improvement cuts rework, you also free up engineering resources who can work on added products.

Note that as you extrapolate from your original estimates, you may have less certainty when calculating business returns. Just remember that these are areas that other parts of the organization must deal with every day. Sales and finance people often must make similar estimates. Since they do, it would be wise to make sure they participate. When you do, you will extend your Figure 12-2 coverage and increase your organization's understanding of your improvement's value. If you don't, the affected groups could resent whatever estimates you make.

This extended example shows how modest efforts can leverage into significant business revenues. By extending your business understanding of your process improvement to your customer's value chain, you will both better plan your improvement and communicate its value to others. When you do, continue to emphasize that these returns require widespread adoption. This will take planning and perseverance.

Scurvy proposal (addendum 1): "Such increased revenue from the 50 other voyages planned in the next two years would finance the building of 10 additional warships. Using these to accompany our merchant fleet would eliminate the ten ships and cargo we lose each year to the Portuguese. The net result of these added savings will increase our profits another 50 percent."

EXTENDING VALUE DISCUSSIONS TO YOUR BUSINESS FUTURE _____

The previous sections discussed value examples from several perspectives. From a cost recovery view, a modest software process improvement saved hundreds of engineering hours. Extending the example to organizational benefits multiplied these savings into much larger increased revenue. Figure 12-5 further extended the value chain to customer needs. That example suggested that such an analysis would help you to better focus and market your products to serve customer needs. Similar analyses will help you to better understand the value of *your* process improvements. They will also help you to more effectively communicate this value to accelerate adoption.

Sometimes you will also need to relate proposed improvements to changing business needs. Some years ago, Hayes and Wheelwright created a product/process model to link marketing and manufacturing strategies to make better decisions. [7] Their model was a matrix showing product structure evolving from low volume/low standardization to high volume/high standardization on one axis against process structure evolving from job shop manufacturing to continuous flow on a second axis. Interesting insights can be gained by looking at improvements, using a similar model for a business with products having high software content. Figure 12-7 adapts the model in this way. Appendix C shows a more complete version and discusses how the original model was adapted.

The circles with arrows showing movement suggest evolutionary patterns that have happened or seem to be happening. There is nothing inherent in any of them that requires them to be where they are. Rather, market and business forces have pushed them from a natural starting point in the upper-left corner to where they are today. There is enough industry experience that the bubbles for applications software, communications software, spreadsheets, and operating systems seem easy to position. HP trends suggest other bubbles and arrows for electronic instruments, computer peripherals, and tools. Let's look at the instrument business discussed in the earlier cost/benefit examples from the perspective of Figure 12-7.

This business sells low volumes of multiple products. In the past, each product has had few dependencies on the others or on connected computers. This suggests that the electronic instrument bubble in Figure 12-7 is positioned right for this business's current state. What are some points you might make to your business leaders that would convince them their business is moving as shown? You might describe at least four technologies that are driving your business to change.

- Embedded computers with large memories have rapidly enabled designers to create instruments that do much more than in the past. (*Increased capability leads to added markets and higher volume.*)
- Interface standards have made computer/instrument connections efficient and commonplace. (*Interfaces to computers lead to releases tied to computer hardware and software changes.*)

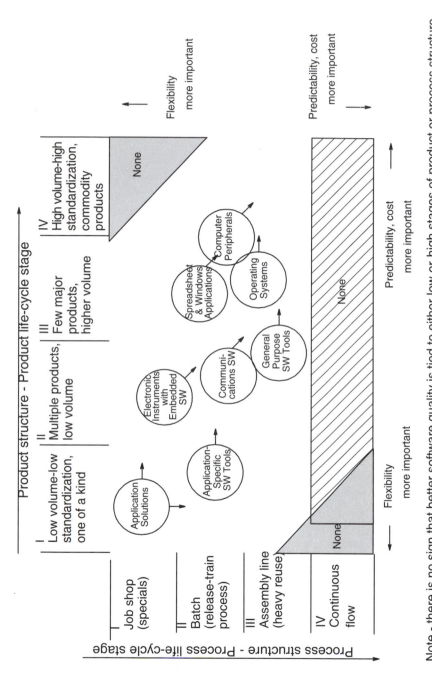

Figure 12-7 Software product/process matrix showing suggested evolutionary trends (Adapted and reprinted by permission of *Harvard Business Review*. An exhibit from "Link Manufacturing Process and Product Life Cycles" by Robert H. Hayes and Steven C. Wheelright. (Jan.-Feb. 1978). Copyright ©1978 by the President and Fellows of Harvard College; all rights reserved.)

Product structure - Product life-cycle stage

| I Low volume-low standardization, one of a kind | II Multiple products, low volume | III Few major products, higher volume | IV High volume-high standardization, commodity products |

Flexibility more important

Predictability, cost more important

None

None

Application Solutions

Application-Specific SW Tools

Electronic Instruments with Embedded SW

Communi-cations SW

General Purpose SW Tools

Spreadsheet & Windows Applications

Operating Systems

Computer Peripherals

None

Predictability, cost more important

Flexibility more important

Process structure - Process life-cycle stage

I Job shop (specials)

II Batch (release-train process)

III Assembly line (heavy reuse)

IV Continuous flow

Note - there is no sign that better software quality is tied to either low or high stages of product or process structure.

228

- Inexpensive graphics and color terminal interfaces have provided designers more powerful and flexible user interfaces. *(Greater user power leads to added markets and higher volume.)*
- Many customers are now also personal computer users and would like both instrument connections to personal computers and access to other applications. *(Added computer interfaces lead to both higher sales volume and increased motivation to reuse designs and code across platforms.)*

The sum of these trends creates pressures to provide customers more functionality inside instruments, a greater variety of interconnections, and very different user interfaces on multiple computer platforms - all via software. Businesses that recognize such trends early and lead competitors in adapting to the trends are the ones that will survive and prosper. Leaders of such businesses recognize that movement along either product or process axis of Figure 12-7 is enabled by new *abilities* that must be grown or acquired.

Remember that core competence gives you the abilities that lead to competitive advantage. When you position your improvement as helping to build or maintain a needed core competence, then its value appears even stronger to your business leaders. For example, Figure 12-8 (from Chapter 3)

Figure 12-8 Core-competence structure for instrument systems business

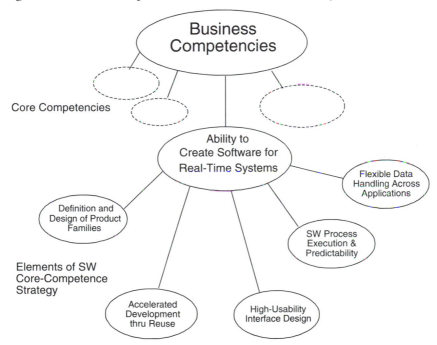

shows strategic needs for our electronic instrument business example. The earlier specifications improvement example is a key starting point toward every core-competence element in the figure. Having a superior ability for determining customer requirements and converting that knowledge into good specifications will influence and improve product-family definition. It will facilitate reuse. It is absolutely necessary for highly usable interfaces. It plays a key role in smoother software process execution. And it is necessary for better data handling. Not only do the previous examples show large business returns for the immediate future, this model also expands management thinking from a conventional product focus to include an improved specifications process as a clear requirement to lead the competition along the path suggested in Figure 12-7.

Businesses evolve and some key process improvements enable that evolution. If your process improvement is such a key, your challenge will not be in justifying value. Rather, it is more likely to be in good planning and risk management, and in showing rapid, measurable progress toward the new competencies driving your business future.

*Scurvy proposal (addendum 2): "The increasing size of our fleet will naturally be accompanied by increased revenues. The Crown can use these to fight our enemies, increase the empire, and consolidate its influence over large parts of the newly discovered lands."**

CONCLUSION

While the problem of adoption is not new, rapidly changing times emphasize its importance. The explosion of the variety and complexity of software applications makes the software field one of the most rapidly changing fields in history. As a result, we often hear about "change management"—the current popular term for attacking adoption issues. It brings adoption research evidence, particularly in the fields of agriculture and medicine, that shows that having a good idea is not enough. Even clearly identified savings won't ensure widespread adoption of a great improvement. You have to convince, guide, and encourage people.

This chapter has focused on understanding and communicating value both in persuasive terms and matched to different target audiences. This is a necessary step in successfully accelerating process-improvement adoption.

---

* "The effectiveness of lemons in keeping sailors in good health for record periods at sea was demonstrated by Admiral Nelson (1758-1805) during the Napoleonic Wars, when the British Navy consumed over a million gallons of juice. Indeed, French writers have claimed recently that their navy was not defeated as a result of British skill or bravery, but by their lemons." [8]

Apply your understanding of value to position your change by

- Investment worth—What are the costs, benefits, and customer value?

- Business advantage and urgency—Is your change fundamental to your current business? Is it something that gives you a strong competitive advantage? Is it an enabler for entry into another business? In other words, does it help you to gain and sustain needed software core competence?

- Organizational readiness—Even though this area was not in the scope of this chapter, don't forget it. How much and how widespread is enthusiasm for your change? Will your change eliminate obvious organizational pain? How believable is existing proof for your change? Are there distractions that will get in the way of adoption? Use the methods from Chapters 5 and 6 to help you here.

Determine the audience you must convince, and adapt the form of value you present to meet the needs of individuals, small groups, a development organization, or a business team. With this framework, you will know what needs to be done, how your business will benefit, and the readiness of people to move ahead.

A major challenge in today's rapidly changing software development world is understanding which improvements will yield the greatest value for your business. An even greater challenge is to convince others of that value effectively and to hold their attention despite shifting business and organizational conditions. The examples here give you the abilities to quantify value and to express it in different ways so that others will understand it in their terms. Your challenge is to take these abilities and successfully use them to convince your "navy" to eliminate "software scurvy." Just remember that while getting your improvements to stick may seem to drag out over a few year's time, your knowledge of their value and their urgency to your business survival will guarantee that you will be successful in far less time than it took to cure scurvy.

BIBLIOGRAPHY

1. Mosteller, F., "Innovation and Evaluation," *Science 211*, (1981), pp. 881-886.

2. Rogers, E., *Diffusion of Innovations*, 3rd Edition, New York: Macmillan Publishing, 1983.

3. Grady, R., *Practical Software Metrics for Project Management and Process Improvement*, Englewood Cliffs, N. J.: Prentice-Hall, Inc., 1992, pp. 129-130.

4. Smith, P., and Reinertsen, D., *Developing Products in Half the Time*, New York: Van Nostrand Reinhold, 1991.
5. Von Braun, C., "The Acceleration Trap," *Sloan Management Review*, Vol. 32, No. 1, (Fall, 1990), pp. 49-58.
6. Von Braun, C., "The Acceleration Trap in the Real World," *Sloan Management Review*, Vol. 32, No. 4, (Summer, 1991), pp. 43-52.
7. Hayes, R., and S. Wheelwright, "Link Manufacturing Process and Product Life Cycles," *Harvard Business Review*, (Jan.-Feb., 1979), pp. 133-140.
8. Bynum. W., and R. Porter, *Companion Encyclopedia of the History of Medicine*, Vol. 1, London and N.Y.: Routledge, 1993, p. 469.

13

*Key Lessons from Adoption of a Software Engineering Best Practice**

Buying a house is one of the biggest decisions that you ever make. When my wife and I bought our house, we worried about a lot of things. One was that the house was used and that it had a radiant (hot water) heating system. We had been told that some systems used the wrong kind of pipe and that those systems had to be replaced after 15 years. Although we were told that the pipes in the house were ok, we decided to include a heating-system inspection in the contract.

It turned out that the system didn't have the right pipes, and they had to be replaced. The $25 inspection fee was the best investment we ever made. The sellers had to buy a new heating system that cost over 100 times the inspection cost.

Most software inspections won't yield a return on investment (ROI) of 100 to 1. Depending on your business though, some can, and our data suggests that you can expect a yield of about 10 to 1 (not of total engineering costs, rather compared to what you would spend finding and fixing the same defects in test).

This is the story of HP's adoption of one key engineering practice and the insights we have gained. These lessons will give many of you who are

---

* Portions of this chapter were originally published by R. Grady and T. Van Slack as "Key Lessons in Achieving Widespread Inspection Use," *IEEE Software,* (July 1994), pp. 46–57. © 1994 IEEE.

directly or indirectly responsible for software process improvements more confidence in the steps you need to take to successfully install and propagate any effective software engineering practice.

Figure 13-1 shows three versions of an S-shaped curve of technology adoption that researchers have shown typically occurs. [1] The leftmost curve shows rapid adoption and the fastest ROI. The other curves show much slower adoption rates. The figure illustrates that the adoption rate of a new practice can vary significantly. It also suggests four recognizable stages defined in this chapter. We believe that HP's inspections program has progressed all the way to the Standardization Stage—the fifth ring of the spiral model for process-improvement adoption introduced in the first chapter. This chapter gives the exciting story of how this happened and talks about how our experiences help us understand what actions will help to accelerate adoption of many other practices.

Figure 13-1 Technology adoption model showing three different adoption rates

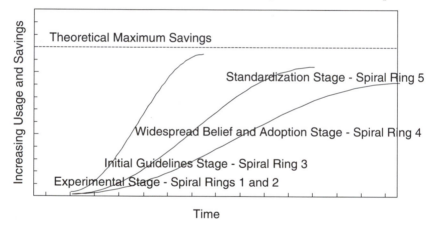

There are several key questions that are addressed here. What were the most important lessons learned? What characterizes the four stages? What situations led to failures or successes? And most important, how can we apply the lessons learned to speed the adoption of other proven practices?

BACKGROUND: WHAT IS AN INSPECTION?

It is easy to identify three major influences on HP software inspections. The first of these is historical. All engineers do reviews of some sort. In HP, two of the more obvious hardware-related reviews were for designs and for printed circuit boards. Both of these were motivated by the need to reduce very costly cycle times that also delayed time to market. It is not surprising that our early software walkthroughs were modeled after hardware reviews.

The second major influence was the historical article published by Michael Fagan in 1976, "Design and Code Inspections to Reduce Errors in Program Development." [2] This article introduced the term "software inspections," and it widely influenced industry. For the first time, it presented summary data that helped managers to better visualize and anticipate inspection results. It also described the processes well enough that commercial classes soon followed. HP's first internal classes were created in the late 70s, and they were widely taught in the early 80s.

The third influence was Tom Gilb. [3] He extended Fagan's inspection process in several important ways that represented a timely philosophical match with HP thinking. First, he was a strong proponent of inspecting early life-cycle artifacts more than code. Second, he extended Fagan's application of metrics to include measures of the inspection process itself. Finally, he described how to use these measures to motivate process improvement. In 1990, HP combined these improvements with our accumulated experience with Fagan's methods to revise the inspection classes that are internally taught today.

A Brief Summary of the Current HP Inspection Process

The HP Inspection Process is a process for conducting a formal review of a document by a document owner and a team of peers. This is led by a process chairperson, the moderator. The primary goal of the inspection process is to help the document owner and the organization develop a high-quality product cost effectively. Inspections ensure that documents are clear, self-explanatory, correct, and consistent with all related documents. Five roles are defined. Sometimes one person acts in more than one role.

- *Inspectors* find items (errors, omissions, inconsistencies, and areas of confusion) in a target document and issues (items that are beyond the scope of an inspection team).
- *Scribe* records items and issues found both before and during a logging meeting.
- *Owner* owns a document; identifies and fixes defects.
- *Moderator* manages the process; facilitates an inspection; reports statistics to the Chief Moderator; reports inspection's status and logged issues to management.
- *Chief Moderator* owns the inspection process; gathers and reports statistics across all inspections; drives inspection process improve-

ments; serves as a focal point for changes to inspections standards and checklists.

Some divisions also continue to use the *reader* role (a person who paraphrases a document during a logging meeting), particularly for complex code documents.

Figure 13-2 shows the seven distinct steps of the inspections process, what happens, the people involved, and the time spent. This well-defined process represents a transformation of HP's earlier reviews and walkthroughs to an engineering process. Figure 13-3 shows how the process outputs are used to improve our products, inspections process, and development processes.

Occasionally the inspections process varies. For example, some divisions hold more formal meetings than others. In general, HP's culture leads to divisional autonomy and less formality than in many other companies. One aspect that the current HP Inspection Process emphasizes, though, is that informality must not extend to the recording and tracking of meeting results.

Figure 13-2 HP inspections process steps and characteristics

	Planning	Kickoff	Preparation	Logging Meeting	Cause/ Prevention	Rework	Follow-up
What	Plan Inspection & Create Packet	Brief Team	Find Items & Issues	Find & Log Items & Issues	Brainstorm Cause(s) & Recommend Action(s)	Verify & Fix Defects	Release Document
Who	Moderator & Owner	Team	Team	Team	Team	Owner & Moderator	Moderator & Owner
Time	2 hrs	1/2 hr	2 hrs	1 1/2 hrs	1/2 hr	???	1/2 hr

The process step that varies the most is the cause/prevention step. Few divisions have successfully done this step prior to rework. The most successful adaptors of this step ask the engineers who fix the defects to enter causal information and brief recommended actions when fixes are done. Then, a separate failure-analysis activity takes data both from multiple inspections and from other test results to analyze and brainstorm solutions to frequently occurring or expensive problems.

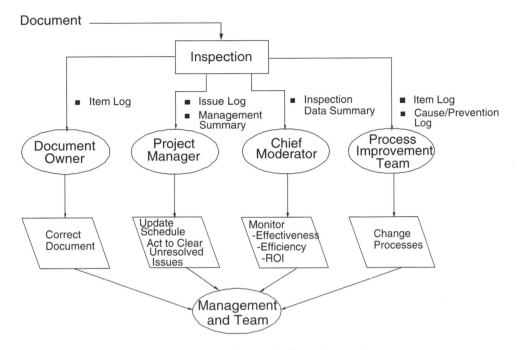

Figure 13-3 Using the results from inspections

The HP inspections process is the result of over 20 years of experience and improvements. The roles, steps, and results are well understood and effective. The process works.

Now let's map the evolution of the program onto the four stages shown in Figure 13-1. From this we can better understand how adoption grew and how the program's success can be repeated by other process-improvement programs.

HP'S EXPERIMENTAL STAGE (1976–1982)—SPIRAL RINGS 1 AND 2

In researching HP's early inspections experiences, we gained an appreciation for how hard it is for archaeologists to reconstruct early history without any written records. In our case, we can at least summarize the memories of the people who were doing software work then, but their recollections are bound to be both fuzzy and biased.

Earlier, we briefly described the first HP software reviews that evolved from hardware reviews. Here we expand on the period immediately following the publication of Fagan's article. [2] The first thing that the article did was to provide a common point of departure for different HP groups. What were once isolated reviews initiated by former hardware engineers and project managers now became more organized efforts supported by managers in quality assurance and, occasionally, R&D.

At this time, only a few HP divisions had quality-assurance people with a software background. Fagan's article gave even the nonsoftware quality people something specific to work on with software people. Fagan's checklists were leveraged along with the roles of moderator and code readers with different points of view. Much of this time period also saw an emphasis on code inspections.

There were some comparisons with Fagan's published metrics for engineering times, defect-finding rates, and defect types. Few of these matched Fagan's data closely enough for people to feel very positive about their results. Some of the startups resulted in failures. Many of the groups trying to do inspections had little more than Fagan's article. For some project teams, this was not enough to reshape team dynamics that included strong egos and tendencies to criticize. Word of some of these failures often spread even faster than success stories.

The groups that believed in inspections, tuned their processes, and survived this initial startup period became the advocates for better company support. It was clear to them that better training, documentation, and a supportive atmosphere were a part of successfully applying inspections.

Lessons Learned

This first time period was when HP struggled with inspections to move around the first rings of the spiral model for process-improvement adoption. Our experiences tell us:

- Initial use of new processes, methods, or tools heavily depends on visionary people who can look at someone else's results and see how they can be locally applied. Often this means having the right person in the right place at the right time.
- For a division to lead in the adoption of best practices, it must foster visionary attempts and not penalize failures. A risk-averse environment is not one that results in leadership.
- Early success is fragile. Establishing a support infrastructure can make the difference between success and failure, and it can be difficult to convince people to try again.

ESTABLISHING INITIAL HP GUIDELINES (1983–1988)—SPIRAL RING 3

This period marked a transition in HP not only for inspections but also for the use of many other software best practices. Events are easier to reconstruct due to the creation of the HP Software Engineering Lab (SEL) in 1983 and Software Engineering Training (SET) in 1984. SEL started the Software Engineering Productivity Conferences (SEPCs) in 1984, and SET started a newsletter, *SET News*. Their written records help us to reconstruct this period's key events and lessons.

An evolved version of an internal HP software inspections class was piloted in 1983. SET was created to propagate just such practices through training. They expanded class availability to the point that over 150 engineers took the class just in 1984, and they also offered train-the-trainer sessions. [4] The SEPC proceedings help us to understand the outcomes from this training.

In the first SEPC, a paper showed one group's ways of adapting Fagan's checklists for a specific HP division. [5] By 1985 there was already a shift to reporting results in measurable terms. Figure 13-4 is a bar chart of the most commonly reported metric results, defects found per hour of time invested. [6-16] Each bar summarizes the results reported in one SEPC paper. The hours include preparation, inspection, and moderator times. In those cases where the article gave a breakdown of defects by severity, the detail is shown. A "major" defect is one that would cause a product malfunction if left unfixed.

Most of the bar variation is probably caused by varying definitions and different software types and business applications. These variations did not matter much, because the repeated success stories were strong reinforcing arguments that inspections did work. The SEPC conferences played a key role in building inspections momentum.

Figure 13-4 Defect-finding rates reported in HP SEPC conference proceedings

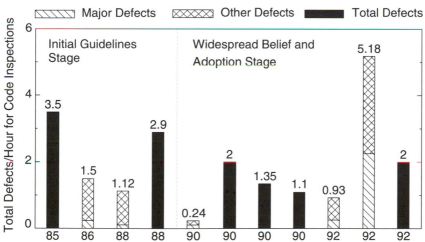

Each bar gives results reported for a different division in a SEPC paper. Multiple bars for a year are from multiple papers.

Two other key events occurred in 1984. The first was a two-day management course called "Quality Software: The Management Role." This course was particularly important because most of HP's R&D managers had hardware backgrounds, not software. Their decision-making styles often presumed development process familiarity, while their knowledge base no longer included that familiarity.

All HP R&D managers took this course over the next 1 1/2 years. Taught mostly by their peers, it exposed many of them to a much better understanding of what software developers do. This understanding led to stronger management support for needed process improvements.

The other 1984 event was the creation and staffing of the job of Productivity Manager in most HP divisions. This new job's primary responsibility was to speed the adoption of best practices within a division. These Productivity Managers formed a basic infrastructure to actively support divisional R&D improvements.

The final key event in the 1983–1988 time frame occurred in 1986. Our company president announced a software 10X improvement program. [17] This program challenged all HP R&D product labs to improve two key quality metrics—12-month postrelease defect density and open critical/serious defects—by a factor of ten.

Combined with documented success stories, an infrastructure that provided a divisional conduit to support change, and freshly fanned flames of management commitment, the 10X challenge gave added motivation to adopt best practices quickly. For inspections, this was reflected in a 1987 quality manager survey. It showed that inspections were a clear first choice for helping divisions to achieve their 10X goals. [18]

Lessons Learned

The period of 1983–1988 was an exciting time for HP software developers. Among other things, it marked an increased, more consistent use of inspections. These were clear signs that we were making the transition to more rapid adoption that signaled movement through the third spiral ring to the fourth ring. Some of the key lessons learned were:

- A high-level, compelling vision (the 10X goals, in this case) directly tied to business challenges helps ensure strong management sponsorship.
- Management training contributes to strong, sustained sponsorship.
- Clearly defined, local, process-improvement responsibility speeds best-practice adoption.

- An effective way to widely communicate successes helps both to speed the rate of successful adoption and to speed the rate of making best practices even better.
- Readily available training is necessary to speed technology adoption, but it is not sufficient to sustain use (see below).

A Retrospective from One Division

Despite all the positive influences, there still were failures as well as successes. Let's look at the use of inspections by two different project teams within one division. Both team's firmware R&D engineers attended the 1984 version of the Software Inspections course, which taught the Fagan method. It included the reader role, discussed problems that can arise in inspection meetings, and how to achieve group consensus on defects. But it included little about how to use metrics to control or improve the inspections process, and there wasn't any infrastructure yet to support teams trying to use inspections.

Team 1 used the method for code, and it helped them find defects. However, they felt that they weren't getting the ROI they should, but they didn't know why (they didn't collect any process metrics). Gradually they stopped using inspections. First, the project manager thought that they were too slow and people intensive. Second, the team felt that inspecting noncode documents (requirements, specifications, designs, and test plans) took too long and didn't uncover enough major defects.

Team 2 used the method for code inspections and, like Team 1, tried to use the method for noncode documents. They experienced similar results, but instead of dropping inspections they set about improving the process. First they eliminated the reader role. Instead of having a person paraphrase the document, they had the moderator just step the team through the document. They adjusted the speed to the potential for defects. This helped the team to focus the meeting on the document sections that had the most problems, and they achieved a better defect-finding rate.

Team 2 also experienced unproductive meeting discussions. To solve this, they eliminated discussing whether potential defects were really defects. An inspector could report and log any problem. After the meeting, the document author reviewed the log to decide if they needed any follow-up discussion. This again sped up the meeting and increased the number of potential major defects reported.

Finally, Team 2 had inspectors report their preparation time and the number of defects they found at the start of each inspection meeting. This helped ensure that every inspector spent enough time reviewing the document before the meeting. All these process changes resulted in more successful noncode inspections.

Despite both teams being in the same division, only Team 2 took the initiative to adjust the process to improve it. This happened in many parts of HP. Training by itself was *not* enough to ensure success, and an unsuccessful experience made it difficult to get groups like Team 1 to try inspections again.

WIDESPREAD BELIEF AND ADOPTION (1989–1994)—SPIRAL RING 4 _____

By 1989, the 10X program was far enough along that divisions were reporting and corporate was summarizing data reasonably consistently. While some progress could be seen, pressure had increased on the divisions to show how they planned to achieve the goals. An internal, corporatewide survey showed that all HP divisions were doing some form of inspections, although only 19 percent regularly did software design reviews. The survey also showed strong confidence in inspections. Over 30 divisions picked inspections as a key practice on which to focus their efforts to achieve their 10X goals. While some were working hard to use inspections widely, only five had plans for inspections training. It seemed clear that renewed corporate consulting efforts could help improve the divisions' results.

HP kicked off a new initiative specifically designed to

- improve the efficiency and effectiveness of inspections by implementing a moderator certification program, revising the training course, and implementing a companywide technology transfer plan.
- improve division awareness and commitment by developing a business case for inspections, gaining R&D management commitment by visits, marketing inspections, and monitoring division performance.

Four Corporate Quality people worked part-time in close partnership with key practitioners to meet these goals. Early 1990 started with an internal HP Inspections Practitioner's Workshop to share and summarize best practices. An outside consultant attended and adapted these practices into an existing class. This formed the basis of a Moderator Training Class that soon followed. Meanwhile, an HP person created a "Management Pitchkit" on the business reasons for doing inspections.

These efforts culminated in a "Blitz Campaign" to promote inspections and the new training class. Both Michael Fagan and Tom Gilb spoke at that summer's SEPC, and some of the key Practitioner's Workshop presenters wrote four excellent papers. [10-13] Some of the data they included was shown in Figure 13-4. The Blitz Campaign created the awareness of the need for people to upgrade their skills and management commitment to do so. This, in turn, created demand for corporate, group, and divisional productivity and quality assurance people to provide the means to do these upgrades.

HP responded by assigning both a full-time Corporate Inspections-Program Manager and a full-time training specialist in one of the largest HP Groups (a Group is a grouping of divisions in related businesses). A key partnership formed. Corporate provided guidance and funding. The Group championed the improvements, adapted the Moderator-Training Class for effective learning through practice, and modernized the Inspections Class. This HP Group felt that having these classes delivered externally was too expensive, so they planned to deliver them using internal people. Figure 13-5 shows that significant numbers of engineers were receiving the new training by early 1991.

These results did not come easily, though. The corporate approach to certify moderators was based on the premise that there is one "best" way to do inspections. All we should have to do is push people toward it. But HP's divisions are independent, and they did not respond well to standardization. They didn't want to just be told what wasn't right, particularly in those cases where they saw their inspections as working. They wanted flexibility in using any best methods.

Conversely, divisional people did want process improvement help. They particularly faced a constant struggle to hold management commitment to continuous improvements. What the divisions wanted was consulting support tailored to the various Figure 13-1 adoption phases.

Figure 13-5 Cumulative inspection training

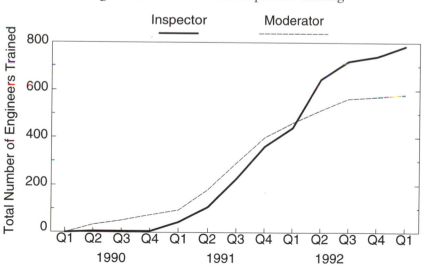

Meanwhile, the training specialist also had problems. One of the first pilot classes "exploded," because engineers's expectations were poorly set. The specialist experienced the same reactions that the corporate program manager had, only at the engineer level. Class needs hadn't been defined ahead, and the instructional materials weren't easy to adapt on-the-fly. Also, a manager had set up the class for a group but then gave the engineers mixed signals regarding the class's importance versus other activities.

Other classes included attendees who had tried inspections and not found them useful. No one had told them how the methods in the new class might correct earlier problems. So the training specialist came to the same conclusion as the corporate program manager: Consulting was needed to assess where a division was and to create an environment for success *before* training was done.

The consulting approach worked. It had to be adapted to each division, but with each different division meeting, the customer needs became clearer and our ways of satisfying them improved. The needs usually fell into three broad categories.

- Organizational commitment. Somebody—a key manager or key engineers—needed convincing that inspections could and should be done sooner instead of later.
- Advice and training on improving inspections. Often a local inspections champion was using a process that wasn't good enough for people to feel that it was indispensable.
- Help in adapting the updated inspections approach to the division.

We then developed a consulting model structured to match and meet customer needs, provide appropriate training, and follow up until the customer succeeds. It has five basic steps:

- Define the organizational business objective for doing inspections.
- Evaluate and influence the organization's readiness to do inspections.
- Create an infrastructure for success by identifying a local, interested person as Chief Moderator (who will also act as a champion).
- Benchmark the current process.
- Adjust the process, train people, and consult to ensure success.

Figure 13-5 shows that many engineers were receiving inspections training. Our 1983–1988 experiences were that the number of people trained is only a weak predictor of successful best-practice adoption, though. We wanted a stronger indicator, so we created a survey whose goal was to determine the percent penetration and effectiveness of inspections across HP. We defined a division's "degree of penetration" as the percentage of projects that held four or more inspections during a project's life. This number had worked well at one division that asked teams to do four inspections before judging their worth. We felt that teams that did at least four inspections would not only continue to do them, but they would also decide to increase the number of inspections in the future.

We also had consulted more with larger labs, so we wanted to see if they had higher penetration. We arbitrarily broke the data into four, different size groupings. These groupings helped us to validate that we had consulted with the divisions with the greatest potential needs (we had consulted with about 70 percent of the two largest groupings). Figure 13-6 shows both the average penetration for different lab sizes and the percent of the total HP population in each category. For example, labs with over 75 software engineers represent over 50 percent of HP's total software engineers, and they did four or more inspections on 63 percent of their 1994 projects.

Figure 13-6 HP 1994 inspections penetration by number of division software developers

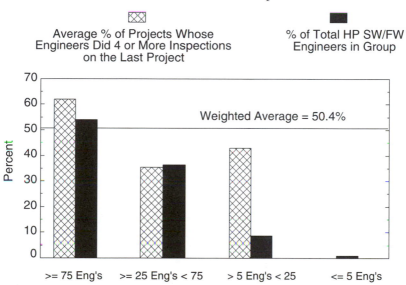

The 1989 survey showed that all divisions were doing inspections. However, it didn't ask how many projects did them, or about how many were done per project. The 1994 data in Figure 13-6 more clearly shows that about half of the projects were either not using inspections or were just starting out. Fortunately, this graph is a lagging indicator. Many of the people trained in 1993–94 were working on projects that just hadn't completed four inspections yet. While the average penetration strongly increased from 32 percent in 1992 to 50.4 percent in 1994, there still was much room for improvement.

The survey data does contain some encouraging signs. Years of research show that the "S-shaped diffusion curve takes off at about 10 to 25 percent adoption," [1] and over 60 percent of the responding divisions had already achieved 25 percent penetration. Those that haven't are groups that can best benefit from continued consulting.

We also strongly encourage early life-cycle document inspections, because these inspections help uncover defects that are very expensive if not found until later. We now analyze what percentage of different documents are inspected each year. In this case, our data only tells us whether projects inspected at least one noncode document of each type. Figure 13-7 shows our success in those divisions that had high inspections penetration. For example, 53 percent of the projects in divisions with greater than 25 percent penetration did at least one design inspection. When all reporting divisions are included, the average is still 40 percent. This is much better than the 1989 average of 19 percent. It suggests that the recent training and consulting have helped to increase early document inspections.

Figure 13-7 HP 1994 inspections usage by document type (divisions with ≥25% projects that did 4 or more inspections)

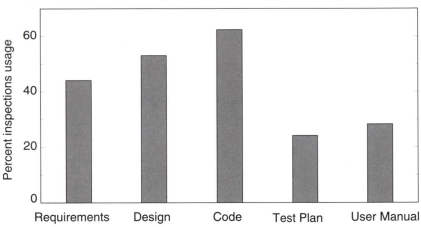

For this diagram, a project "used" inspections for a particular document type when at least one document of that type was inspected.

The survey clearly shows that inspections use is increasing, but the rate of increase varies. Because we are interested in how proven technologies such as this one can be adopted faster, we looked more closely at one HP Group that has been very active during the last few years. This Group had a full-time person responsible for inspections, and people who regularly both scheduled and led training. They also had high-level management support. One of their Group's key goals was to reduce rework, and using inspections was a major strategy to do this. Figure 13-8 shows the dramatic difference in the increased number of inspections done by that Group (74 percent) compared with the rest of HP (21 percent) from 1991 to 1992.

Figure 13-8 Increasing divisional use of inspections
(overall 35% increase from 1991 to 1992)

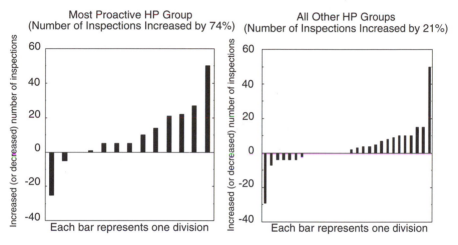

What about differences between the most improved divisions and the ones that remained unchanged or actually did fewer inspections? There were many contributing aspects, but the most consistent one was the presence or absence of a divisional Chief Moderator. For example, in the left chart of Figure 13-8 the rightmost six bar divisions all had a Chief Moderator. It is clear that a good divisional infrastructure is as important as the Group and corporate ones.

Lessons Learned

During this time period, we finished progressing around the spiral model's fourth ring. While the period of "widespread belief and adoption" will still continue in many HP divisions, there are some important lessons we can take advantage of.

- Training and process guidelines are not sufficient. Consulting with objectives tailored to divisions is also required. Find champions (for inspections, Chief Moderators) and sponsors. Work with divisions after training to ensure success.

- Few divisions can start with an optimal process. Learn the divisions' immediate wants and their long-term plans. Understand their processes and organizational constraints.
- Program-focused infrastructure (Group-level people with full-time inspections responsibility, in this case) makes a big difference in the adoption rate.
- Good management process metrics are necessary to achieve and sustain widespread use and effectiveness (see below).

Another Retrospective

The experiences in two divisions show how our thinking has gone beyond just implementing inspections to how inspections affect our products. The first of these is about the steps that led to one division's rapid, successful inspections adoption. [19] This division's code volume was growing rapidly. Fortunately, they had good historical labor and defect metrics, so the Quality Manager could make a strong case that future projects were in jeopardy unless they changed their practices. The proposal was to do inspections to substantially reduce their testing effort and schedule.

The convincing didn't stop there. They took one of the cleanest modules written by one of their best engineers after they thought it was done, and did an inspection. The inspection uncovered three significant problems. This helped to build strong engineering support, as well. This division was one of the first to integrate real work products into the training instead of canned examples. This, combined with their emphasis on training intact work groups, helped to speed their adoption rate.

Finally, as with other past successes, there was a strong champion. In three years, the division has done over 180 inspections. The average time to find and fix major defects using inspections continues to be over 10 times better than their old test-method times. They are getting more complex products to market far sooner than they would have by using their old process.

The second story is about a division that already had widespread lab inspections use that remained high even through several reorganizations. [20] Inspections typically found 60 to 70 percent of their defects. A review of their postrelease critical/serious defects raised some doubts, though. The trend showed no significant improvement.

To learn more, they asked 13 project managers a set of questions. They probed backgrounds, reasons for doing inspections, details about the inspections, the data collected, and what follow-up occurred. They learned that a strong belief system had kept inspections alive. There was enough positive data that the basic beliefs continued, but their process was stagnant. It focused on code and other back-end work products. Entry and exit criteria had relaxed, and there was seldom any attempt to use inspections data to drive process changes.

Questioning the process was a healthy exercise. The results created both motivation and direction for change. The key changes included a greater front-end emphasis and stronger metrics to drive process improvements and to monitor their inspections process.

STANDARDIZING A PRACTICE—SPIRAL RING 5

It's not clear that there ever will be a single "standard" HP inspections process, but this is not the issue. What matters is that every project use some variation of the standard in an efficient, cost-effective way. This section reflects our continuing plans, based on the lessons learned, to optimize our process.

The critical leadership roles during all other HP inspections stages were those of champion and sponsor. This stage is no different. *The first part of the standardization plan is to continue to proactively identify and help champions and sponsors.* They will provide the technical and organizational leadership necessary for each group to assume long-term process ownership and responsibility.

We must arm these champions and sponsors with strong, persuasive messages. *The second part of the standardization plan is to reinforce management awareness with a strong inspections business case.* Many success stories have been presented at the SEPCs. Some of these stories have gone beyond measuring inspections defect-finding rates to comparing them with defect-finding rates in systems test. [9,11,13,14,16] While these rates vary from 4.4 times better up to 20 times better, they all make a strong business case.

Figure 13-9 shows a cost-benefit summary for design inspections, developed from well-documented HP and industry results. These numbers are for first-time application of design inspections on a six-person, 50,000 non-comment source statement project. For brevity, the detailed assumptions and calculations aren't included, but they are published elsewhere. [21] The ROI is a simple ratio of engineering time benefits to costs (1759/(48 + 25 + 96) = 10.4). Potential added revenue from quicker time to market improves the ROI even more.

ITEMS	COSTS	BENEFITS
Training	48 Engineering hours $1650 (= approx. 25 Eng. hours)	
Startup costs	96 Engineering hours .5 Months	
Reduced defect find/fix time		1759 Engineering hours
Reduced time to market		1.8 Months

ROI > 10:1 in first year and increases in subsequent years.

Figure 13-9 Cost/benefit analysis of design inspections

This is a much better return than many other R&D investments provide. In addition, there is little risk, and you needn't wait long for the initial investment to be paid off. Note that the training and startup costs occur only once per team, although there will be a small, ongoing cost for a Chief Moderator. This type of analysis is important, because later adopters of new practices are more conservative and need stronger persuasion. While justification details may not interest them, they often won't be convinced unless they know someone has done the work.

A software organization's management, like the most successful 1992 HP Group's management, must believe that inspections are important enough to develop them as a key part of their software core competence.

The third part of the standardization plan is to continue building an infrastructure strong enough to achieve and hold software core competence. We've seen that such an infrastructure maximizes the adoption rate and increases the odds that inspections are optimally done. Three infrastructure layers contribute complementary aspects of success for HP: corporate, group, and divisional. Their key roles are to train, consult, communicate, improve, and *be responsible for the inspections process.*

The fourth part of our standardization plan is to measure the extent of adoption. We believe that consistently improving inspections use will visibly reduce defects and development times. We needed a measure that would tie inspections results as closely as possible to such improvements. We approached this by creating a measure consisting of three adoption components.

- *Depth (percentage of projects using inspections)*—Some minimum number of project inspections are necessary to signify that a project team seriously believes in inspections. (It is four now, but it may change.)

- *Breadth (weighted percentage of documents inspected)*—A weighting factor that accounts for the fact that inspecting early project work products (requirements, designs) yields better returns than inspecting late ones (code).

- *Inspections process maturity*—Not all inspections are equal. Today's inspections process is much more effective than Fagan's first method. We will use a simple weighting factor based on an "inspections maturity model" (refer to Appendix D for details).

We have tried combining these aspects several different ways. All these attempts successfully separated the divisions we judge as "most effective" in terms of inspections from those that are "least effective." Figure 13-10 shows our results, based on annual survey data. It gives you both a sense of how widely divisions vary and how many divisions responded to the survey. The bars are in ascending order.

Figure 13-10 HP 1994 extent of inspections adoption

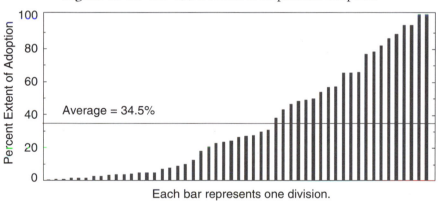

Each bar represents one division.

The formula that we used to prepare Figure 13-10 and continue to use is (refer to Appendix D for details):

Extent of Adoption = Insp. Process Maturity × (% Projects Using
+ Weighted % Documents Insp.) × constant

Imperfect as this metric is, it gives a baseline against which to track year-to-year progress. For example, the metric shows an increase from 20 percent adoption in 1992 to 34.5 percent adoption in 1994. Most importantly, it includes the three major aspects that our experience shows contribute to reduced costs and development time.

CONCLUSION

Software inspections have taught us a lot about technology adoption. This chapter's major sections gave an overview of HP's inspection process and then stepped through our experiences with the four technology adoption stages originally shown in Figure 13-1. Table 13-1 summarizes the key lessons we learned in each stage.

Table 13-1 Key contributors to successful HP divisional adoption of inspections and to making a transition to the next stage

	Experimental Stage	Initial Guidelines Stage	Widespread Belief and Adoption Stage
BUSINESS FACTORS		Compelling Vision (10X)	Recognition of need for core competence
ORGANIZATIONAL READINESS	Local improvement infrastructure	Company-wide infra-structure (productivity managers) Company-wide comm-unications (SEPC)	Inspections infrastructure (company, group, divisional levels) and metrics Needs assessment - organizational plans, readiness, constraints Consulting to set stage for success
PEOPLE FACTORS	Visionary people (champions) No penalties for failures (sponsorship)	Management training (sponsors) Local adaptation	Proactive identification of champions and sponsors

Where then is HP on its S-shaped curve? First we must compute the theoretical maximum savings. We estimate that roughly one-third of all software costs are rework and that inspections can save 60 percent of these costs. For a company the size of HP when we started tracking adoption, a conservative potential savings was $105 million *per year* (refer to Appendix D for details).

Next, we estimate how much the inspections program is already saving. This is done by using data from our 1994 survey, separately estimating savings for each document type, and then adding these results. HP is now in the fifth ring of the spiral model for process improvement. We estimate a total HP inspections savings in 1994 of $31.1 million. Figure 13-11 shows our progress from the time we started tracking up to that point.

These are very rough calculations, but they give us a way to translate our extent-of-adoption measure to companywide savings. Note that when we translate these savings to a lab of 100 engineers, they yield a bonus of over 4 engineers to work on things other than rework (*in every lab across the entire company!*).

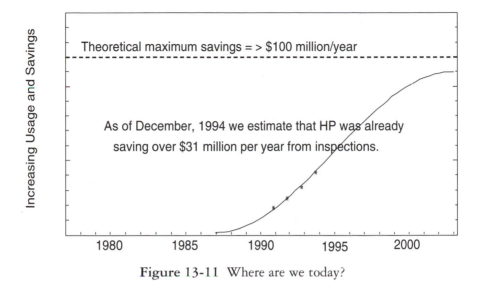

Figure 13-11 Where are we today?

It's no wonder that a U.S. government study concluded that it took an average of 15 to 20 years for new software technology to get to the point that it could be popularized and disseminated. [22] It has taken HP over 15 years to use inspections widely, and we feel that we still have almost 70 percent of the benefits yet to gain. It is too late to speed up the earlier phases for inspections, but it is not too late to apply what we have learned.

HP has created a set of Software Initiative (SWI) programs to accelerate companywide adoption of a small number of software best practices, including inspections. These initiatives play a key role by providing timely help to divisional pilot projects for these best practices. The initiatives also provide the corporate-level infrastructure that we learned was key to speeding technology adoption.

It is through experiences like those we described here that we learn how to do things better in the future. These are elements of success. We now have a model for how technology adoption occurs, we know what to do to accelerate improvements, and we've seen examples of typical problems we can expect. These experiences can be and are being applied to accelerate adoption of other best practices, and we've seen that the returns for such investments can be huge.

BIBLIOGRAPHY

1. Rogers, E., *Diffusion of Innovations*, 3rd Edition, New York: Macmillan Publishing, 1983.

2. Fagan, M., "Design and Code Inspections to Reduce Errors in Program Development," *IBM Systems J.*, Vol. 15, No. 3, (1976), pp. 182-210.

3. Gilb, T., *Principles of Software Engineering Management*, Reading, MA: Addison-Wesley, 1988.

4. *SET News*, (Dec. 1984). (Not available outside HP.)

5. Smith, C. H., "Five Computer Language Inspection Checklists," *HP Software Engineering Productivity Conference Proceedings*, (April 1984), pp. 1-30 to 1-56. (Not available outside HP.)

6. Decot, D., and B. Scott, "Inspections at DSD - Automating Data Input and Data Analysis," *HP Software Engineering Productivity Conference Proceedings*, (Aug. 1985), pp. 1-79 to 1-89. (Not available outside HP.)

7. Altmayer, L., and J. DeGood, "A Distributed Software Development Case Study," *HP Software Productivity Conference Proceedings*, (April 1986), pp. 1-54 to 1-62. (Not available outside HP.)

8. Shirey, G., "Code Inspections: Doing the Right Thing the Right Way," *HP Software Engineering Productivity Conference Proceedings*, (Aug. 1988), pp. 129-140. (Not available outside HP.)

9. Temple, Y., J. Malin, D. Miller, and E. Torres, "Tools of the Trade: Structured Design, Reuse, and Inspections," *HP Software Engineering Productivity Conference Proceedings*, (Aug. 1988), presentation slides. (Not available outside HP.)

10. Blakely, F., and Mark Boles, "A Case Study of Code Inspections," *HP Journal*, (Oct. 1991), pp. 58-63.

11. Hilgendorf, D., and J. Nissen, "A Code Inspections Success Story," *HP Software Engineering Productivity Conference Proceedings*, (Aug. 1990), pp. 415-426. (Not available outside HP.)

12. Nishimoto, A., "Evolution of an Inspection and Metrics Program at MPD," *HP Software Engineering Productivity Conference Proceedings*, (Aug. 1990), pp. 527-537. (Not available outside HP.)

13. Tillson, T., and J. Walicki, "Testing HP SoftBench: A Distributed CASE Environment: Lessons Learned," *HP Software Engineering Productivity Conference Proceedings*, (Aug. 1990), pp. 441-460. (Not available outside HP.)

14. MacLeod, J., "Implementing and Sustaining a Software Inspection Program in an R&D Environment," *HP Journal*, (June 1993), pp. 60-63.

15. Mallette, D., "Inspections by Telephone," *HP Software Engineering Productivity Conference Proceedings*, (August 1992), pp. 203-212. (Not available outside HP.)

16. Rodriguez, S., "Software Inspections," *HP Software Engineering Productivity Conference Proceedings*, (August 1992), pp. 193-202. (Not available outside HP.)

17. Grady, R., and D. Caswell, *Software Metrics: Establishing a Company-Wide Program*, Englewood Cliffs, N. J.: Prentice-Hall, Inc., 1987, p. 79.

18. LeVitt, D., "A Survey of HP Best Engineering Practice," *HP Software Engineering Productivity Conference Proceedings*, (May 1987), pp. 4-173 to 4-179. (Not available outside HP.)

19. Dickmann, D., "Integrating Inspections into the Development Environment," *HP Software Engineering Productivity Conference Proceedings*, (August 1992), pp. 179-181. (Not available outside HP.)

20. Shirey, G., "How Inspections Fail," *Software Practitioner*, Vol. 3, No. 3 and 4, (May-Aug 1993).

21. Grady, R., *Practical Software Metrics for Project Management and Process Improvement*, Englewood Cliffs, N. J.: Prentice-Hall, 1992, pp. 130, 180-181, 190-194.

22. Redwine, S., and W. Riddle, "Software Technology Maturation," *IEEE 8th Conf. on Software Eng.*, (Aug. 1985), pp. 189-200.

14

Your Mileage
May Vary

For years, new U.S. cars have been labeled with estimated miles-per-gallon of gas you should expect for city and highway driving. This started after gasoline prices dramatically went up in the 1970s. It was a way to encourage both car buyers and makers to pay more attention to using less gas.

Naturally, lawyers got involved when car makers started including these figures in ads, so you now often hear the phrase "your mileage may vary." This phrase and many others have even led to a new class of jobs—speed speakers. These announcers can say an incredible amount of legal nonsense in a very short time. You can almost visualize them using a magnifying glass to read the fine print in their script.

After describing many successful process improvements, I feel compelled to give my version of "your mileage may vary," though I'm certainly not motivated to do so by any legalities. Rather, I use the phrase to emphasize methods you can use to improve your "mileage," or success rate, when making your own improvements. Software process improvement is very complicated, so I will also show symbols to highlight helpful methods as a useful way to remember them when needed.

A spiral model for process improvement was the first model introduced in the book. Its significance should be clearer now. Software process improvement is an unending journey. While each improvement can be viewed as a tactical project, you must follow through with others to remain competitive.

If we were to unwrap the spiral into a linear model, it might look like Figure 14-1 below. We start moving toward a desired future state from a current state. Sometimes we encounter roadblocks, but gradually we move ahead with solutions. An intermediate state represents an acknowledged success. But we don't stop there, so the dots represent other projects, or later progressions from current to intermediate states for other spiral loops. I'll reemphasize the key successful techniques discussed in the book in the following sections, starting with the future desired state.

DEFINE PROCESS IMPROVEMENT IN TERMS OF THE STRATEGIC FUTURE

The starburst at the right of Figure 14-1 is your starting point. It represents your organization's strategic future, so the first way to improve your "mileage" (chances for, and speed of, success) is to define that future clearly. The most succinct definition of a future desired state is a vision. Several chapters discussed its role related to core competence, gaining commitment, widespread adoption, and particularly in creating an environment for success.

Figure 14-1 The software-improvement journey

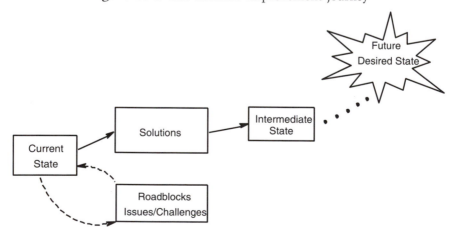

Improving Mileage #1:
Understand Business Needs Well.

A process that adds structure and commitment to your organization's vision is
the core-competence planning process.
Its major contribution is that it elevates
process-improvement thinking to a
strategic level. It also expands top management's competitive view from a traditional product focus to include key
abilities the organization needs to create
those products. Ideally, the core-competence planning process is as strong as
your business-planning process. It produces a well-written plan, and you
review and update it yearly.

Just as business planning isn't always ideal, core-competence planning
isn't either. Don't let this discourage you. Think of core-competence planning as a spiral process, also. Even the first loop of a spiral will help strength-
en your process improvements, and each update of your plan will be even
better.

GET A CLEAR PICTURE OF YOUR CURRENT STATE

Once you have a good picture of your desired future, there are three key
methods by which to gain a similar understanding of your current state.

Improving Mileage #2:
Understand Your Software
Development Costs and Their
Leverage Points.

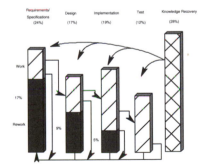

The software-improvement investment
model gives you a simple way to model
major development, rework, and
knowledge recovery costs. It helps to

- give your management a better
  understanding of how software developers work,
- change people's opinions of the relative importance of proposed
  improvements, and
- set realistic expectations for proposed cost savings.

You get an even better picture of improvement opportunities when you also analyze your major defect sources, using HP's software failure-analysis model. This information is especially powerful when you combine it with the investment-model information. It

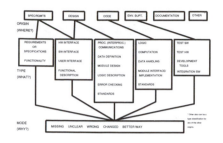

- further clarifies costs,
- gives you an excellent way to evaluate the potential of proposed improvements, and
- gives you an effective way to track and communicate the successful changes that you make.

Improving Mileage #3:
Understand Your Organization's Readiness for Change.

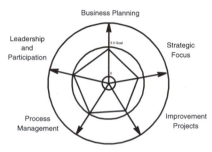

The third way to get a clear picture of your current state is to do an assessment that is well matched to your organization's needs. Pick one that matches your business needs, level of sponsorship, scope of needed change, and your best guess of organizational readiness. An assessment does three key things for you. It

- gives you a reference point of current strengths and opportunities,
- motivates people to change, and
- models how to approach improvements.

It isn't easy to get a clear picture of an organization's readiness for change. An assessment can be one of your best tools to evaluate a complex sociological system and start it moving toward improvement.

AVOID AND MINIMIZE POTENTIAL ROADBLOCKS _____

Process-improvement projects face complex sociological issues not normally faced in product projects. Extra analysis and planning can go a long way in helping to avoid roadblocks.

Improving Mileage #4:
Understand Your Business and Organizational Forces.

Division A

			Positive	Neutral	Negative
Business	Strategic	Vision / Business Strategic Focus / Core Competence			
Business	Tactical	Customer Perceptions / Market Share / Product Cycle Time / Profitability			
Organizational	Strategic	Organizational Maturity / Process Improvement / Infrastructure			
Organizational	Tactical	Organizational Inertia / Stability / Cost/Time Alignment			

More than any other tool included here, a force-field analysis of management commitment gives your best snapshot of potential varying "mileage." For example, look at the two force fields at the right. How successful are the two organizations? How successful would you be in making improvements in them?

Division B

			Positive	Neutral	Negative
Business	Strategic	Vision / Business Strategic Focus / Core Competence			
Business	Tactical	Customer Perceptions / Market Share / Product Cycle Time / Profitability			
Organizational	Strategic	Organizational Maturity / Process Improvement / Infrastructure			
Organizational	Tactical	Organizational Inertia / Stability / Cost/Time Alignment			

The forces clearly suggest that you should expect to be more successful with division A, and this has also been our experience. That doesn't mean that division B can't or won't improve. It also doesn't mean that they are in trouble. They have successful products and are working on a new, exciting product line. The big advantage of having a force-field analysis view is that it helps steer you toward simple risk-minimizing strategies like the ones suggested in Chapter 5.

Improving Mileage #5:
Understand the Origins of Resistance to Change.

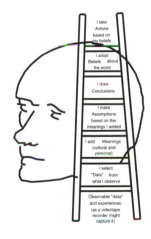

People develop reasonable beliefs based on experiences. Proposed changes can be dissimilar enough to their past experiences that when they try to draw analogies, the analogies won't reflect probable outcomes. One way to avoid being judgmental about such derived beliefs is to think of their resistance as a "standard reason" not to do things. This can help you open your viewpoint so you can think about both your and their ladders of inference. Resulting discussions will help you both to create ways to remove roadblocks.

Improving Mileage #6:
Strengthen Plans.

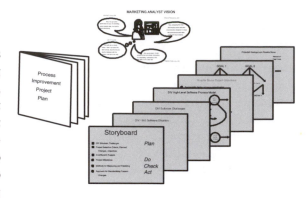

More complex projects require better planning and risk management, and even the simplest process improvement isn't easy. Thus, you especially need to plan to motivate people and to optimize their working environment. Process improvements also more fully use the plan/do/check/act cycle. This requires activities that many team members aren't experienced with. These added risks mandate at least a minimal, written, process-improvement plan.

COMMUNICATE SOLUTIONS TO MAXIMIZE SUCCESS

Moving any project or organization toward a future desired state includes increasingly more detail as you firm up plans and do individual projects. This detail evolves in a series of presentations and usually includes investment-return estimates that you must effectively communicate to various groups. It also includes convincing reports of intermediate results.

Improving Mileage #7:
Storyboard Your
Improvement Project Early.

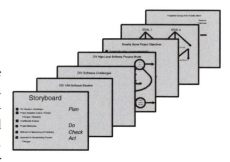

You will need to effectively describe your project and its benefits often. A good approach is to imagine its completion early and create a storyboard that envisions how that will appear. This is a powerful way to describe your project clearly as part of the organization's future desired state. Another useful tool that ensures strong ties to business goals is the goal/question/metric (GQM) process. These ties lead to more easily accepted communications.

Improving Mileage #8:
Set Reasonable Expectations for Results.

The first part of setting reasonable improvement expectations is to cal- culate cost savings. This is a dou- ble-edged sword. If you don't do these estimates or if the way you commu- nicate them makes them seem low, your project is unlikely to be approved. If you estimate too high, your project may be cancelled, because you aren't believed. Also, if your estimates are high and you are allowed to finish, your project may still be considered a failure.

Doing a cost-savings analysis early in your planning forces you to doc- ument assumptions. This analysis enables you to make your intermediate steps and improvement gains clearer. These will generally be both believable and high enough to help ensure your needed approvals.

Improving Mileage #9:
Frame Expectations for Different Audiences.

A key step both in gaining and holding project sponsorship is to translate your cost savings into benefits. The methods in Chapter 12 will help you to do this. They will also help you to gain broader organizational support and to overcome pockets of resistance.

Improving Mileage #10:
Reinforce Success with Measured Results.

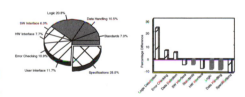

There is nothing like quantified intermediate results to eliminate doubts and solidify support. By imagining how your results will look during your initial planning/storyboarding, you will ensure that you collect the right data to report successes confidently.

YOUR IMPROVEMENT FUTURE

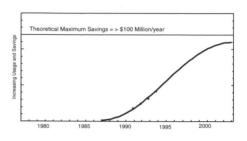

The spiral model suggests that all the results presented in the book are intermediate results. Even the most completely adopted practice—inspections—isn't fully mature yet. The many examples of success have taught us alternative ways to approach improvements more effectively. They have also given us the confidence that we can succeed.

The spiral model emphasizes looking toward a future desired state. When we hear "your mileage may vary," we first think of cars, yet there is a much more dramatic example. Imagine a space shuttle. At liftoff, its miles-per-gallon of fuel is very low. However, as its fuel burns, its miles-per-gallon of fuel quickly improves. There is less weight to lift, the atmosphere gets much thinner and provides less resistance, and ejected booster rockets reduce weight even faster. This is an exciting image for software process improvement.

Your mileage will vary, too. In many ways, we have relearned in the software arena what was previously learned in sociological studies of other fields, such as agriculture and medicine. Despite solid evidence that new crop rotation and fertilizing techniques were clearly superior, and that boiling water or new drugs provided significant benefits, it still took many years for these improvements to be accepted.

These examples might discourage some, but I find it exciting. It gives us confidence in sociological tools and methods that have already been proven effective. As we continue to mature software engineering, improvement techniques will get even better, and we will also understand our sociology better. While there will always be new challenges, our past successful process improvements will help us around a continuing improvement spiral for our profession. It is my fervent belief and desire that the examples and methods in this book will help with your software process-improvement journey, too.

Appendix A
Cost Model of Major Software Development/ Maintenance == Components ==

The basic components of the Management Model of Major Software Development/Maintenance are described in Chapter 4. The spreadsheet below was used to create the chapter's model, which is repeated here as Figure A-1 (except that percentages include decimal values reflected in the spreadsheet instead of being rounded). The spreadsheet was also designed so that some of the basic assumptions driving the model could be easily changed and explored. These assumptions are set in the first section of the spreadsheet. For example, by changing the maintenance, enhancement, and development percentages (cells B4, B5, B6, which are now set to 20/35/45), the two alternate models in Figures A-2 and A-3 result. The percentage split in Figure A-2 (48/32/20) might be found in some Information Technology (IT) development groups. The percentage split in Figure A-3 (20/0/80) might be found in some firmware development groups. Using the model this way has enabled us to estimate returns from process-improvement investments. (See Chapter 8)

A complete description of all the model's cell contents are also included here in case you want to enter it and adapt it for your own use.

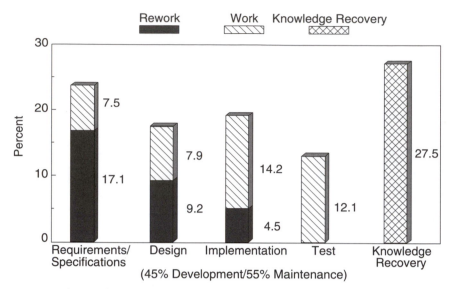

Figure A-1 A management model of major development/
maintenance cost components

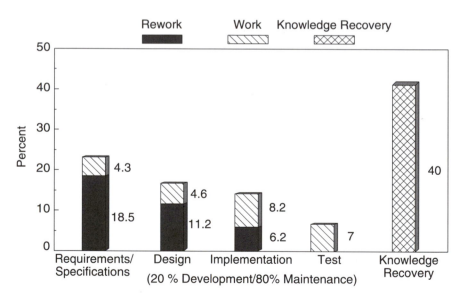

Figure A-2 Potential management model of major information technology
development/maintenance cost components

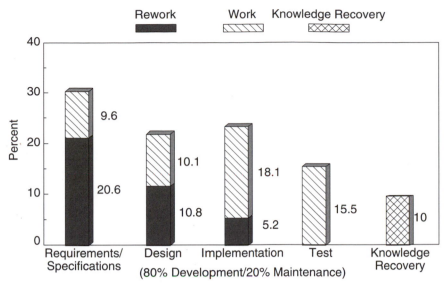

Figure A-3 Potential management model of major firmware development/maintenance cost components

12/29/96

Dev %	18.0	19.0	34.0	29.0	100.0
		%Prg.Und.	%Non PU		
Maint. %	20.0	0.5	0.5		
Enhance %	35.0	0.5	0.5		
Devel %	45.0				
Doc %	20				
Insp %	10				

	Rqmts/Spec	Design	Coding	Test	Understanding	Total
Work	5.3	5.5	9.9	8.5	22.0	51.2
Doc.	1.5	1.6	2.8	2.4	5.5	13.8
Insp.	0.8	0.8	1.4	1.2		4.2
R/S Rwr	3.8					3.8
Design Rw	2.3	1.6				4.0
Code Rwr	3.4	2.3	1.4			7.1
Test Rwr	2.9	2.0	1.2	0.0		6.0
Maint Rwr	4.8	3.3	2.0			10.0
Total Rwr	17.1	9.2	4.5	0.0		30.8
					27.5	
Total	24.6	17.1	18.7	12.1	27.5	100.0
Devel.	8.1	8.6	15.3	13.1		45.0
Enhance	3.2	3.3	6.0	5.1		17.5
Dev + Enh	11.3	11.9	21.3	18.1		62.5
Dev+Enh-Rw	7.5	7.9	14.2	12.1		41.7

Failure-Analysis Data by Percent (Not Including Environment Support, Documentation, or Other)

Test (5/87)	7.3	16.7	74.7	1.3	100.0
10/88	36.0	32.5	26.3	5.2	100.0
5/90	12.7	23.2	58.5	5.6	100.0
2/92	24.2	20.2	55.6		100.0
7/92	25.0	36.8	38.2		100.0
Maint (8/89)	18.5	33.9	44.8	2.8	100.0
11/91	15.6	54.5	29.9		100.0
Average	19.9	31.1	46.9	2.1	100.0
Mult.	109.4	48.0	19.2	7.7	
	2177.1	1493.5	899.7	16.3	4570.2
Normal.	0.48	0.33	0.20	0.00	1.0
FA-All (83)	40.7	35.6	23.7		100.0
1/89	11.7	45.5	25.4	17.4	100.0
2/92	34.7	40.8	24.5		100.0
Average	29.0	40.6	24.5	5.8	100.0

Failure-Analysis Data by Defect Count for Seven Divisions

	Rqmts/Spec	Design	Coding	Env. Supt	Document	Total
Totals	537	852	1049	30	47	2515.0
Percentage	21.4	33.9	41.7	1.2	1.9	100.0
Multiplier	109.4	48	19.2	1.0	1	
	2335.9	1626.1	800.8	1.2	1.9	4765.9
Norm. Perc.	49.0	34.1	16.8	0.0	0.0	100.0

The references below in the left column (A1, A2, B2, . . .) refer to the spreadsheet cell locations.

Basic Model Assumptions

A1: '12/29/96   Control Date
A2: 'Dev %'s   Avg. from 152 HP projects [1]
B2: 18
C2: 19
D2: 34
E2: 29
H2: @SUM(B2..E2)
C3: '%Prg.Und.   Described in one article (based on two others); [2]
                             later mildly supported [3, 4]
D3: '%Non PU
A4: 'Maint. %   Avg. from outside HP [5, 6, 7, 8] This is defect-
                             fixing part of maintenance.
B4: 20
C4: 0.5
D4: 1-C4
A5: 'Enhance %   Avg. from outside HP [5, 6, 7, 8] This is
                             adaptive/perfective part of maintenance.

B5: 35
C5: 0.5
D5: 1-C5
A6: 'Devel %   Avg. from outside HP [5, 6, 7, 8]
B6: 45
A7: 'Doc %   Assumed percentage of work and rework.
B7: 20
A8: 'Insp %   Assumed percentage of work and rework.
B8: l0

Development and Maintenance Detail

Bl0: 'Rqmts/Spec
Cl0: 'Design
Dl0: 'Coding
El0: 'Test
Fl0: 'Understanding
Hl0: 'Total
All: 'Work
Bll: (B26-B12-B13)   Rqmts/Spec (Dev+Enh - Doc - Insp - R/S Rwrk)
Cll: (C26-C12-C13)   Design (Dev+Enh - Des Rwrk - Doc - Insp)
Dll: (D26-D12-D13)   Coding (Dev+Enh - Code Rwrk - Doc - Insp)
Ell: (E26-E12-E13)   Test (Dev+Enh - Test Rwrk - Doc - Insp)
Fll: +F22-F22*B7/100   PU Work = PU Total - PU Doc
Hll: @SUM(Bll..Fll)   Total Work
Al2: 'Doc.
B12: +B26*B7/100   Rqmts/Spec (Dev+Enh) * Doc%
Cl2: +C26*B7/100   Design (Dev+Enh - Des Rwrk) * Doc%
Dl2: +D26*B7/100   Coding (Dev+Enh - Code Rwrk) * Doc%
El2: +E26*B7/100   Test (Dev+Enh - Test Rwrk) * Doc%
Fl2: +F22*B7/100   PU Doc = PU Total * Doc% (assumed % same as
                                     for development)
Hl2: @SUM(B12..F12)   Total Doc Work
Al3: 'Insp.
Bl3: +B26*B8/100   Rqmts/Spec (Dev+Enh) * Insp%
Cl3: +C26*B8/100   Design (Dev+Enh - Des Rwrk) * Insp%
Dl3: +D26*B8/100   Coding (Dev+Enh - Code Rwrk) * Insp%
El3: +E26*B8/100   Test (Dev+Enh - Test Rwrk) * Insp%
Fl3: '
Hl3: @SUM(B13..F13)   Total Insp. Work

Each phase rework component is assumed to be one-third of the development + enhancement task total. For the design, code, and test tasks, the rework is further broken down to attribute portions to defects introduced in earlier tasks. These breakdowns are derived using assumptions based on (1) numbers of defects measured in six HP divisions and (2) relative costs of fixing defects reported by Boehm, Moller, and HP. [9, 10]

A15: 'R/S Rwr

B15: +B25/3   Total Rqmts/Spec Rwrk = Rqmts/Spec (Dev + Enh)/3 (assumed 1/3 rework)

H15: @SUM(B15..F15)

A16: 'Design Rwr   Divide total Design Rework proportionally among current and previous defect sources.

B16: +B39*H16/(B39+C39)

C16: +C39*H16/(B39+C39)

H16: (C23+C24)/3   Total Design Rwrk = Design (Dev + Enh)/3 (assumed 1/3 rework)

A17: 'Code Rwr   Divide total Code Rework proportionally among current and previous defect sources.

B17: +B39*H17/(B39+C39+D39)

C17: +C39*H17/(B39+C39+D39)

D17: +D39*H17/(B39+C39+D39)

H17: (D23+D24)/3   Total Code Rwrk = Code (Dev + Enh)/3 (assumed 1/3 rework)

A18: 'Test Rwr   Divide total Test Rework proportionally among current and previous defect sources.

B18: +B39*H18/(B39+C39+D39+E39)

C18: +C39*H18/(B39+C39+D39+E39)

D18: +D39*H18/(B39+C39+D39+E39)

E18: +E39*H18/(B39+C39+D39+E39)

H18: (E23+E24)/3   Total Test Rwrk = Test (Dev + Enh)/3 (assumed 1/3 rework)

A19: 'Maint Rwr   Maint (defect-fixing part)% * non-PU% * norm. for defect #'s and relative phase-fix costs.

B19: +B39*B4*D4

C19: +C39*B4*D4

D19: +D39*B4*D4

H19: @SUM(B19..F19)

A20: 'Total Rwr

B20: @SUM(B15..B19)

C20: @SUM(C15..C19)

D20: @SUM(D15..D19)

E20: @SUM(E15..E19)

H20: @SUM(B20..E20)

F21: +F22   Copy of PU sum for bar chart

A22: 'Total   Total = Work + Doc + Insp + Test + Total Rwrk (for phase)

B22: @SUM(Bll..B19)

C22: @SUM(Cll..Cl9)

D22: @SUM(Dll..Dl9)

E22: @SUM(Ell..El9)

F22: +B4*C4 +B5*C5   Total PU = Maint PU*%PU + Enhance PU*%PU

H22: @SUM(B22..F22)

A23: 'Devel.   Devel = Devel % * phase %

B23: +B6*B2/100

C23: +B6*C2/100

D23: +B6*D2/100

E23: +B6*E2/100

H23: @SUM(B23..E23)   Should be the same as assumed Devel % (at top)

A24: 'Enhance   Enhance = Enhance % * Non PU % * phase %

B24: +B5*D5*B2/100

C24: +B5*D5*C2/100

D24: +B5*D5*D2/100

E24: +B5*D5*E2/100

H24: @SUM(B24..E24)   Should be the same as assumed Enhance % * non-PU % (at top)

A25: 'Dev + Enh   Simple sum of Dev + Enh (for each phase)

B25: +B23+B24

C25: +C23+C24

D25: +D23+D24

E25: +E23+E24

H25: @SUM(B25..E25)

A26: 'Dev+Enh-Rwr   Assume work part is 2/3, rework is other third

B26: +B25*2/3

C26: +C25*2/3

D26: +D25*2/3

E26: +E25*2/3

H26: @SUM(B26..E26)

Failure-Analysis Data from Seven HP Divisions, Applied as Multipliers to Defect Data

The average of these is different from Figure 4-4, since these count each division equally, whereas Figure 4-4 takes a simple average of the total defects. The model here does this to try to ignore the effects of large amounts of data from one or two divisions. See below for the source of Figure 4-4 data.

B28: 'Failure-Analysis Data by Percent (Not Including Environment
                    Support, Documentation, or Other)
A29: 'Test (5/87)   First 5 divisions' defect data from system/
                    integration test activities
B29: 7.3
C29: 16.7
D29: 74.7
F29: 1.3
G29: @SUM(B29..G29)
A30: ' 10/88
B30: 36.0
C30: 32.5
D30: 26.3
E30: 5.2
G30: @SUM(B30..G30)
A31: '   5/90
B31: 12.7
C31: 23.2
D31: 58.5
E31: 5.6
G31: @SUM(B31..G31)
A32: '   2/92
B32: 24.2
C32: 20.2
D32: 55.6
G32: @SUM(B32..G32)
A33: '   7/92
B33: 25.0
C33: 36.8
D33: 38.2
G33: @SUM(B33..G33)
A34: 'Maint (8/89)   Next 2 divisions' data from maintenance/
                    postrelease activities

B34: 18.5
C34: 33.9
D34: 44.8
E34: 2.8
G34: @SUM(B34..G34)
A35: '   11/91
B35: 15.6
C35: 54.5
D35: 29.9
G35: @SUM(B35..G35)
A36: 'Average   Average % defects introduced in major
                      development activities
B36: @SUM(B29..B35)/7
C36: @SUM(C29..C35)/7
D36: @SUM(D29..D35)/7
E36: @SUM(E29..E35)/7
H36: @SUM(B36..G36)
A37: 'Mult.   Relative cost to fix defects in postrelease
                      compared to fixing in phase introduced [1, 9, 10]
B37: 109.4
C37: 48
D37: 19.2
E37: 7.68
B38: +B36*B37   Defect % * relative cost multiplier
C38: +C36*C37
D38: +D36*D37
E38: +E36*E37
H38: @SUM(B38..D38)
A39: 'Normal.   Normalize defect % * relative cost factors to add
                      up to 1
B39: +B38/H38
C39: +C38/H38
D39: +D38/H38
E39: +E38/H38
G39: @SUM(B39..D39)

Failure Analysis Data from Two HP Divisions that Collected Data from All Development Stages

This analysis is for reference purposes only to compare with above test and maintenance averages; data not used above.

A41: 'FA-All (83)
B41: 40.7
C41: 35.6
D41: 23.7
G41: @SUM(B41..G41)
A42: '   1/89
B42: 11.7
C42: 45.5
D42: 25.4
E42: 17.4
G42: @SUM(B42..G42)
A43: '   2/92
B43: 34.7
C43: 40.8
D43: 24.5
G43: @SUM(B43..G43)
A44: 'Average
B44: @SUM(B41..B43)/3
C44: @SUM(C41..C43)/3
D44: @SUM(D41..D43)/3
E44: @SUM(E41..E43)/3
H44: @SUM(H41..H43)/3

Failure Analysis Data from Seven HP Divisions

This data is used for Figure 4-4.

A46: 'Failure-Analysis Data by Defect Count for Seven Divisions
B47: 'Rqmts/Spec
C47: 'Design
D47: 'Coding
E47: 'Env. Supt.
H47: 'Document
A48: 'Totals
B48: 537   Sum by defect origin of data from 7 divisions.

C48: 852

D48: 1049

E48: 30

F48: 47

H48: @SUM(B48..F48) Total defects

A49: 'Percentage

B49: 100*B48/H48 Get new percentage by dividing origin count by

C49: 100*C48/H48 total defects and then multiplying by 100.

D49: 100*D48/H48

E49: 100*E48/H48

F49: 100*F48/H48

H49: @SUM(B49..F49)

A50: 'Multiplier Use same weighting factors as above.

B50: +B37

C50: +C37

D50: +D37

E50: 1

F50: 1

B51: +B49*B50 Multiply origin defect percentages by weighting factors.

C51: +C49*C50

D51: +D49*D50

E51: +E49*E50

F51: +F49*F50

H51: @SUM(B51..F51)

A52: 'Norm. Perc. Normalize origin defect percentages back to 100 percent.

B52: 100*B51/H51

C52: 100*C51/H51

D52: 100*D51/H51

E52: 100*E51/H51

F52: 100*F51/H51

H52: @SUM(B52..F52)

Bar Chart: A Management Model of Major Development/Maintenance Cost Components

X-Axis Labels:	B10 - F10
Range, Label, Legend A:	B20 - F20
Range, Label, Legend B:	B26-F26
Range, Label, Legend C:	B21-F21

BIBLIOGRAPHY

1. Grady, R., *Practical Software Metrics for Project Management and Process Improvement,* Englewood Cliffs, N. J.: Prentice-Hall, Inc., 1992, pp. 42,49,53.
2. Corbi, T., "Program Understanding: Challenge for the 1990s," *IBM Systems Journal,* Vol. 28, No. 2, (1989), pp. 294-306.
3. Dekleva, S., "Software Maintenance: 1990 Status," *Software Maintenance: Research and Practice,* Vol. 4, (1992), pp. 233-247.
4. Henry, S., and M. Humphrey, "A Controlled Experiment to Evaluate Maintainability of Object-Oriented Software," *Proceedings of the IEEE Conference on Software Maintenance,* San Diego, Calif., (1990), pp. 258-265.
5. Lientz, B., and E. Swanson, *Software Maintenance Management,* Reading, Mass.: Addison-Wesley, 1980.
6. Albran, A., and H. Nguyenkim, "Analysis of Maintenance Work Categories through Measurement," *Proceedings of the IEEE Conference on Software Maintenance,* Sorrento, Italy, (1991), pp. 104-113.
7. Foster, J., "Program Lifetime: A Vital Statistic for Maintenance," *Proceedings of the IEEE Conference on Software Maintenance,* Sorrento, Italy, (1991), pp. 104-113.
8. Rubin, H., E. Yourdon, and H. Battaglia, "Industry Canada Worldwide Benchmark Project," *Conf. on the Appl. Software Metrics,* Orlando, Fla., (Nov. 1995), pp. 51-52.
9. Boehm, B., *Software Engineering Economics.* Englewood Cliffs, N. J.: Prentice-Hall, Inc., 1981, p. 40.
10. Moller, K. H., "Increasing of Software Quality by Objectives and Residual Fault Prognosis," *First E.O.Q.C. Seminar on Software Quality,* Brussels, Belgium, (April 1988), pp. 478-488.

Appendix B

Core-Competence Planning Notes

If you've ever participated in or been responsible for creating or updating a business plan, you know it's an imprecise, time-consuming, discussion-filled process. Yet its output is crucial to a business's success. Business plans also change, evolve, and improve, so plans for new or young businesses are less complete and less well defined than for mature businesses.

Core-competence (CC) plans are intended to be of strategic importance similar to business plans, so they should be approached with a similar mindset and dedication. Meeting participants should be like those who would work on a business plan: the organization's manager and functional staff, key marketing and R&D specialists, and one or two strong facilitators. Remember that the process is not intended to be rigid, although later steps generally build on results of earlier steps.

The schedules below are included to give you some idea of relative timings. All times are approximations that have varied considerably from organization to organization. Times are most affected by tactical business issues that affect meeting attendees' participation and attention spans. When extra meetings are needed, plan to add an extra 20 minutes at the start to set the stage and refresh memories from the last meeting. Be sure to also plan 10 to 15 minutes at the end of each meeting for wrap-up and action items.

We prototyped this process several times as we developed it. You should probably do so at least once before really doing it with your business team.

Sample First-Day Schedule

8:30– 8:45	Present objectives, discuss approach, final outcome, tentative schedule.
8:45– 9:00	Briefly discuss core-competence definition and process.
9:00–10:00	**Step 1.** Gain agreement on working definition for vision statement; also agree on other step 1 contents of CC plan: value proposition, basis for sustainable competitive advantage, other referred documents, who plan is written for.
10:00–10:15	Break.
10:15–11:15	**Step 2.** Brainstorm an initial list of potential CCs.
11:15–11:30	Break.
11:30–12:00	Group the potential CCs.
12:00– 1:00	Lunch.
1:00– 2:00	Test CCs with inclusion/exclusion tests. Record "leadership"/"fundamental" thoughts. Get consensus on two to five key CCs.
2:00– 2:15	Break.
2:15– 3:30	**Step 3.** Create CC structures for each CC (define principal strategic elements).
3:30– 4:30	Create two or three CC element definitions.
4:30– 4:45	Review meeting results; assign tasks to be done before next meeting.

It is useful to separate the core-competence sessions by a week or more. This allows time for the group to informally discuss their results and to do preparatory work for the next session(s). Depending on your progress in the first day of meetings, here are some possibilities for homework between day 1 and day 2.

- Define core-competence elements.
- List key processes.
- Gather competitive information related to core-competence elements
- Fill in parts of the table "Competitive analysis of core-competence elements."

Sample Second-Day Schedule

You might consider breaking this day into two half-days. This has the advantage of giving added time for homework.

8:30– 8:45	Review where you are in process, discuss approach for day, final outcome, and tentative schedule.
9:00–10:00	**Step 4.** Brainstorm key processes and one pivotal job.
10:00–10:15	Break.
10:15–11:00	Complete step 4.
11:00–12:00	**Step 5.** Evaluate strengths and weaknesses.
12:00– 1:00	Lunch.
1:00– 3:00	**Step 6.** Target areas for short- and long-term improvements.
3:00– 3:15	Break.
3:15– 4:15	**Step 7.** Define improvement objectives.
4:15– 4:30	**Steps 8 and 9.** Summarize resource requirements; recommend person responsible for creating and executing plan.
4:30– 4:45	Review meeting results; assign tasks to be done before next meeting.

If you broke this day into two half-days, here are some possibilities for homework between the two sessions.

- Make CC graphic representations like Figure 3-3 for all the CCs showing their associated solution components.
- Complete the assessments relative to competition for all CC elements and solution components (the first three columns of Table 3-1).
- Create first-pass suggestions for improvements needed (column 4 of Table 3-1).

Appendix C

Software Product/Process Matrix

The modified Hayes and Wheelwright model used in Figure 12-7 was simplified from the original. [1] The original also included key management tasks and the dominant competitive modes. Figure C-1 shows a more complete version.

The product structure axis maps well to software. Software products often start as low-volume applications and evolve to more generalized solutions. The process structure axis also maps well, except there is no continuous flow equivalent for software. The triangular shadings in the model were in Hayes and Wheelwright's original model. The rectangular shaded box was added for software.

The most significant model change is to the labels on the arrows along the two major axes. In the original model, the axes were labeled from the viewpoint of product specialization. Both axes started from flexibility and quality emphases and moved to dependability (which they further defined as reliability and predictability) and cost. This had to change for software. There is no sign that better software quality is tied to either low stages of product or process. We might even be tempted to claim the opposite—that better software quality (or reliability) is tied to higher stages of either prod-

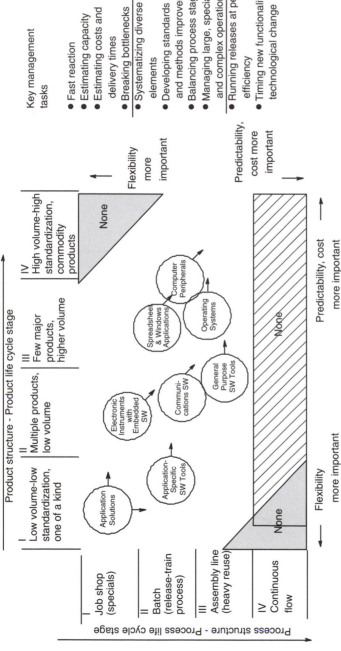

Figure C-1 Software product/process matrix showing suggested evolutionary trends (Adapted and reprinted by permission of *Harvard Business Review*. An exhibit from "Link Manufacturing Process and Product Life Cycles" by Robert H. Hayes and Steven C. Wheelright. (Jan.-Feb. 1978). Copyright ©1978 by the President and Fellows of Harvard College; all rights reserved.)

uct or process. However, there are too many exceptions to make such a claim today. The Figure C-1 model makes no quality assumptions.

The key management tasks and the dominant competitive modes are also largely the same as they were in the original model. These are generally business related, so only minor changes were made to eliminate hardware-specific items and terminology.

BIBLIOGRAPHY

1. Hayes, R., and S. Wheelwright, "Link Manufacturing Process and Product Life Cycles," *Harvard Business Review,* (Jan.-Feb., 1979), pp. 133-140.

Appendix D

Extent-of-Adoption Metric

Definition of Equation Components for Extent of Adoption

We created the Extent-of-Adoption measure to gauge companywide progress against the three key program emphases: process maturity, depth of use, and breadth of use. The intent was for each of three factors to have roughly equal affects under "normal" conditions. The metric can range from 0 to 140, but we set all calculated values greater than 100 to a maximum value of 100.

> Extent of Adoption = Insp. Process Maturity × (% Projects Using
> + Weighted % Documents Insp.) × constant

Insp. Process Maturity = a constant from 1 to 14 based on the five-level model below

% Projects Using = % of projects that did four or more inspections on their last project. We picked the number four because one division had great success by asking teams to do four inspections before judging their effectiveness.

Weighted % Documents Insp. = (5.7 × % req. + 2.5 × % design + 2 × % test plans + % code) /11.2. Several studies have measured the relative costs of fixing different types of defects. We will use weighting factors based on their results. [1] These factors are then multiplied by the percent inspections use for each document. For Figure 13-10, we used the percent use shown in Figure 13-7, although a simple survey was the data source. Because the survey only asked for the presence or absence of inspections for different document types on projects, the results overstate actual use. Weighted % Documents Insp. has a factor of 11.2, so that its values also vary from 0 to 100.

constant = 0.05; this value fits Extent of Adoption into a range of 0 to 100 when the Insp. Process Maturity factor is at level 3 (weight of 10) and the % Projects Using and Weighted % Document Insp. are at their maximum values.

There is no scientific basis for assuming that level 2 is three times better than level 1, or level 3 is ten times better, and so on. The assigned maturity weights and their mathematical use in the Extent-of-Adoption metric are intended only to identify trends. As with all metrics that are created for one purpose, there is always the potential that some people might use this one for other purposes. To minimize the extent of potential distortions, we did a series of sanity checks. We tested all combinations of the three factors at their high and low conditions. We then asked ourselves if the results seemed reasonable. To us, they did.

Inspections Assessment Maturity Model

The Inspections Assessment Maturity Model details the practices that early HP adopting divisions used to improve their peer-review processes. Model levels 1 and 2 are not really inspections, they are informal peer desk reviews to formal walkthroughs. Level 3 is an industry-typical inspection process. Level 4 is a best-practice inspection process. Level 5 links formal inspections to a defect-prevention activity.

Level 1: Initial/Ad hoc (Level weight = 1)

- No established objective for doing reviews.
- Individual peer review/desk checking to informal walkthroughs being done.
- No process documentation, training, or process infrastructure.

Level 2: Emerging (Level weight = 3)

- Informal objective to find and remove defects.

- Informal and formal walkthroughs being done.
- Process may be documented, some trained practitioners, and some awareness of need for infrastructure.

Level 3: Defined (Level weight = 10)

- Stated objective to find and remove defects.
- Formal inspections recommended on major projects.
- Process documented, moderators trained, process infrastructure in place, metrics collected.
- Standards, templates, and checklists may not exist.

Level 4: Managed (Level weight = 12)

- Stated objective to improve the defect detection-and-removal process earlier in the life cycle.
- Formal inspections required on key documents for all major projects.
- Process metrics used to improve process, defect-cause information collected.
- Standards, templates, and checklists exist for all key document types.

Level 5: Optimizing (Level weight = 14)

- Stated objective to prevent defect introduction.
- An organizational standard exists—and is adhered to—that defines which documents will be inspected under what conditions.
- Defect cause information is used in root-cause analysis to target changes to development process.

Estimated Actual and Projected HP Inspections Savings

We derived the 1994 estimated savings of $31.1 million using the formula:

Est. $ savings/year = % Total costs saved × Rework % × Efficiency factor (.5) × Total eng. costs

% Total costs saved—percentage for a work-product component only. It peaks at 100%.

Rework %—comes from an internal average total HP software development cost model. HP's estimated total rework is 33 percent. It is broken down into the work-product components shown in Table D-1.

Efficiency factor—Capers Jones says this varies from 30 percent to 75 percent. [2] Assume 50% for 1994 because our average maturity level estimates were almost 3 (2.71).

Total eng. costs—assuming 3,500 R&D software engineers at a cost of $150,000 per engineering year, total cost is $525 million.

Maximum possible savings from inspections—this is computed from the total engineering cost formula to be $525M × 33% × 60% = $105M. (Some of this maximum will be saved through other engineering techniques, so while this is a theoretical maximum, the practical maximum will be somewhat less. Also, while inspections substantially reduce costs, they don't totally eliminate them. We use a 60% efficiency factor to simulate these combined effects.)

The total savings are the sum of the savings from four major work products. This is estimated by taking the increased percent of different types of inspections, times their assumed components of total software costs (a rework percent times total costs), times an assumed 1994 efficiency factor of 50 percent. For example, design savings would be 39% × (11% × $525M) × .5 = $11,261K. These are very rough calculations, but they give us a way to translate our extent-of-adoption measure to company-wide savings. The estimated 1994 percentages came from the 1994 Inspections Survey. Because the survey only asked for the presence or absence of different inspection types on projects, the results overstate actual use. The efficiency factor of only .5 at least somewhat makes up for this. Table D-1 summarizes the savings estimates.

Table D-1 Estimated yearly savings attributable to HP software inspections

Work Product	Estimated Starting Point	Estimated 1994	Total Costs Saved	Rework	Estimated Savings Per Year
Specifications	1%	34.3%	33.3%	17%	$14,860,000
Design	1%	40.0%	39.0%	11%	$11,261,000
Code	5%	48.1%	43.1%	4%	$4,526,000
Test Plans	1%	18.7%	17.7%	1%	$465,000
Total				33%	$31,112,000

BIBLIOGRAPHY

1. Grady, R., *Practical Software Metrics for Project Management and Process Improvement*, Englewood Cliffs, N. J.: Prentice-Hall, 1992, p. 130.
2. Jones, C., *Programming Productivity.* New York: McGraw-Hill, 1986, p. 179.

Appendix E
Software Process-Improvement Reference
— *Bibliography* —

Like the book's main sections, this annotated bibliography is organized into Plan, Do, Check, and Act. This organization is somewhat artificial, since most of the references also touch on other areas besides the ones in which they're placed. My main criteria for picking references for annotation were either that they discussed a particular topic very well or that they offered an unusual insight or "Aha!" to me. I hope that my classification of them will help you to fill in some gaps you might find in my discussions.

PLAN

1. Humphrey, W., *Managing the Software Process*, Reading, Mass: Addison-Wesley, 1989.

   This book helped create ideas and discussions during the exciting, early stages of recent software process improvement thinking. It not only describes the SEI software process maturity model and much of the thinking behind the model, it also motivates and gives practical suggestions for improving processes.

2. Prahalad, C., and G. Hamel, "The Core Competence of the Corporation," *Harvard Business Review*, (May-June 1990), pp. 79-91.

This has been a very influential article for high-level managers, although it never clearly defines "core competence." I believe it is influential because many organizations in the 80s followed out-sourcing strategies and learned that such strategies caused them to lose entire markets. Many managers are looking for satisfactory explanations. Regardless of the cause, core competence has been a very powerful concept when communicating with managers in HP.

3. Irvin, R., and E. Michaels III, "Core Skills: Doing the Right Things Right," *McKinsey Quarterly*, (Summer 1989), pp. 4-19.
   While the Prahalad and Hamel article seems to be better known, I find that this article is better written and more helpful. Irvin and Michaels use the term "Core Skills," instead of core compe-tence, but the concepts all seem the same. The examples are excel-lent, and their five "secrets" are useful.

4. Schaffer, R., and H. Thomson, "Successful Change Programs Begin with Results," *Harvard Business Review*, (Jan.-Feb. 1992), pp. 80-89.
   This outstanding article presents a single important message well: focus on results, not activities. Its practical advice is worth pass-ing on to your top managers and periodically reviewing.

5. Silver, B., "TQM vs. the SEI Capability Maturity Model," *Software Quality World*, Vol. 4, No. 2, (1992), pp. 18-26.
   This excellent article challenges the CMM from the Total Quality Management (TQM) viewpoint. It views some of the flaws as: ignoring TQM, cultural issues and software support, institution-alizing QA groups instead of a QA mentality, encouraging orga-nizations to postpone statistical process control and defect causal analysis, discouraging continuous process improvement for some activities after achieving certain levels, and not attaching perfor-mance measures to capabilities. These challenges can be useful because they can help people in strong, quality-oriented organi-zations to see how the CMM might be used to complement cur-rent organizational activities to strengthen software.

DO

6. Dion, R., "Elements of a Process Improvement Program," *IEEE Software*, (July 1992), pp. 83-85.
   This article describes the exciting results of Raytheon's process improvement program over four years. It also describes their

approach and the key steps they took, including the kinds of improvements, the training courses and tools they used, and the quantified results they achieved. (These results are discussed in Chapter 11.)

7. Humphrey, W., T. Snyder, and R. Willis, "Software Process Improvement at Hughes Aircraft," *IEEE Software*, (July 1991), pp.11-23.
This article was one of the first that attempted to strongly justify process improvements tied to progress against the CMM. I feel it is only partially successful, since it has no compelling graphic image, and its main ROI conclusion is based on an internal cost performance index that isn't explained well. Its CMM discussion is excellent, though, and does a good job of setting expectations for anyone considering a similar approach.

8. Weller, E., "Lessons from Three Years of Inspection Data," *IEEE Software*, (Sept. 1993), pp. 38-45.
This article was picked as the best *IEEE Software* article in 1993 for good reasons. It summarizes the results of over 6,000 software inspections at Bull in a variety of ways. Its data can help other organizations to set expectations for inspection times, defect finding rates, and how to approach processes. (Some of these results are discussed in Chapter 11.)

9. Lawrence, P. "How to Deal with Resistance to Change," *Harvard Business Review*, (Jan.-Feb. 1969), pp. 160-176.
This is an excellent "classic" article that talks about some experiments that involved varying degrees of worker participation in changes. The results clearly showed more rapid and effective acceptance of changes when workers were more involved in the changes and how they would happen.

10. Embar, C., "Strategic Visioning," *Crosstalk*, (Nov./Dec. 1995), pp. 5-9.
While this article's title suggests that it is limited to visioning, it also has valuable advice about strategic planning. The visioning discussion is particularly good.

CHECK

11. Grady, R., *Practical Software Metrics for Project Management and Process Improvement*, Englewood Cliffs, N. J.: Prentice-Hall, Inc., 1992.
The essence of "Check" is measurement, so software metrics books and articles will help you here. The most effective measures will

both serve project uses and process-improvement uses. *Practical Software Metrics* offers many examples of both uses from real projects. The second half of the book also goes into more process-improvement measurement detail than this book does, including chapters on "proven" software engineering practices, failure analysis, business justification of six different software engineering practices, and metrics for measuring the health of a software business.

12. Herbsleb, J., A. Carleton, J. Rozum, J. Siegel, and D. Zubrow, "Benefits of CMM-Based Software Process Improvement: Initial Results," *Technical Report, CMU/SEI-94-TR-13*, (Aug. 1994).

    This SEI report was done in response to many requests that the SEI show quantitative evidence that process improvements and increasing maturity levels make good business sense. It does a very good job of bringing together good success stories. I found the part with case studies to be the most valuable. I thought the aggregated results less useful, and even somewhat misleading. Their summary might lead you to believe that you could expect all of the presented results simultaneously. I believe that different benefits will be driven more or less on a case-by-case basis. Viewed this way, the table entries are still very promising.

13. Katz, A., "Measuring Technology's Business Value," *Information Systems Managment*, (Winter 1993), pp. 33-39.

    This excellent article describes a range of business-related IT metrics and their use by a variety of businesses that responded to a survey. The metrics both emphasize some differences in how IT is viewed compared to R&D and provide some insights into how process-improvement investments could be viewed.

14. Bollinger, T., and C. McGowan, "A Critical Look at Software Capability Evaluations," *IEEE Software*, (July 1991), pp. 25-41.

    This 1991 analysis of the SEI Software Capability Evaluation is particularly good because it effectively illustrates the potential dangers of thinking of a strong improvement model (the CMM) as a "report card." Such dangers are possible with all high-level strategic measurements, if individuals decide to meet the "words" of a goal rather than the "spirit." The authors also describe the earlier version of the CMM well and flag other real flaws (design of CMM toward large organizations that create relatively consistent products, danger of organizations stagnating for fear of becoming less mature, and the difficulty of consistent evaluations).

15. Humphrey, W., and B. Curtis, "Comments on 'A Critical Look,'" *IEEE Software*, (July 1991), pp. 42-46.

    It was a great move by *IEEE Software* to add an SEI reply along with the Bollinger and McGowan article. Humphrey and Curtis do a very good job of defusing some of the SCE criticisms and turning you back to the philosophical intent of the CMM.

ACT _____

16. Rogers, E., *Diffusion of Innovations*, 3rd Edition, New York: Macmillan Publishing, 1983.

    I encourage anyone who becomes seriously involved with technology transfer or adoption to read this book. It is undoubtedly the origin of the majority of concepts taught today under the umbrella of "change management." More importantly, its many and varied stories reinforce some of the most important sociological learnings about people undergoing change in a wide range of different fields. It will help you to better understand all aspects of plan/do/check/act.

17. Raghavan, S., and D. Chand, "Diffusing Software Engineering Methods," *IEEE Software*, (July 1989), pp. 81-90.

    This outstanding article summarizes many of Everett Rogers's key diffusion learnings and makes many persuasive connections to what needs to be done to apply these learnings to software engineering.

18. Basili, V., G. Caldiera, F. McGarry, R. Pajerski, G. Page, and S. Waligora, "The Software Engineering Laboratory—An Operational Software Experience Factory," *ACM Proc. Intn'l. Conf. on Software Engineering*, (May 1992), 370-381.

    The NASA/Goddard efforts have been successfully guided for over 20 years by Frank McGarry and Vic Basili. This excellent article discusses some of their key approaches (GQM, Quality Improvement Paradigm, Experience Factory) and briefly summarizes some of their key results.

19. Billings, C., J. Clifton, B. Kolkhorst, E. Lee, and W. Wingert, "Journey to a Mature Software Process," *IBM Systems Journal*, Vol. 33, No. 1, (1994), pp. 46-61.

    The Space Shuttle software systems have also evolved for many years. This article describes the evolution of their software processes since the 1960s. (Some of their results are also discussed in Chapter 11.)

COMPLETE ALPHABETIC LISTING

Articles described earlier are marked in bold type and with "**" in front of the authors' names.

1. Abernathy, W., and K. Wayne, "Limits of the Learning Curve," *Harvard Business Review*, (Sept.-Oct. 1974), pp. 109-119.
2. Abreu, F., and W. Melo, "Evaluating the Impact of Object-Oriented Design on Software Quality," *Third Intn'l Software Metrics Symposium*, Berlin, Germany, (Mar. 1996).
3. Adler, P., and A. Shenbar, "Adapting Your Technological Base: The Organizational Challenge," *Sloan Mgmt. Review*, Vol. 32, No. 1, (Fall 1990), pp. 25-37.
4. Albran, A., and H. Nguyenkim, "Analysis of Maintenance Work Categories through Measurement," *Proc. of the IEEE Conf. on Software Maintenance*, Sorrento, Italy, (1991), pp. 104-113.
5. Aoyama, M., "Beyond Software Factories: Concurrent-Development Process and an Evolution of Software Process Technology in Japan," *Information and Software Technology*, Vol.38, No.3, (March 1996), pp.133-143.
6. Bamford, C., and W. Deibler II, "Comparing, Contrasting ISO 9001 and the SEI Capability Maturity Model," *IEEE Computer*, (Oct. 1993), pp. 68-70.
7. Bartlett, P., P. Robinson, T. Hains, and M. Simms, "Use of Structured Methods for Real-Time Peripheral Firmware," *Hewlett-Packard Journal*, (Aug. 1989), pp. 79-86.
8. Basili, V., "Viewing Maintenance as Reuse-Oriented Software Development," *IEEE Software*, (Jan. 1990), pp. 19-25.
9. **Basili, V., G. Caldiera, F. McGarry, R. Pajerski, G. Page, and S. Waligora**, "The Software Engineering Laboratory-An Operational Software Experience Factory," *ACM Proc. Intn'l. Conf. on Software Engineering*, (May 1992), 370-381.
10. Basili, V., and S. Green, "Software Process Evolution at the SEL," *IEEE Software*, (July, 1994), pp. 58-66.
11. Basili, V., and H. D. Rombach, "Tailoring the Software Process to Project Goals and Environments," *IEEE Ninth Intn'l Conf. on Software Engineering*, Monterey, CA, (April 1987), pp. 345-357.
12. Basili, V., M. Zelkowitz, F. McGarry, J. Page, S. Waligora, and R. Pajerski, "SEL's Software Process-Improvement Program," *IEEE Software*, (Nov. 1995), pp. 83-87.
13. Benno, S., and Frailey, D., "Software Process Improvement in DSEG-1989-1995," *Texas Instruments Technical Journal*, Vol.12, No.2, (Mar.-Apr. 1995), pp.20-28.

14. **Billings, C., J. Clifton, B. Kolkhorst, E. Lee, and W. Wingert**, "Journey to a Mature Software Process," *IBM Systems Journal*, Vol. 33, No. 1, (1994), pp. 46-61.

15. Bilotta, J. and J. McGrew, "What Do You Do First? What Do You Do Next? The Scaling of Level 2 Practices," *1996 Software Engineering Process Group Conf.*, (May 1996).

16. Boehm, B., "Improving Software Productivity," *IEEE Computer*, (Sept. 1987), pp. 43-57.

17. Boehm, B., *Software Engineering Economics*. Englewood Cliffs, N. J.: Prentice-Hall, Inc., 1981, p. 40.

18. **Bollinger, T., and C. McGowan**, "A Critical Look at Software Capability Evaluations," *IEEE Software*, (July 1991), pp. 25-41.

19. Brassard, M., *The Memory Jogger Plus+(TM)*, Methuen, Mass: GOAL/QPC, 1989.

20. Brodman, J., and D. Johnson, "What Small Businesses and Small Organizations Say About the CMM," *Proc. of the 16th Intn'l. Conf. on Software Engineering*, (1993), pp. 331-339.

21. Brooks, F.,*The Mythical Man-Month*, Reading, Mass: Addison-Wesley, 1975.

22. Brooks, F., "No Silver Bullets—Essence and Accidents of Software Engineering," *Computer*, (April 1987), pp. 10-18.

23. Capper, N., R. Colgate, J. Hunter, and M. James, "The Impact of Object-Oriented Technology on Software Quality: Three Case Histories," *IBM Systems Journal*, Vol. 33, No. 1, (1994), pp. 131-157.

24. Card, D., "The Rad Fad: Is Timing Really Everything?," *IEEE Software*, (Sept. 1995), pp.19-22.

25. Card, D. with R. Glass, *Measuring Software Design Quality*, Englewood Cliffs, N.J.: Prentice-Hall, Inc., 1990.

26. Cassafer, D., "Implementing KAIZEN (Continuous Improvement) through Retrospectives," *HP 1992 Software Engineering Productivity Conf. Proc.*, (Aug. 1992), pp. 13-21. (Not available outside HP.)

27. Cattaneo, F., A. Fuggetta, and L. Lavazza, "An Experience in Process Assessment," *ACM 0-89791-708-1/95/0004*, (1995), pp. 115-121.

28. Corbi, T., "Program Understanding: Challenge for the 1990s," *IBM Systems Journal*, Vol. 28, No. 2, (1989), pp. 294-306.

29. Crosby, P., and C. Reimann, "Criticism and Support for the Baldrige Award," *Quality Progress*, (May 1991), pp. 41-44.

30. Culver-Lozo, K., "Rapid Iteration in Software Process Improvement: Experience Report," *IEEE Proc. of the 3rd Intn'l Conf. on the Software Process*, (Oct. 1994), pp.79-84.

31. Curtis, B., "A Mature Look at Maturity Assessment," *Conf. on the Application of Software Measurement 1995*, Orlando, Fla., (Nov. 1995).

32. Curtis, B., and M. Paulk, "Creating a Software Process Improvement Program, *Information and Software Technology*, Vol.35, No.6-7, (June-July 1993), pp.381-386.

33. Curtis, B., and J. Statz, "Building the Cost-Benefit Case for Software Process Improvement," TeraQuest Metrics, Inc., Austin, Texas, 1995.

34. DeMarco, T., and T. Lister, *Peopleware*, New York: Dorset House, 1987.

35. Deming, W. E., *Out of the Crisis*, Cambridge, Mass: MIT Center for Advanced Engineering Study, 1986.

36. Dickmann, D., "Integrating Inspections into the Development Environment," *HP Software Engineering Productivity Conf. Proc.*, (August 1992), pp. 179-181. (Not available outside HP.)

37. **Dion, R., "Elements of a Process Improvement Program," *IEEE Software*, (July 1992), pp. 83-85.

38. Dion, R., "Process Improvement and the Corporate Balance Sheet," *IEEE Software*, (July 1993), pp. 28-35.

39. Edgar-Nevill, V., "Evaluation of the SEI Software Capability Model within an Information Systems Context; In Pursuit of Software Quality," *Proc. of Second Intn'l Conf. on Software Quality Mgmt. SQM 94*, (July 1994), p.263-278.

40. El Emam, K., and N. Madhavji, "Does Organizational Maturity Improve Quality?" *IEEE Software*, (Sept. 1996), pp. 109-110.

41. **Embar, C., "Strategic Visioning," *Crosstalk*, (Nov./Dec. 1995), pp. 5-9.

42. Fenton, N., S. Pfleeger, and R. Glass, "Science and Substance: A Challenge to Software Engineers," *IEEE Software*, (July, 1994), pp. 86-95.

43. Feurer, R., K. Chaharbaghi, and J. Wargin, "Analysis of Strategy Formulation and Implementation at Hewlett-Packard," *Management Decision*, Vol. 33 No. 10, (1995), pp. 4-16.

44. Fiore, P., F. Lanubile, and G. Visaggio, "Analyzing Empirical Data from a Reverse Engineering Project," *Reverse Engineering Newsletter*, (1996), pp. Rev-8 to Rev-14.

45. Foster, J., "Program Lifetime: A Vital Statistic for Maintenance," *Proc. of the IEEE Conf. on Software Maintenance*, Sorrento, Italy, (1991), pp. 98-103.

46. Fuggetta, A., and G. Picco, "An Annotated Bibliography on Software Process Improvement," *SIGSOFT Software Engineering Notes*, Vol.19, No.3, (July 1994), p.66-68.

47. Garvin, D., "How the Baldrige Award Really Works," *Harvard Business Review*, (Nov.-Dec. 1991), pp. 80-93.

48. **Grady, R., *Practical Software Metrics for Project Management and Process Improvement*, Englewood Cliffs, N. J.: Prentice-Hall, Inc., 1992.

49. Grady, R., "Successfully Applying Software Metrics," *IEEE Computer*, (Sept. 1994), pp. 18-25.

50. Grady, R., and D. Caswell, *Software Metrics: Establishing a Company-Wide Program*, Englewood Cliffs, N.J.: Prentice Hall, 1987.

51. Grady, R., and T. Van Slack, "Key Lessons in Achieving Widespread Inspection Use," *IEEE Software*, (July, 1994), pp. 46-57.

52. Graves, S., W. Carmichael, D. Daetz, and E. Wilson, "Improving the Product Development Process," *Hewlett-Packard Journal*, (June 1991), pp. 71-76.

53. Griss, M., "Software Reuse: From Library to Factory," *IBM Systems Journal*, Vol. 32, No. 4, (1993), pp. 548-566.

54. Haase, V., R. Messnarz, G. Koch, H. Kugler, and P. Decrinis, "Bootstrap: Fine-Tuning Process Assessment," *IEEE Software*, (July, 1994), pp. 25-35.

55. Halliday, M., I. Bhandari, J. Chaar, and R. Cillarege, "Experiences in Transferring a Software Process Improvement Methodology to Production Laboratories," *Journal of Systems Software*, Vol. 26, (1994), pp. 61-68.

56. Hayes, R., and S. Wheelwright, "Link Manufacturing Process and Product Life Cycles," *Harvard Business Review*, (Jan.-Feb. 1979), pp. 133-140.

57. Henry, J., and B. Blasewitz, "Process Definition: Theory and Reality," *IEEE Software*, (Nov. 1992), pp. 103-105.

58. Henry, J., S. Henry, and L. Matheson, "Improving Software Maintenance at Martin Marietta," *IEEE Software*, (July, 1994), pp. 67-75.

59. Henry, S., and M. Humphrey, "A Controlled Experiment to Evaluate Maintainability of Object-Oriented Software," *Proc. of the IEEE Conf. on Software Maintenance*, San Diego, CA, (1990), pp. 258-265.

60. **Herbsleb, J., A. Carleton, J. Rozum, J. Siegel, and D. Zubrow**, "Benefits of CMM-Based Software Process Improvement: Initial Results," *Technical Report, CMU/SEI-94-TR-13*, (Aug. 1994).

61. Hofman, B., "ISO 9000 Audits vs. SEI Assessments: How Do They Compare," *5th Annual SEPG National Meeting*, Costa Mesa, CA, April 29, 1993.

62. Hollis, J., "Establishing A Peer-Review Process for Work Products," *HP Project Mgmt. Conf. Proc.*, (April 1996). (Not available outside HP.)

63. Humphrey, W., *A Discipline for Software Engineering*, Reading, Mass: Addison-Wesley, 1995.

64. **Humphrey, W.**, *Managing the Software Process*, Reading, Mass: Addison-Wesley, 1989.

65. **Humphrey, W., and B. Curtis**, "Comments on 'A Critical Look'," *IEEE Software*, (July 1991), pp. 42-46.

66. **Humphrey, W., T. Snyder, and R. Willis**, "Software Process

Improvement at Hughes Aircraft," *IEEE Software*, (July 1991), pp.11-23.

67. Hutchings, T., M. Hyde, D. Marca, and L. Cohen, "Process Improvement That Lasts: An Integrated Training and Consulting Method," *Comm. of the ACM*, Vol.36, No.10, (Oct. 1993), pp.104-13.

68. **Irvin, R.**, and E. Michaels III, "Core Skills: Doing the Right Things Right," *McKinsey Quarterly*, (Summer 1989), pp. 4-19.

69. Ishikawa, K., *Guide to Quality Control*, Tokyo: Asian Productivity Organization, 1976.

70. *ISO 9000-3, Guidelines for the Application of ISO 9001 to the Development, Supply, and Maintenance of Software*, Intn'l Organization for Standardization, Geneva, (June 1, 1991).

71. *ISO 9001, Quality Systems—Model for Quality Assurance in Design/Development, Production, Installation, and Servicing*, Intn'l Organization for Standardization, Geneva, 1987.

72. Jervis, P., "Innovation and Technology Transfer—The Roles and Characteristics of Individuals," *IEEE Trans. on Engineering Mgmt.*, Vol. EM-22, No. 1, (Feb. 1975), pp. 19-27.

73. Jones, C., "The Economics of Software Process Improvement," *IEEE Computer*, Vol.29, No.1, (Jan. 1996), pp.95-97.

74. Jones, T., and W. Sasser, "Why Satisfied Customers Defect," *Harvard Business Review*, (Nov.-Dec. 1995), pp. 88-99.

75. Kaplan, R., and D. Norton, "The Balanced Scorecard—Measures that Drive Performance," *Harvard Business Review*, (Jan.-Feb. 1992), pp. 71-79.

76. Kaplan, R., and D. Norton, "Putting the Balanced Scorecard to Work," *Harvard Business Review*, (Sept.-Oct. 1993), pp. 134-147.

77. **Katz, A.**, "Measuring Technology's Business Value," *Information Systems Managment*, (Winter 1993), pp. 33-39.

78. Kelly, J., J. Sherif, and J. Hops, "An Analysis of Defect Densities Found During Software Inspections," *Journal of Systems Software*, Vol. 17, (1992), pp. 111-117.

79. Krasner, H., "The Payoff for Software Process Improvement (SPI): What It Is and How to Get It," *Software Process Newsletter*, pp. 3-8.

80. Lawlis, P., R. Flowe, and J. Thordahl, "A Correlational Study of the CMM and Software Development Performance," *Crosstalk*, (Sept. 1995), pp. 21-25.

81. **Lawrence, P.**, "How to Deal with Resistance to Change," *Harvard Business Review*, (Jan.-Feb. 1969), pp. 160-176.

82. LeVitt, D., "A Survey of HP Best Engineering Practice," *HP Software Engineering Productivity Conf. Proc.*, (May 1987), pp. 4-173 to 4-179. (Not available outside HP.)

83. Lim, W., "Effects of Reuse on Quality, Productivity, and Economics,"

IEEE Software, (Sept. 1994), pp. 23-30.

84. Lipke, W., and K. Butler, "Software Process Improvement: A Success Story," *Crosstalk*, Vol. 38, (1992), pp. 29-31.

85. Lofgren, G., "Quality System Registration," *Quality Progress*, (May 1991), pp. 35-37.

86. Lowe, D., and G. Cox, "Implementing the Capability Maturity Model for Software Development," *Hewlett-Packard Journal*, (Aug. 1996), pp. 6-14.

87. Lutz, R., "Targeting Safety-Related Errors During Software Requirements Analysis," *SIGSOFT '93 ACM 0-89791-625-5/93/0012*, (Dec. 1993), pp. 99-106.

88. MacLeod, J., "Implementing and Sustaining a Software Inspection Program in an R&D Environment," *Hewlett-Packard Journal*, (June 1993), pp. 60-63.

89. Mayobre, "Reuse-Oriented Software Development at Grenoble Networks Division," *HP Software Engineering Productivity Conf. Proc.*, (Aug. 1992), pp. 113-123. (Not available outside HP.)

90. McWilliams, B., "The New Value Brokers," *Computerworld Client/Server Journal*, (Oct. 1995), pp. 29-32.

91. Melo, W., L. Briand, and V. Basili, "Measuring the Impact of Reuse on Quality and Productivity in Object-Oriented Systems," *U. of Maryland Tech. Report CS-TR-3395*, (Jan. 1995).

92. Moller, K. H., "Increasing of Software Quality by Objectives and Residual Fault Prognosis," *First E.O.Q.C. Seminar on Software Quality*, Brussels, Belgium, (April 1988), pp. 478-488.

93. Mosteller, F., "Innovation and Evaluation," *Science*, Vol. 11, (1981), pp. 881-886.

94. Nakhai, B., and J. Neves, "The Deming, Baldrige, and European Quality Awards," *Quality Progress*, (April 1994), pp. 33-37.

95. Onoma, A., and T. Yamaura, "Practical Steps Toward Quality Development," *IEEE Software*, (Sept. 1995), pp. 68-76.

96. Paulish, D., and A. Carleton, "Case Studies of Software Process Improvement Measurement," *IEEE Computer*, (Sept. 1994), pp. 50-57.

97. Paulk, M., "How ISO 9001 Compares with the CMM," *IEEE Software*, (Jan. 1995), pp. 74-82.

98. Paulk, M., B. Curtis, M. Chrissis, and C. Weber, "Capability Maturity Model, Version 1.1," *IEEE Software*, (July 1993), pp. 18-27.

99. Paulk, M., W. Humphrey, and G. Pandelios, "Software Process Assessments: Issues and Lessons Learned," *Proc. of the Intn'l. Software Quality Exchange*, (1992), pp. 4B41-4B58.

100. Paulk, M., C. Weber, B. Curtis, and M. Chrissis, *The Capability*

Maturity Model: Guidelines for Improving the Software Process, Reading, Mass: Addison-Wesley, 1995.

101. Perry, D., N. Staudenmayer, and L. Votta, "People, Organizations, and Process Improvement," *IEEE Software*, (July, 1994), pp. 36-45.

102. Pfleeger, S., and H. Rombach, "Measurement-Based Process Improvement," *IEEE Software*, (July, 1994), pp. 8-11.

103. **Prahalad, C., and G. Hamel**, "The Core Competence of the Corporation," *Harvard Business Review*, (May-June 1990), pp. 79-91.

104. *Quality Maturity System Review Process Handbook*, Hewlett-Packard Part No. 5959-1663, Sept. 1994, p. 3. (Not available outside HP.)

105. **Raghavan, S., and D. Chand**, "Diffusing Software Engineering Methods," *IEEE Software*, (July 1989), pp. 81-90.

106. Redwine, S., and W. Riddle, "Software Technology Maturation," *IEEE 8th Conf. on Software Engineering*, (Aug. 1985), pp. 189-200.

107. Reinertsen, D., "Whodunit? The Search for the New-Product Killers," *Electronic Business*, (July 1983), pp. 35-37.

108. Riddle, W., "The Magic Number Eighteen Plus or Minus Three: A Study of Software Technology Maturation," *ACM SIGSOFT Software Eng. Notes*, Vol. 9, No. 2, (April 1984), pp. 21-37.

109. Rix, M., "Case Study of a Successful Firmware Reuse Program," *HP Software Engineering Productivity Conf. Proc.*, (Aug. 1992), pp. 125-137. (Not available outside HP.)

110. Roberts, E., "Managing Invention and Innovation," *Research/Technology Mgmt.*, Vol. 31. No. 1, (Jan./Feb. 1988), pp. 3-21.

111. Robinson, P., and P. Bartlett, "CPB's Use of Structured Methods for Real-Time Peripheral Firmware," *HP Software Productivity Conf. Proc.*, (August 1988), pp. 285-295. (Not available outside HP.)

112. **Rogers, E.**, *Diffusion of Innovations*, 3rd Edition, New York: Macmillan Publishing, 1983.

113. Rooijmans, J., H. Aerts, and M. van Genuchten, "Software Quality in Consumer Electronics Products," *IEEE Software*, Vol.13, No.1, (Jan. 1996), pp.55-64.

114. Rosenbaum, S., and B. du Castel, "Managing Software Reuse—An Experience Report," *ACM 0-89791-708-1/95/0004*, (1995), pp. 105-111.

115. Rout, T., and P. Briggs, "An Assessment-Based Approach to Process Improvement in Software Testing," *Proc. of AQUIS '93. 2nd Intn'l. Conf. on Achieving Quality in Software*, (Oct. 1993), pp.391-406.

116. Rubin, H., "Software Process Maturity: Measuring Its Impact on Productivity and Quality," *IEEE Proc. of 1993 15th Intn'l. Conf. on Software Engineering*, (May 1993), pp.468-476.

117. Rubin, H., E. Yourdon, and H. Battaglia, "Industry Canada Worldwide

Benchmark Project," *Conf. on the Appl. Software Metrics*, Orlando, Fla., (Nov. 1995), pp. 51-52.

118. Saiedian, H., and R. Kirzara, "SEI Capability Maturity Model's Impact on Contractors," *IEEE Computer*, (Jan. 1995), pp. 16-25.

119. **Schaffer, R., and H. Thomson**, "Successful Change Programs Begin with Results," *Harvard Business Review*, (Jan.-Feb. 1992), pp. 80-89.

120. Scholtes, P., *The Team Handbook*, Madison, Wis.: Joiner Associates, Inc., 1988.

121. Scott, G., "Can Software Engineering Afford to Improve the Process?" *ACM SIGSOFT, Software Engineering Notes*, Vol. 17, No. 2, (Apr. 1992), pp. 39-42.

122. Senge, P., A. Kleiner, C. Roberts, R. Ross, and B. Smith, *The Fifth Discipline Fieldbook*, New York: Doubleday, 1994.

123. Shirey, G., "How Inspections Fail," *Software Practitioner*, Vol. 3, No. 3 and 4, (May-Aug 1993).

124. **Silver, B.**, "TQM vs. the SEI Capability Maturity Model," *Software Quality World*, Vol. 4, No. 2, (1992), pp. 18-26.

125. Smith, P., and D. Reinertsen, *Developing Products in Half the Time*, New York: Van Nostrand Reinhold, 1991.

126. Stark, G., L. Kern and C. Vowell, "A Software Metric Set for Program Maintenance Management," *Journal of Systems and Software*, Vol. 24, (1994), pp. 239-249.

127. Stark, M., "Impacts of Object-Oriented Technologies: Seven Years of Software Engineering," *Journal of Systems and Software*, Vol. 23, (1993), pp. 163-169.

128. Stewart, T., "Rate Your Readiness to Change," *Fortune*, (Feb. 7, 1994), pp. 106-110.

129. Sudman, S., and N. Bradburn, *Asking Questions: A Practical Guide to Questionnaire Design*, San Francisco, Calif.: Jossey-Bass, 1985.

130. Tanaka, T., K. Sakamoto, S. Kusumoto, K. Matsumoto, and T. Kikuno, "Improvement of Software Process by Process Description and Benefit Estimation," *ACM 0-89791-708-1/95/0004*, (1995), pp. 115-121.

131. Taramaa, J., and V. Seppanen, "A Roadmap from Configuration to Application Management," *Proc. of Conf. on Software Quality Mgmt.*, Southampton, UK: Comput. Mech. Publications, (April 1995), Vol.1, pp. 111-120.

132. Thamhain, H., and D. Wilemon, "Building High Performing Engineering Project Teams," *IEEE Trans. on Engineering Mgmt.*, Vol. EM-34, No. 3, (Aug. 1987), pp. 130-137.

133. Thomson, H., and P. Mayhew, "The Software Process: A Perspective on Improvement," *Computer Journal*, Vol.37, No.8, (1994), p.683-690.

134. Tichy, W., P. Lukowicz, L. Prechelt, and E. Heinz, "Experimental Evaluation in Computer Science: A Quantitative Study," *Journal of Systems Software*, Vol. 28, (1995), pp. 9-18.

135. Visaggio, G., "Process Improvement through Data Reuse," *IEEE Software*, (July, 1994), pp. 76-85.

136. Von Braun, C., "The Acceleration Trap," *Sloan Mgmt. Review*, Vol. 32, No. 1, (Fall, 1990), pp. 49-58.

137. Von Braun, C., "The Acceleration Trap in the Real World," *Sloan Mgmt. Review*, Vol. 32, No. 4, (Summer, 1991), pp. 43-52.

138. **Weller, E.**, "Lessons from Three Years of Inspection Data," *IEEE Software*, (Sept. 1993), pp. 38-45.

139. Weller, E., "Using Metrics to Manage Software Projects," *IEEE Software*, (July, 1994), pp.27-33.

140. Whitney, R., E. Nawrocki, W. Hayes, and J. Siegel, "Interim Profile Development and Trial of a Method to Rapidly Measure Software Engineering Maturity Status," *Technical Report CMU/SEI-94-TR-4*, Pittsburg: Carnegie-Mellon Univ., (March 1994).

141. Willis, R., "Technology Transfer Takes 6 +/- 2 Years," *IEEE CH1883-8/83/0000/0108*, (1983), pp. 108-117.

142. Witkin, L., "The Renoir Project at PSD: Reflections on Our Experiences," *HP Software Engineering Productivity Conf. Proc.*, (May 1987), pp. 1-87 to 1-104. (Not available outside HP.)

143. Wohlwend, H., and S. Rosenbaum, "Schlumberger's Software Improvement Program," *IEEE Trans. on Software Engineering*, Vol. 20, No. 11, (Nov. 1994), pp. 833-839.

144. Zimmer, B., "A Case Study in Process Improvement," *Profile: Software Quality and Productivity at Hewlett-Packard*, (Dec. 1990). (Not available outside HP.)

145. Zimmer, B., "Software Quality and Productivity Analysis at Hewlett-Packard." (Not available outside HP.)

Index